C0-BKV-968

TRAVELER'S GUIDE BOOK

to

EUROPE And ASIA

MARK ATLAS'

TRAVELER'S GUIDE BOOK

to

EUROPE And ASIA

Your Passport to

MAKING IT ABROAD

Robert Speller & Sons, Publishers, Inc.
New York, New York 10010

© 1973 by Mark Altschuler

Library of Congress Catalog Card No. 72-82766
ISBN 0-8315-0133-2

Second Edition

Printed in the United States of America

TABLE OF CONTENTS

FOREWORD

Dear Traveler,

During my recent trip around the world (through Australia and 50 countries in Europe, Asia and Africa), I observed many of my fellow Americans from the Hilton set to the hitchhikers falling victim to false rumors. I saw both misled tourists and budget-minded travelers fall prey to con-games, go broke in tourist traps, and end up in hospitals and jails. (There are over 1,000 young Americans in foreign jails at the present time.) I became acutely aware that there is no guide book which advised American tourists and travelers what to expect, both good and bad, throughout the entire tourist trail from Morocco to Moscow and Athens to Australia.

Almost all of the existing guide books go no further than recommending restaurants and hotels.

The first section of this book consists of general information and helpful tips to tourists and travelers alike. The back, or map, section which contains a synopsis of each country as well as statistical information gives the tourist some idea of what to expect and, most important, dispels rumors about the respective countries.

All travelers about to embark on their journeys should ask themselves: "Why am I traveling? What is my goal?" I have found that oftentimes in finding our goals, we double our efforts while losing sight of our aims. Most travelers get into trouble when they forget the purpose of their trip. They hear of an exotic place, change their itinerary without thinking of the expense or the consequences, and later find themselves broke or worse.

To keep abreast of the ever changing travel information, the last page is a post card addressed to the author so that you the traveler can add-to and up-date the information for future editions.

Remember your aims. Stay within your budget and return home safely to tell about your travels.

See you in the world

SUMMER TRAVEL REPORT

If there seem to be fewer young travelers in Europe this year than there were in 1970 and 1971, there are two reasons for it.

1. European cities have accepted the fact that young travelers are here to stay, so they are catering to their needs. For example, instead of sleeping in the streets in Amsterdam and crowding the tourist information office looking for a place to stay, everyone now flocks to Vondel Park, which is a designated "sleep-in" area set up by the Amsterdam government.

2. Another reason the crowds seem to have disappeared in Europe is that it seems to be only a stopping-off place for the more adventurous young travelers who are heading to Eastern Europe, North Africa, the Middle East and Asia.

The summer Olympics in Munich attracted many thousands of tourists, made accommodations impossible to find and caused many inconveniences. Many summer travelers avoided the area because of this. Whereas hitchhiking was once commonplace on the West German autobahn, this year many young travelers reported getting tickets and having to pay fines for hitchhiking.

If you are not attending a world event, it is a good idea to avoid the area because of inflation and a lack of accommodations.

With the travel trend moving toward Asia, novice ravelers face a great challenge. Many of them, attracted by drugs, are unaware of the false rumors they are following. Reliable sources told me that last Spring the West European and American Embassies in Afghanistan were sending home at least one coffin a week as the result of an overdose.

But don't let this deter you. Asia is still quite inexpensive by American standards, and these countries are the greatest to visit.

WARNING: Phoney air charter agencies stranded another thousand young Americans in Europe again this year. Be cautious!!! (See chapter on Transportation Charter Flights)

Prices, schedules and statistical information in this book are current as of this writing but are subject to change without notice.

ACKNOWLEDGEMENTS

In no way have any companies or organizations mentioned in this book provided me with any financial or promotional assistance. They are mentioned solely on merit for their contributions in providing valuable services for Americans abroad.

To the personnel of the foreign consulates based in New York and to my fellow American travelers whose stimulating questions provoked research, I wish to extend my thanks.

I also wish to acknowledge the following for supplying much of the information in this book:

American Express Company, 65 Broadway, N.Y., N.Y. 10006

American Youth Hostels, Inc., 20 West 17th St., N.Y., N.Y. 10011

International Air Transport Association, 211 E. 43rd St., N.Y., N.Y. 10017

Pan American Airlines, 200 Park Ave., N.Y., N.Y. 10017

Perera Company, Inc, 29 Broadway, N.Y., N.Y. 10006

Trails West/American Trails, Great Neck, N.Y. 10023

Travel Information Bureau, P.O. Box 105, Kings Park, N.Y.

U.S. Department of Health, Education and Welfare, Washington, D.C.

U.S. Office of Special Counsel Services, Washington, D.C.

U.S. State Department, Washington, D.C.

And the following individuals:

Editing: Linda Myers
Typing: Gloria Sperazza
Maps: Richard Poggioli

PRE-TRAVEL CHECK LIST

1. Leave the following information with a relative or close friend:
   Passport number and personal information
   Travelers' check numbers
   Names and numbers of credit cards
   Checking account numbers (See Passports & Documents.)
2. Make arrangements to have money sent to you in case of emergency. (See Money.)
3. In case of emergency leave your itinerary with a close friend, relative, or at your place of business. (See Mail.)
4. Students traveling during the summer: make arrangements for the fall semester before leaving, and return home in time for registration. Also check to see if you can receive any credits for your travel experience.
5. Arrange for the post office to hold your mail, or ask a trusted friend or neighbor to collect it daily and to keep an eye on things.
6. Stop paper and milk delivery. Notify police that you are leaving. Install an automatic light that goes on at night.
7. Pay bills, rent and insurance premiums, or leave checks for same.
8. Clean your apartment or house. Disconnect radio, TV, and other electrical appliances. LOCK THE DOOR.
9. Board your plants and pets.
10. If leaving for more than a month or two, disconnect the battery cables in your car.
11. If leaving your car in a long-term parking lot at an airport or pier, make sure you don't lose the claim check or the keys. While on your trip, keep the claim check with your important papers—not in your pocket, or lock claim check in the glove compartment of your car.

TO MY PARENTS

Who proved that the generation gap exists only in the minds of the uninvolved.

PASSPORTS AND OTHER DOCUMENTS

What documents are important to me?

Whether you are a tourist or a hitchhiking student, you will need your passport, world health certificate and currency or travelers' checks. You may also need: airline and/or rail tickets, health and/or accident insurance identification card, student card, youth hostel card, credit cards, military ID cards and driver's license.

What is a passport?

A passport is an official document that identifies the bearer's nationality and citizenship. It requests that the bearer be given protection, lawful aid and safe passage while traveling or living in foreign countries recognized by the Federal government.

Who needs a passport?

Anyone who wishes to travel outside of the continental United States, Alaska, Hawaii or U.S. possessions, such as Puerto Rico. Special arrangements between the United States and Canada and between the United States and Mexico enable travelers to enter and exit without need of passport.

Where can I apply for a passport?

You can apply at a Passport Agency (located in Boston, Chicago, Honolulu, Los Angeles, Miami, New Orleans, New York, Philadelphia, San Francisco, Seattle and Washington. D.C.) or before a clerk of any probate court or before a designated postal clerk. Look in your local telephone book for Passport Agency or court addresses, or contact your local post office for the nearest postal facility accepting passport applications.

What is required to obtain a passport?

You must prove that you are a citizen of the U.S. Bring proof of citizenship or naturalization in the form of a birth certificate, baptismal certificate or previous passport. NOT ALL BIRTH CERTIFICATES ARE ACCEPTABLE. Call the Passport Agency to make sure.

You will need two 2½ x 2½-inch photographs taken within six months of your application. Black and white or color are acceptable. Photographs must be full-face on unglazed paper with a light background. Vending machine photos are not acceptable.

Your passport picture should present you as well-groomed. When applying for visas, your passport photo may be the controlling factor in approval or denial.

Who may be included in a passport?

The husband or wife of the bearer.

Unmarried minor children, including step-children and adopted children. (A minor is under 18 years of age.)

Unmarried minor brothers or sisters.

It is advisable for each member of a family to have an individual passport. Many times members of a family will split up while traveling, then meet again at a later date. Thus, with only one family passport some members are left without identification. Should the passport be lost, all would suffer the consequences and inconveniences.

How much does a passport cost?

Ten dollars ($10), payable by certified, personal or travelers' check, or money order. There is also a two dollar ($2) fee for handling of your application at the local level. In most cases a mailing charge of 50¢ is added.

How long does it take to receive a passport?

Normally about two weeks. However, from early spring to midsummer it can take 3 to 6 weeks, depending on the area of the country in which you reside.

In an emergency present your airline or boat ticket or other proof of intent to depart, to your county passport agency. Your passport will be ready overnight.

(AVOID DELAYS IN GETTING VISAS—PLAN IN ADVANCE OF YOUR DEPARTURE DATE.)

Can I get a passport by mail?

Only if you have had a passport issued in your name within eight years of your new application. You cannot get one by mail if your current passport was issued before your eighteenth birthday, or if you want an additional member of the family included.

How long is a passport valid?

Five years from date of issue.

Is it O.K. to travel with a passport ready to expire?
Can I get it renewed while abroad?

Yes, as long as it is valid. Go to the nearest American Embassy office.

If you are planning a trip and your passport will expire before you return to the U.S.A., apply for a new one prior to your departure. Applying for a new passport while abroad can be extremely inconvenient.

How do I renew my passport?

Present your current valid passport to your nearest Passport Agency. Follow the same procedure used when applying for the original passport. Two photos, the fee and the application are still required, but your passport will serve as your identification.

When must I present my passport?

To embassy officials when applying for a visa; to customs officials; to airlines when buying a ticket to a foreign country and again at departing; during legal money exchanges; and when purchasing duty-free goods. Sometimes hotels will hold your passport for the length of your stay.

What happens if my passport is stolen or lost?

THIS IS VERY SERIOUS.

A passport is your freedom; without it you are stranded with no identity. You cannot leave the country, cash travelers' checks or change money, nor can you check into a hotel.

The first thing to do is notify local authorities. Next, notify the nearest American embassy or consulate.

Your passport is the most important of all your documents. Everyone from the Hilton set to hitchhikers should be fearful of loss or theft. Your first concern is preventing loss or theft; your second is replacing it as fast as possible.

You must prove who you are in order to get a new passport. Each year embassies all over the world are plagued with English-speaking foreigners claiming to be John Does from Cincinnati, who have lost their passports and want new ones. That the embassies are cautious in issuing new passports is understandable. You are under suspicion until you prove who you are.

If you have identification, such as a birth certificate or a driver's license, it will facilitate matters. Most important, keep a record of your passport number and place of issuance. After an embassy has checked you out thoroughly, you will be issued a temporary three-month passport. Your case will entail further investigation.

Your passport and health certificate should be kept together and carried with you at all times. You will always need both when entering and exiting a foreign country. NEVER leave them in your room. NEVER carry them in your back pocket or in any other place accessible to pickpockets or thieves.

It is best to make two records of your passport and travelers' check numbers, date and place of issuance. Leave one copy with a relative or a friend back home. Keep the other copy in your luggage. As a further precaution, write your passport number and travelers' check numbers on the back of your belt.

Is it O.K. to carry my passport in my luggage?

No. Your passport must be easily accessible at all times, i.e., customs, border checks, train conductors, etc.

Where is the best place to carry my documents?

For tourists, a plain billfold or a passport case can be used for all your papers. Use a paper clip to fasten your health card to the last page of your passport.

Never keep any documents, currency or checks in your back pocket, nor leave them in an unguarded suitcase or in your hotel room. If you do not wish to carry them, check them along with other valuables at your hotel desk.

Students and hitchhikers should take more elaborate steps for the safety and protection of their valuables. A cloth (or leather) pouch, as in Figures 1 and 2, is worn around the neck or around the waist. The belt pouch, as in Figure 3, slides on the belt like an eyeglass case. Figure 4 is a military pocket.

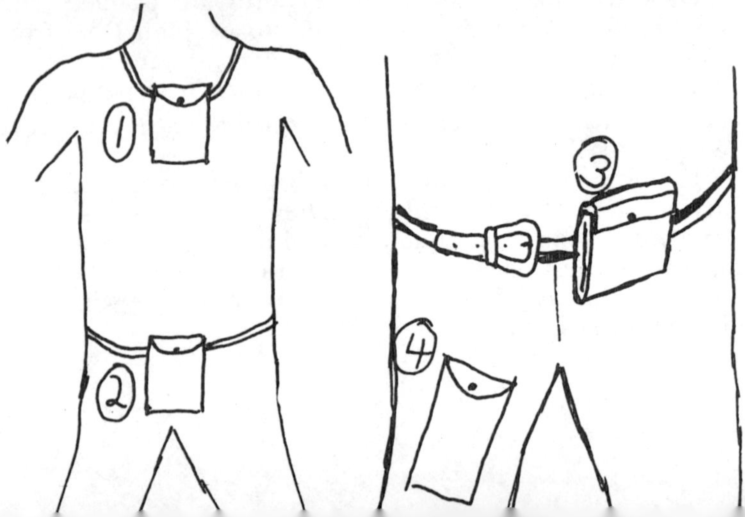

Passport and other papers should be wrapped in a plastic bag before being put into a pouch: this will protect them from dirt and moisture. These pouches can be purchased in the sporting goods departments of many stores. Tailors will make them for a very small fee.

When camping out or staying in youth hostels, passports and other valuables should be kept with you in your sleeping bag.

Another very popular item with young travelers is the hippie-type shoulder sack. Almost all the travelers I ever met who had experienced thefts carried this type of gear. It is easily put aside and forgotten and readily accessible to pick-pockets.

GIRLS CARRYING PURSES: BE SURE TO KEEP AN EYE ON THEM AND BE SURE THEY HAVE ZIPPERS OR STRONG CATCHES.

What is the World Service Authority?

An organization which issues a world passport based on the philosophy of the United Nations Universal Declaration of Human Rights, Article 13:

"(1) Everyone has the right to freedom of movement and residence within the borders of each state."

"(2) Everyone has the right to leave any country, including his own, and to return to his country."

Holding this passport makes you a "Citizen of the World." However, you still retain your U.S. citizenship.

This passport has been recognized by thirteen nations and is on file with seventy-seven others. For further information write to: World Service Authority, Schillerstrasse 10, Basle, Switzerland.

TUDENT IDENTIFICATION CARD

What is it?

A student identification card indicates that the bearer is registered at an institute of learning.

What are its uses?

It will make available various discounts at hotels, restaurants, and places of entertainment. It will give you free or reduced admissions to many museums.

In most places throughout the world only the International Student Identification Card will be accepted. This card is available at: Council on International Educational Exchange, 777 United Nations Plaza, New York, N.Y. 10017. Tel: 212-661-0310.

SOFA, 1560 Broadway, New York, N.Y. 10036. Tel: 212-586-2080. SOFA requests a photo copy of your local ID card, one photograph, a self-addressed stamped envelope, plus $2.00.

International Student Visitors Service, 866 Second Ave., New York, N.Y. 10017 (cost $2.00) Tel: 212-421-6680.

American Union of Students, 127 East 27th St., New York, N.Y. accepts members between the ages of 18 and 35 who are still students or recent graduates. Membership costs $10.00 annually, which includes other AUS services.

International ID cards may be obtained in London, Amsterdam and nearly every major city in Europe. Any tourist information center will supply you with addresses of student organizations.

Can non-students utilize these cards?

No. However, a driver's license, credit card, military ID card or any similar document will enable you to bluff your way through most box offices and entrances. Sometimes no one will bother to check whatever card you use.

Non-students will find it easy to purchase forged ID cards throughout the world. A black marketeer is your best bet. (See Black Market) A forgery costs $3.00 to $5.00 depending on where you are.

YOUTH HOSTEL CARD

What is it?

A valid card from the American Youth Hostel Association will enable you to enjoy the services of youth hostels throughout the U.S. and the world. Cards are valid for one year. There is no age limit; in some areas, regulations prohibit anyone over 25 years from staying at a hostel.

YHA fees are as follows: $5.00, 18 years old or under; $8.00 18-20 years; $10.00, 21 years and older.

TIP: It is less expensive to join a Youth Hostel Organization in Europe; the cost there is approximately $6 to $8 U.S. However, it is advisable to purchase a youth hostel card before leaving the U.S., as the card is not always available in

European hostels. To obtain a card write to: American Youth Hostels Inc., DeLaplane, Virginia 22025 (Also available at local hostels)

To obtain a card write to American Youth Hostel Association, 20 West 17th St., New York, N.Y. 10011.

TIP: It is less expensive to join a youth hostel organization in Europe; cost there is approximately $6.00.

AIRLINE, BOAT, BUS AND TRAIN TICKETS

Tickets should be kept with other important documents, i.e., passport, health certificate, currency. Ticket serial numbers should be recorded and kept in an easily accessible place. In event of loss, notify local authorities and the appropriate ticket office.

If you lose an airline ticket and cannot reach the company that issued it, any major international airline will help you. You must prove who you are and give correct details regarding where and when you purchased the lost ticket, and serial numbers if known.

The same details should be given in case of loss of boat tickets. Refunds for lost bus and/or rail tickets are rare.

Your passport number is usually recorded on the face of your Eurailpass; no refund is possible in the event of loss or theft. (For further information, see Transportation).

INTERNATIONAL DRIVER'S LICENSE

This is requ red to drive *legally* in most countries throughout the world. To obtain one from your local automobile association, you need a valid driver's license, two photographs and $3.00.

YOUR LOCAL DRIVER'S LICENSE MUST ACCOMPANY YOUR INTERNATIONAL PERMIT AT ALL TIMES.

It is possible to obtain a driver's license in some foreign countries by presenting your American license and passing a written examination.

MILITARY IDENTIFICATION

If you are registered with the Selective Service or if you are a member of the Reserves, you are legally required to notify your local draft board of change of address or of intent to travel abroad. Young men celebrating their 18th birthday while traveling abroad must register within 30 days with the Selective Service at the nearest United States Embassy or representative of same.

Draft cards and/or other military identification should be carried with you at all times. In the event of loss or theft, be sure to notify local and American authorities in the area.

VISAS

What is a visa?

A visa is an official signature or an endorsement on a passport, showing that it has been examined and approved and that the bearer may enter the country or pass through it. A visa gives the same basic information as an invitation to a country club dance: the name of the bearer, the time of arrival, the length of stay, and the purpose of the visit.

Where do you get a visa?

In the United States go to the consulate or representative of the country you wish to visit, situated in the following cities: Washington, D.C., New York, New Orleans, Los Angeles, San Francisco, and Chicago. If you cannot visit one of these consulates personally, many travel agents will obtain the proper visas for you for each country you plan to visit.

What is a Visa Agency?

You can find a visa agency through your local travel agent. You simply send your passport and a list of the countries you wish to visit to a visa agency, and they do the rest of the legwork. They add a service charge to the cost of each visa. Remember: visas to many countries are free. If you have the time to get a visa by yourself, do so.

Can I get a visa after I have left the United States?

Yes. The tourist who is on a one or two-week vacation is advised to have all visas arranged before leaving the United States. The traveler with more time on his hands, such as the college student and hitchhiker, should pick up visas as he goes. Tourists information centers in major foreign cities will supply you with a list of the names and addresses of consulates to see for visas.

You will also find that traveling to various sections of town to see the consulates will add to your sightseeing pleasure. The consulates will supply you with any information and will answer any questions.

Visas are less expensive when purchased outside the continental United States.

What requirements are necessary to obtain a visa?

Many countries in Asia and Eastern Europe require three things: (1) proof of reasonable means of support; (2) an onward ticket, or through passage; (3) a visa for the next country on your itinerary.

What is meant by reasonable means of support?

You must be able to prove that you can sustain yourself while visiting. Many countries will require you to show $10 a-day for every day that your visa is valid. For example, on a 30-day visa you must show $300. However, you are not required to spend any specific amount.

What is meant by onward ticket?

Before you receive a visa you must prove that you have a prepaid boat, plane, or railroad ticket to leave. This will prevent you from becoming stranded.

Some countries will stamp your ticket NON-TRANSFERABLE, thus preventing you from selling it. Other countries will record your ticket number in your passport with a special stamp, thereby making it impossible for you to sell your ticket.

When is it best to get visas in advance?

For all countries you plan to visit in Eastern Europe and Asia. For example, let's say you've purchased an airline ticket from New York to Budapest, Prague and Moscow. You would not be allowed to enter Budapest until you have shown that you have visas for Prague and Moscow.

Which Asian countries do not require visas in advance?

Israel, India, Malaysia, Thailand, Hong Kong, and Singapore offer visas to American travelers at port of entry. (See map chapters for additional information.)

Do I need a visa for every country?

No. Most Western European countries do not require visas. In fact, it is as easy to go from Switzerland to Italy as it is to go from New York to New Jersey. Traveling through Western Europe is much like traveling through the United States. Passports are stamped only when entering or exiting a country. The stamp of each country has its own distinct size, shape, and color. It is a good idea to ask for these stamps at each border. If you are not keeping a diary, they serve as an excellent log of your travels.

How many types of visas are there?

Very many. There are four basic types of visas: transit, tourist, multiple entry tourist, and work.

What is a transit visa?

A transit visa is issued when you are passing through a country and not intending to stay very long. For example, to travel from Turkey to Yugoslavia or vice versa by land, you must cross Bulgaria. At the Bulgarian border you must show proof that you will be allowed to enter the country which is your destination—either Yugoslavia or Turkey. (In this case, possession of an American passport constitutes proof.) Border officials will then issue you a transit visa allowing you a specified number of days to pass through Bulgaria.

What is a tourist visa?

A tourist visa is good for only one journey to a country, after which it must be renewed.

What is a multple entry tourist visa?

This type of visa, issued in countries such as South Korea, Taiwan, and Japan is good for 48 months or for the life of the passport, whichever expires first. It allows a tourist a 30, 60, or 90-day visit, depending on the country. The tourist can return any time within the 48 month period without filling out new forms and encountering similar inconveniences.

In some cases, a multiple entry visa is a must. For example, if going from India to Nepal and back to India.

What is a work visa?

Work visas are extremely hard to get, because there is much unemployment throughout the world. It is advisable to get a work visa in America before you leave. It is difficult to obtain work visas within most countries of the world. (See chapter on Working Abroad.)

How much does a visa cost?

In many cases, with an American passport, visas are free. In some countries, such as Laos, Cambodia, Hungary, Poland and others, a fee is charged, often as much as $5.00. In many countries, postage stamps are permanently affixed to your visa, as a receipt for the fee you have paid.

In many Eastern European countries, not only do you pay for a visa but, you must convert and spend money for each day you are there. (This is called token money) In cases like this, it is wise to get the shortest visa possible; it is fairly easy to extend it.

Token money cannot be converted back to dollars. If you get a seven-day visa, you will be required to spend $35 at $5 a day. Should you leave after three days, you would have $20 of unspent local money left over. If you get a two-day visa and extend it day by day, you won't get stuck with a large amount of non-negotiable local currency.

Which countries require token money?

Hungary, $5.00 per day; Czechoslovakia, $5.00 per day; Poland, $9.00 per day; East Berlin, $1.50 per day. (For more information see Map chapter).

What is the best type of photo for a visa?

Photographs from vending machines are acceptable in most countries. (For more information, see chapter on Photos.)

What if I run out of passport pages for my visas?

It is not likely that you'll run out of space in your passport. If you do, go to an American Embassy or consulate for additional pages.

Does it matter which passport page a visa is put on?

No. It is a good idea to use a blank page. Stamps are often overlapped. Many times a new stamp is put on top of a still valid visa, making it hard to read.

What length visa is best?

Except for the type where daily token money is charged, it is advisable to get a visa with the longest possible time period. Example: if you are entitled to a 30-day visa and have the money to cover it, don't ask for a two-week visa; you'd have to go through unnecessary red tape to extend it if you decide to stay longer.

Can a visa be extended within a foreign country?

In most cases, yes, with a slight service charge. For example, in Indonesia, it costs $15 to extend a visa for even one day.

In other countries, such as Hungary and Czechoslovakia, the daily token money is the only requirement for extending a visa.

In some of the Asian countries, such as Singapore and Malaysia, you simply must have a good reason for staying longer.

If I have met all requirements—money, prepaid transportation, proper visas—is it possible to be denied entry to a country?

Absolutely, because of physical appearance. (See American Image).

Are there any other reasons I might be denied entry to a country?

Many countries have no diplomatic ties with their neighbors. If you have the stamp of a given country on your passport, you might not be allowed into a neighboring country. If you have the stamp of South Vietnam on your passport, you will not be allowed into any Communist country and vice versa.

What is a loose visa?

It is issued by a country, such as Israel, having political difficulties with other countries. An Israeli stamp on your passport would deny you entry into Arab countries and countries of Arab sympathizers, such as Russia. Therefore, Israel issues a loose visa, which is later removed from your passport, leaving no record of your visit.

HEALTH

What precautions should I take before leaving home?

If you have not had dental and medical checkups recently, get them before you leave. Once you leave the States, medical treatment can be expensive, and a good doctor may be hard to find.

If you must carry any medicines with you, make sure they are clearly labeled and that you have a prescription for each one.

If you are allergic to any medications, such as penicillin, or if you are a diabetic or have any conditions or handicaps that require special or emergency care, make sure you have such identification with you at all times. It can be a dog tag around your neck, a bracelet, a card in your wallet, or a slip of paper clipped in your certificate of vaccination booklet or onto the back page of your passport.

When leaving the London-Paris-Rome circuit for any other parts of Europe or Asia, you will find minor stomach disorders or intestinal viruses very common. A change of food, water, and climate can play havoc with your system. There are a number of patent medications available to combat these illnesses, but it is always best to check with your doctor before leaving. Never take a friend's prescription.

TIP: What most travelers don't seem to realize is that a change in your environment can not only cause diarrhea (Montezuma's revenge) but can also cause constipation. Be sure to carry a reliable laxative.

Can I get health insurance to cover me abroad?

Yes. First, find out if your present health insurance policy covers you while you are abroad. Secondly, health insurance can be obtained from a number of companies, such as Allstate or Continental Casualty Co., which includes health and baggage insurance in its policies. Most companies do not sell baggage insurance without medical insurance. For more information contact the nearest Allstate or Continental Casualty Co. office.

The American Youth Hostel Association offers travel insurance at reasonable rates for its members. Write: AYH, National Campus, Delaplane, Virginia 22025.

IMMUNIZATION

I have met some people who wanted to travel abroad but shuddered at the thought of getting the required shots. Since almost every country in the world has adopted the World Health Organization's standards and regulations, certain vaccination certificates for smallpox, cholera and/or yellow fever are necessary.

It is the opinion of the author that if you plan to leave Western Europe (the London-Paris-Rome circuit), you should be vaccinated for smallpox.

According to medical authorities, and my left arm, the smallpox immunization is not an injection but a drop of serum placed on the skin and a few painless scratches, after which a scab usually forms within a few days.

Recently the requirements for smallpox immunizations have been lifted. The following information was supplied by the Department of Health, Education and Welfare and is a public health service recommendation on smallpox vaccinations (as of October 1, 1971).

"Effective immediately a Smallpox Vaccination Certificate as a condition of entry into the United States shall be requested only of those persons who, within the preceding 14 ays have been in a country reporting a smallpox infected ea(s).

"At present these countries are: Botswana, Democratic Republic of the Congo, Ethiopia, India, Indonesia, Malaysia, Muscat and Oman, Nepal, Pakistan (West), and the Sudan. Those persons not in possession of a valid Smallpox Vaccination Certificate may be issued a surveillance order and placed under surveillance by the State and/or local health departments.

"It is the recommendation of the Public Health Service that persons planning travel to Brazil, to any country in Africa, or to any country in Southeast Asia be vaccinated against smallpox for their own protection."

All immunizations must be recorded in the official WHO Certificate of Vaccination booklet, which is available through your local Board of Health, Passport Office, some local travel agencies and WHO.

Smallpox and cholera vaccinations must not only be recorded, but an additional validation stamp administered by your local board of health must also be added.

According to WHO regulations, vaccination certificates are valid for the following specified time periods:

Smallpox: Must be recorded and validated by your local board of health in health certificate booklet; 1 vaccination—time of validity: not less than 8 days or more than 3 years.

Cholera: Must be recorded and validated by your local board of health in health certificate booklet; 2 shots 7 to 10 days apart—time of validity: not less than 6 days or more than 6 months.

Yellow Fever: Yellow fever shots are required by some nations when a traveler has just arrived from infected areas such as South America and Africa; 1 vaccination—time of validity: not less than 10 days or more than 10 years.

The following immunizations are not required by the WHO regulations. (However, I do recommend them for a prolonged stay in areas where the following have recently been recorded. Always check with your embassy and doctor first).

Typhus: Optional—2 shots 7 to 10 days apart, not valid after 6 years.

Typhoid-Paratyphoid: Optional—but advisable for pro- longed stay in infected areas; 3 shots 7 to 28 days ap-

not valid after 1 year.

Tetanus: Optional—but advisable for prolonged stay in infected areas. 1 shot—valid for 1 year.

Malaria: (Pill) Should be taken for at least 2 weeks prior to entry of infected areas and for one week after leaving same. These pills have no side effects. They come in two strengths for daily or weekly ingestion. Check with your doctor.

NOTE: Typhoid, Paratyphoid, Cholera, and Tetanus vaccinations sometimes cause a slight reaction. You should allow time afterwards for a slight fever and sore arm. If you are really eager to travel and see all the places you have always dreamed of, the few minutes of discomfort are worth it. Before I left on my trip I received eight shots. When I visited countries where smallpox, cholera and other epidemics are commonplace, I was glad I had traded a few moments of pain for the years of agony I might have suffered with these diseases.

Remember, it only hurts for a little while.

SCHEDULING VACCINATIONS WHILE ABROAD

During prolonged travel the validity of your immunization may expire. For example, a cholera vaccination is only valid for six months. Should you stay in an infected area longer than that, you would need another injection for further protection. If possible, schedule your trip so that you are not in an infected or remote area when your immunization expires.

For your own protection, arrange to receive your injection at the cleanest facilities available to avoid contracting a contagious disease. In remote areas the same needle may be used on several patients. Avoid such treatment.

How can I keep abreast of the latest health information while abroad?

Visit or call the embassies of the countries on your itinerary (as you travel). Ask for specific health requirements such as immunizations. Also ask about recent epidemics and any changes in health requirements of which travelers should be aware.

Read *The In[illegible] ational Herald Tribune* and other daily [illegible] wh[illegible] often give information of this type. Ask [illegible] rt, [illegible] s.

an extra 50¢ or a dollar and buy yourself a good meal.

Never eat with your fingers. Even if you wash, the water may be impure.

Food such as bread or sandwiches may be impossible to eat without your hands. Therefore hold it by one corner or the crust. Eat everything except the piece you hold.

Even if you can make it without food and water for a while, you still need a good night's sleep. Be sure to get proper rest.

Keep your clothing as well as yourself clean by washing regularly.

SELLING BLOOD

In many countries where religious beliefs forbid local inhabitants to donate blood, tourists and travelers alike are often offered outrageously high prices for blood. Prices can run anywhere from a few dollars to $30.00 for only 400 c.c. (approximately a pint).

The traveler on a limited budget who is running low on funds may think this is an easy way to pick up cash. It is also an easy way to pick up disease. I have seen many of my fellow travelers come down with hepatitis after donating blood. Medical authorities have told me that this unsanitary practice of using the same needle over and over again is an excellent means of transmitting disease.

Throughout Europe and Asia people commonly sell their blood to raise money to buy drugs. High on dope, low on resistance, lack of nourishing food, they donate blood as often as twice a week in places lacking sanitary facilities. Many Americans have caught various diseases under such circumstances and have been left to die in remote hospitals.

You will probably say, "This could not happen to me," but if you go broke almost 10,000 miles from home, almost anything can happen. I met four young Americans just starting out on their journey, all in good health and with sufficient funds. A month later, 2,000 miles away I met two of the four. Both were ill and nearly broke. I asked about their two companions. I found that one was dead, and the other was in a hospital. It seems they did not know how to handle their finances, and, most important, they were not aware of health hazards.

HELLO MISTER, WANNA BUY MY SISTER

Because of the liberalization of morality and ubiquitous prostitution, there is a worldwide epidemic of venereal disease. One should, therefore, be very particular in choosing his partner for sex and take every precaution to avoid disease.

How do I know if I have VD?

According to a spokesman for the American Social Health Association, two most common venereal diseases in the fast-growing epidemic are syphilis and gonorrhea, which are transmitted only by sexual contact. Only a doctor, after performing a series of tests, can tell if you have VD.

What should I do if I think I have VD?

See a doctor immediately. Do not rely on home remedies or advice from friends. In most countries special VD clinics have been established, and prompt and proper medical attention is readily available.

You must be extremely careful in certain areas, such as Southeast Asia, where it's been said, "If the VC don't get you, the VD will."

IMPORTANT NOTE: Having VD is a criminal offense in some places. According to an article in *Parade Magazine (10/10/71),* "VD is a criminal offense in the Soviet Union". In the Georgian Republic where the law is most strictly enforced, one receives his cure in prison. The penalty for spreading VD is one to five years in prison, depending on whom, and how many, one infects.

The article continues, "The British are using yet another expedient in their campaign to eradicate VD." Many patients, mistakenly believing one shot of penicillin will cure them, give false addresses and cannot be contacted. Therefore, public health officials in Birmingham, England have requested a local radio station to broadcast the name, age, sex and nationality of defaulters on VD treatment. As a result, some patients have returned to complete their cure.

TOILETS

Bathroom facilities throughout the world differ greatly. Toilets (or "Ivory Thrones" as they are affectionately called) are found in abundance throughout Western Europe; tourists staying in hotels there need not fear of being inconvenienced.

However, once you venture into the rural areas of Europe

and into the even more rural areas of Asia and the Middle East, toilets become rarer and rarer. The most popular toilet used in these areas is a porcelain square at floor level with a hole in the center and a footprint on either side. For best results, place feet in appropriate footprints and assume a squatting position directly over the hole in the center. Caution: keep pants clear after the squatting position has been assumed.

At first, you'll probably find this routine somewhat uncomfortable. But it will grow on you, and eventually you'll accept it as being more natural than anything you've previously encountered.

In Paris you will find something which looks like a round metal telephone booth located on the sidewalks near the curb. This is actually a urinal for men.

In many Asian countries men and women enter the public toilets by separate doorways, but they lead to a common room without partitions.

Travelers should also be aware that in many parts of Europe washroom attendants of the opposite sex may enter the washrooms completely unannounced to perform their daily chores.

Of course, in major cities you'll always be able to treat yourself to a grand, old-fashioned, American-style toilet simply by going to an American embassy or to any prestigious hotel. Since many other people will follow this tip, to avoid disease, wipe the top of the toilet seat or spread paper on it prior to using.

A problem faced by many tourists, even in Western Europe, is a lack of toilet paper. The shortage is so severe in the rural areas of Asia and the Middle East that it is advisable to carry your own toilet paper with you. Guard it well; thieves abound. If you do run short, you can "borrow" some from public toilets in railway stations, bus terminals, airports, embassies and large tourist hotels. A certain amount of this "borrowing" is expected annually.

If you should suddenly find yourself in an area where toilet paper is nonexistent, remember that newspapers, magazines, currency, leaves and even pages of a guide book can serve a valuable purpose.

Additional information on health requirements and regulations and advice on precautions to take in each country can be found in the map section of this book.

THE AMERICAN IMAGE

I

Throughout the '30's, '40's and '50's and even into the early '60's there were three basic types of travelers.

First, there were the people who booked their entire trips through travel agents and saw the world through the window of an air-conditioned tour bus. They would travel around the world without ever leaving the comfort of middle class U.S.A.

Secondly, there were the college students, secretaries, teachers and others who would save up for years to travel. They were usually found wandering around Europe with all the popular guide books sticking out of their pockets. In order to live within their budget, they all ate and slept in the recommended places—when there was room. But for some reason they would never be able to stick to their budget. Many found the only thing those soft cover guide books were good for was bathroom stationery in one of those recommended pensions.

The third type of traveler was "The-world-is-my-home" type of guy who hitchhiked, hopped freighters and occasionally worked his way from place to place.

In the 60's with fast, efficient air transportation and reduced student and youth fares, traveling became a year-round adventure for millions. No longer are there three distinct classes of Americans traveling abroad. Now there are two basic groups—tourists and travelers.

A tourist is a person who likes to travel living in the style to which he is accustomed. Tourists usually have travel agents pre-arrange their transportation and hotel bookings. Because of changes in climate, food, and water, the tourist will find that living in larger Western-style hotels will not play havoc with his health. Also tourists can venture out into local towns and villages and mix with people in exotic countries yet return to the security of the hotel and step back into their own way of life at will. For the tourist or businessman on a short one- or two-week trip this is the only way to travel. It allows both safety and comfort in foreign surroundings.

A traveler is anyone other than a tourist. Travelers are

usually on a budget. They take more than the conventional one or two weeks for their journey, most often a month or more. This group includes at one end of the spectrum, students, teachers and secretaries and at the other end hitch-hikers, and hippies. Some travelers go native, eating, sleeping and living with the local people.

However you go abroad, as a tourist or a traveler the information in this book will be valuable to you.

II

Americans are perhaps the most self-conscious people in the world. We worry about our image abroad. When we visit another country, we are just as curious to find out what they think of us as we are to discover what they are like.

It would be unfair to generalize and say that they all hate us or love us. Even people of Communist countries have their own individual opinions about America. People in most parts of the world have seen America only in the movies. All they know is what Hollywood has shown them—that there are cowboys in Texas, gangsters in Chicago and that we are all rich.

Our wealth is obvious because we are able to travel, even though our budgets may be very small. An American hippie living in India might spend only 50¢ a day and may not even carry $50 altogether. By American standards he is poor. However, the average Indian family earns only $70 a year. By their standards that hippie is spending a small fortune. Even a tourist in western Europe spending $10 or $15 a night in a hotel is often spending more than a native of that country can earn in a day.

What most foreigners do not realize is that many traveling Americans worked hard and saved for a long time to take their trip.

What most Americans don't realize is that compared to many we were brought up in a land of plenty.

Our educational system has failed to teach us two things. One is how to make money. The other is, if you should be fortunate enough to make a lot of money, *what in hell to do with it!!!*

This lack of economic common sense has left the American tourist and traveler extremely vulnerable. He is fair game for any con artist who comes along. An American who is naive about the value of the dollar abroad may unconsciously create envy among foreigners and add to the already tarnished image of America. The information in this book by helping you save money will also help change the sucker image Americans have and help you to gain the respect of the foreign merchants.

PRIDE

There is one very important thing that Americans can learn by traveling. No matter how small or politically insignificant a country may be, the people are nationalistic and take a great deal of pride in their homeland. When the late President Kennedy said, "Ask not what your country can do for you but what you can do for your country," people around the world applauded. They saw that Americans were patriotic too. However, with the assassination of President Kennedy and a series of controversial affairs, such as the Vietnam War, student unrest and race riots, our image crumbled.

Despite all the bad publicity we have had, there are still millions of Americans who are proud of their country.

Regardless of your politics, while abroad, you are a roving representative for America. Foreigners will ask questions and hang on your every word. You may be the only American they have ever met. For some you may be the only source of information they will be able to obtain about America.

If you are visiting a country with living conditions far below America's, be tactful. A remark you make in jest might be taken seriously. No matter what their living standard is, foreigners have pride and feelings too. They will naturally be offended if you make disparaging remarks about their country.

Most of all, watch what you say about your own country. Many people have absolutely no respect for a man who criticizes his own homeland. If you have nothing good to say about America, it is best you say nothing at all.

SHOW ME YOUR COLORS NO, YOU SHOW ME YOURS FIRST

Until you speak, you may easily be mistaken for a Frenchman, German, Italian or Canadian. Not everyone who travels is American, so don't be surprised if someone stops you on the street and asks what country you're from. You may find that your nationality will be the controlling factor in the attitude a foreigner will have toward you. It can make you friends as well as enemies. To avoid confrontation with foreigners who are anti-American, many American travelers claim a more neutral nation such as Canada, England or Australia as home.

Whether you are proud of being an American or not, I still recommend being as neutral as possible. In other words, in order to avoid embarrassing confrontations don't show your colors until they show theirs.

You will find it much more rewarding while you travel to meet people and have them like you for yourself rather than for your nationality.

AMERICAN FLAGS AND EMBLEMS

Many people display American flags and emblems on luggage and clothing. Even hitchhikers often hold up a flag instead of their thumbs in order to get a ride. The advantages and disadvantages of displaying emblems and flags could fill a long list. For example, many hitchhikers claim that displaying an American flag has gotten them rides, while others claim that was the reason a car passed them and picked up another hitchhiker displaying the flag of another nation.

NO HIPPIES ALLOWED

Almost every American has his own idea about what a hippie is. But people throughout the rest of the world know only what Hollywood has told them. If an American traveler does not have a GI haircut, shirt and tie, Samsonite luggage, and is not staying in the Hilton, he is automatically a hippie.

I do not consider myself a hippie, but because I was carrying a back pack and not staying in the Hilton, I was classified as a hippie by many people around the world. (Since no one likes to be labeled, and I do not want to offend anyone, try to remember that the term hippie or hippie-type as used in this book applies to anyone of any age or background traveling on a smaller budget than the average tourist. It is in no way meant to reflect on the way a person thinks.)

I have found that anyone who wears levis, or carries a back pack, or even Americans traveling on a budget are often considered hippies. During my travels I have witnessed ridiculous events which confirmed this. For example, I once saw a busload of middle-aged tourists entering Morocco. Their driver was completely bald, yet he had a goatee. He was considered a hippie, and the bus was denied entry.

This happens to many Americans, young and old, when applying for visas or crossing borders. It is a shame, but customs officials judge you by what is on your head instead of by what is inside. This does not occur only in isolated spots. A well organized, international, suppress-the-hippie movement is underway. The rationale for this is that hippies are synonymous with drugs. Political pressure to stop the flow of illicit drug traffic has made it extremely rough on anyone who in even the remotest way resembles a hippie.

Another reason for the suppress-the-hippie movement is economic. Many countries would rather fill their cities with clean-cut American tourists who spend $30 a day than put up with budget-minded, hippie-types who may go broke and cause trouble.

Many countries have not only banned hippies but anyone who is not a tourist. In fact, "No Hippies Allowed" signs are posted in many foreign embassies, and often the sale of boat, air and train tickets is denied to anyone fitting their description.

Some countries have even made it the national policy to keep out hippies. On the bulletin board in the American Embassy in Kabul, Afghanistan, among notices and warnings to travelers was one which read:

> Pakistan Gazette, Saturday, January 31, 1970, Islamabad, the capital. Sub-section I of Section 3 of the Foreign Act of 1946. The Central Government is *pleased* to order that no foreigners who belong to the classification of persons commonly known as hippies or beatniks shall enter into Pakistan without the leave of an officer of customs not below the rank of Inspector.

However, this law is not strictly enforced, and even people classified as hard-core hippies are allowed to pass through Pakistan coming and going to Afghanistan and India.

Many young Americans who are classified as hippies by customs officials are harassed when crossing borders or going through customs checks. Their gear is inspected very carefully, and they are questioned. Often qualifications for entrance to countries are strictly enforced, and hippie-types may be denied entry while other Americans with fewer qualifications for visas are let through. If you come across this situation, know your rights and be polite, yet persistent.

Before trying to cross borders or obtain a visa, make sure you fulfill the necessary requirements. If you do, stand your ground. However, if one of the requirements is that anyone with long hair or beards may not be allowed to enter, as in the case of Morocco, then you must comply with these rules.

The following information should help anyone who may be classified as hippie and is planning to travel. These tips will help you circumvent customs regulations legally, avoid hassels and possibly save your life.

TIPS FOR CROSSING BORDERS AND GOING THROUGH CUSTOMS

Long hair and beards

Since long hair automatically makes you a hippie, you will probably have a hard time crossing borders because many countries discriminate against hippies. The following tricks may be used to elude customs officials:

1. Wet hair and pin it back.
2. Pin it up and wear a hat.
3. Some people have even put an ace bandage around their heads and claimed they were in an accident.

You may have some small chance of entering even with long hair. However, should you be caught trying to trick the officials, you will automatically be denied entry. If gaining entry to a particular country means a lot to you, cut your hair and shave. If it is against your principles to do this, then take your chances.

Luggage and Clothing

Instead of carrying a back pack, just buy a collapsible back pack frame, and strap a small piece of luggage or suitcase to it. When approaching borders, put on a shirt and tie, comb your hair, put the back pack frame in your suitcase and cross the border like a neon-lit tourist. (Always be sure to give the name of a good hotel when asked where you're staying). Once you are inside the country and out of sight of customs officials, it will be safe to return to your original attire.

DRUGS

If you in any way, manner, shape or form resemble a hippie, sooner or later you will be stopped and searched for drugs. If you intend to use drugs consume them when you buy them and don't carry them around, especially across borders.

BEGGARS

Since Americans are thought to be rich, you will be the target for every panhandler and beggar throughout the world. In many countries where unemployment and poverty are commonplace the most popular profession is begging.

It is almost impossible not to have some feelings for these people, and many Americans want to help. But panhandling in America is not quite the profession it is in many foreign countries. Certain sections of foreign cities will be completely dominated by beggars and it will not be uncommon to be approached by ten or more at a time within one block.

If you give each one a handout, you will have a never ending battle on your hands. Even if you don't they will follow you for a block or so anyway. As one drops off, another one will pick you up and follow you asking for money.

Often, giving these people a handout will not help them in the least. Many times I have seen a beggar with 10 starving children spend his last $2.00 to buy a watch from a black marketeer. (He probably had gotten $2.00 from begging or panhandling.)

American tourists often fall in love with a young child who is panhandling. After you have looked into his big sad eyes it is extremely difficult to turn him down. I came across such a case in my travels. An American couple fell in love with a young peasant girl who was dirty and in rags. They wanted to send her to school, replace her rags and see that she was fed. A local inhabitant who spoke English told the tourists that they would have to give the money not to the girl but to her parents. The girl would in no way benefit from this because the parents would spend the money foolishly.

It is hard to say it and it may be even harder for you to do, but never give a handout to a beggar. This may hurt at first when you see a starving, helpless fellow human being, but in no way will sticking your hand in your pocket help the millions of people who are in this position. (If you want to help send a contribution to CARE, UNICEF and others.) After a while begging will become so commonplace that you will feel persecuted by these people and become immune to feeling sorry for them.

If you give handouts, you will not only be wasting your money foolishly, but you will be harming the American image by making them think we are soft touches who do not know the value of a dollar.

GOOD SAMARITANS

Nice people don't usually make news, but in my travels I have found that there are people who will go out of their way even at great expense to help a fellow human being. The following are just a few of the good samaritans we feel are worthy of mention

On February 10, 1970, while waiting for a plane at the Bali Beach Airport in Indonesia, I met Gerry R. of Detroit. Gerry had lost his passport, other documents and money and had spent the last three days at the airport broke and hungry. He was trying to borrow money from tourists to fly a thousand miles to Djkarta, the capital of Indonesia, where he could recover his traveler's checks and passport. Gerry's hippie-type appearance repulsed most of the tourists he approached. It was Mr. Peter H. and his wife from New York City who saw the serious predicament Gerry was in and loaned him $35; $32 for the airline ticket, and $3 for his first meal in three days.

On March 13, 1970, I was in Pusan, South Korea. I was traveling with two other young Americans, including John D. from Buffalo. After a day of sightseeing, John realized a pickpocket had relieved him of all his cash. With no money and no ticket for the boat back to Japan, John then started going to hotels and asking American tourists for help. After two unsuccessful days the boat for Japan was ready to leave, and John had almost given up hope. Only three hours before sailing, he ran into the Reverend John C. After hearing John D.'s story, Reverend C. lent him $20 for the boat fare back to Japan.

On April 8, 1970, while in New Delhi, India, I ran into Miss Joan K. (Doc), who had decided to travel around the world before taking her residency. Aware of the substandard health conditions that exist in many parts of Asia, Joan had brought for her own protection a full medical kit and antibiotics. When she saw many of her fellow Americans passing through this area suffering from hepatitis, intestinal viruses and dysentery, she started dispensing free medical aid to needy travelers. In a short time Joan's medicine supply ran out, leaving her to continue her journey unprotected against illness. Fortunately she made it home safely.

On June 11, 1970, I arrived at the railway station on the outskirts of Warsaw, Poland. It was 6:00 a.m., raining, and no one spoke English. Since I had no local money, I was broke until the banks opened at 9:00. I spent two frustrating hours trying to find someone who spoke English or could change money, so I could take a bus into town. Even though the station was crowded, I could find no one who could help me. Finally a woman passing by stopped to ask if she could be of any help. She not only spoke English, but she gave me a bus ticket into town, told me how to find the tourist information center, and because the banks were not yet open, she gave me about one dollar in Polish money. And to top that, she missed her train while helping me!

So to that nameless Polish woman in the railway station and to all the others mentioned here we say "Thank you" for being good samaritans.

We hope that with the help of our readers this list will continue to grow. If you have been helped, helped someone, or heard of a similar story involving a traveler in need, send the details on the attached post card (last page).

THE AMERICAN WAY

Those of us who have never left the borders of America have learned that there are three ways of doing things: the right way, the wrong way, and the American way.

Those of you who finally venture to another country will find there is yet a fourth way of doing things: THEIR WAY.

Discovering these unique social differences can be the most interesting segment of your journey, and overcoming them can be a great challenge.

"When in Rome, do as the Romans do" is extremely good advice. Trying to jam the American way down the throats of foreigners will embarrass you and your fellow American travelers as well as add to the conceited image Americans have abroad. Also keep in mind that many nations were doing it their way long before America ever existed.

The following is a list of some of the basic social differences found throughout Europe, Asia and Australia.

In some places such as Great Britain, milk and beer are not refrigerated and are drunk at room temperature. There are exceptions, such as in large hotels, etc.

In countries such as Great Britain, and Australia, automobiles have right-hand drive and are driven on the left side of the street. Driving in those countries will, therefore, require some adjustment. However, the most dangerous aspect of traveling in such places is being a pedestrian. Most Americans step off the curb and look to the left before crossing a street. However, in countries with right-hand drive, the traffic will come from the right, so don't look to the left.

Numbers: In all of Europe the number (7) is written with a line through it (7). In France, the number (1) looks much like the written letter L (ℓ)

Dates: The date, January 26, 1971, when written in number form American style looks like 1/26/71. However, in Europe this is written 26/1/71.

Spelling: In many English speaking countries you will find that a word which has the same meaning in America will be spelled differently. For example, in the U.S. we use the word *jail;* in Australia it's spelled *gaol.*

Temperature: America uses the Fahrenheit scale to measure temperature. For example, the boiling point is 212° and freezing is 32°. In Europe, a centigrade scale is used to measure temperature: 100° is boiling and 0° is freezing. (See charts)

Metric: This system is used to measure distance, capacity and weight. For example, to measure distance, 1″ = 2.5 centimeters; 1 mile = 1.609 kilometers. Under capacity, 1 cubic inch = 16.387 cu. cnt; 1 pint = 0.4732 liter, and to measure weight, 1 oz. = 28.35 grams, 1 ton = 907.18 kilograms.

Time: In Europe and Asia the 24-hour clock is used. Under this system the day begins at midnight and the hours are numbered around the clock to 24. Therefore, 8:00 a.m. becomes 0800 hours and 9:00 p.m. becomes 2100 hours; 5:30 p.m. would be 1730 hours.

Money: See chapter on Money.

Religious Beliefs: Have as much respect for others' religious beliefs as you would expect them to have for yours.

TRAVEL PROCEDURE

THE FIRST THING TO DO WHEN YOU GET THERE IS PREPARE TO LEAVE

Travel

Arrive early in the day. This will give you an opportunity to orient yourself. It will give you time to locate the Tourist Information Center, get maps, street and transit, change money, and find accommodations. If you arrive late at night, everything may be closed.

A thrifty traveler travels at night. Example: while taking a night train, plane or boat, you will be able to sleep, thus saving a night's rent.

Upon arrival decide where you are going next and how you will get there. Obtain road maps or train, plane and boat schedules you need.

Money

Financial preparation is necessary, so you will not get caught short and have to change a large sum of money in order to leave a country. (See Money chapter.)

Visas

Make sure you have the proper visas for visiting the next country (including transit visas through other countries on the way if these are required). Ask the nearest embassy or Tourist Information Center where you can get visas if you do not already have them. *This may take you a few days.* Therefore, do it upon arrival and don't wait until the last minute.

Knowing there is no problem in traveling to the next country on your itinerary will allow you to enjoy your stay a lot more, and to leave at the drop of a hat.

When filling out applications for a visa, for the sake of simplicity, always be as neutral as possible.

Make sure you use the same name and address that appears on your passport.

If pictures are required, make sure they are a good likeness of you, are recent and project you as being clean-cut. (See Photos.)

When asked your occupation, simplify your job. Example: if you are an auctioneer, simply say "salesman." The word "professor" is more easily understood in most countries than "teacher." If you are unemployed or cannot think of an understandable job title, simply say "salesman."

Try not to use the classification of student. In most countries that's synonymous with trouble. A good example of this occurred in 1968 when the Russians invaded Czechoslovakia. For a long time afterwards students were not allowed to enter. I wrote "salesman" on my visa application and had no problem gaining entry.

When asked what type of visa you are requesting, simply say "tourist." This is the easiest visa to get.

When asked the purpose of your visa, just say "tourist," "pleasure," or "sightseeing."

The same procedure should be used when filling out embarkation or debarkation cards which are given the traveler at the border or on planes, boats or trains upon entering and leaving a country.

Things to remember about embarkation and debarkation cards:

1. Always print legibly, and make sure you sign the card.
2. "Forename" means first name. "Surname" means last name. Don't confuse the two.

EMBARKATION CARD ALIENS ORDER, 1953 **IB 29A**

Surname (in block letters)
Nom en caracteres gros
Familienname in Druckschrift
Cognome in Stampato

Port of disembarkation

Forenames
Prénoms
Vornamen
Nomi

Date of birth
Date de naissance
Geburtsdatum
Data di nascita

Place of birth
Lieu de naissance
Geburtsort
Luogo di nascita

Sex
Sexe
Geschlecht
Sesso

Nationality
Nationalité
Staatsangehörigkeit
Nazionalità

Occupation
Profession
Beruf
Professione

Number of Passport
Numéro du passeport
Passnummer
Numero del passaporto

(or, if a national identity card is used in lieu of a passport, number of national identity card)

Full address in United Kingdom
Adresse précise en Grande Bretagne
Genaue Adresse in Grossbritannien
Indirizzo presso in Gran Bretagna

Signature
Signature
Unterschrift
Firma

(110010) Wt 3108/965/K10.000

After reading about the international, suppress-the-hippie movement, you will know what I mean when I say that your appearance should conform with the information on visa applications and embarkation cards. Once a visa has been issued, entry to a country may still be denied, should the customs officials not like your looks.

MONEY

How much is it in real money?

Figuring the rate of exchange from dollars into francs, lira, marks, reals or pound notes is frustrating to some tourists. To others this routine probably seems as simple as playing Monopoly. For the money changers who deal with this multitude, it's definitely no game.

When you are traveling, your money is your second most valuable possession (your passport is your first). Every year thousands of American travelers go broke in some far corner of the globe and end up in jails or hospitals, mainly because they have mismanaged their money. Knowing how to control your finances is your biggest asset.

Travelers checks are the safest form of money to carry because they are insured against loss or theft. Sometimes they are more valuable than dollars, bringing a higher rate of exchange. They may be purchased at any major bank in the United States, but American Express, the originator of travelers checks, is probably the best place to go for them.

American Express, unlike most American banks, maintains offices throughout the world. Recovering an American Express Travelers Check lost en route is much simpler than recovering a lost bank check.

Nevertheless, the most sought-after currency in the world is the good old American greenback. Though it is risky to carry large sums of money while traveling, you should carry some American dollars with you. Dollars are more useful than checks when dealing with shopkeepers and black marketeers.

Can I buy foreign money in America?

If you want to buy some foreign currency before you leave America, almost any bank can handle the sale or direct you to the proper bank. Money changing specialists, such as Perera Co. Inc., can supply you with a small envelope of local currency for each country you will be visiting. They can also quote you the current exchange rates.

For additional information write to Perera Co. Inc., 29 Broadway (Perera Bldg.), New York, N.Y. 10006, or telephone (212) 344-7383. Also there is a branch office at Kennedy Airport's International Arrivals Building, Main Lobby, open day and night, seven days a week (tel. (212) 656-8444.)

IMPORTANT NOTE: When you originally change your money into local currency, the bank teller will give you a receipt. You need this receipt in order to change that money back into any other currency. This receipt is most important in countries where the black market thrives (see "Black Market") or in countries where token money is charged for your visa (see "Visas").

When you change money at a bank, you will often be charged a fee which can be between one and three per cent of the amount depending on the country. With travelers checks (except when cashed by the issuing company) an additional tax may also be charged.

Most banks will change only paper money, not coins worth less than a dollar. If you are traveling with friends, pool all your coins and change them into one lump sum—unless you want to keep them for a souvenir.

If you are in a country where it is illegal for a bank to issue American currency, and local currency is worthless outside its borders, take your local money and change it into something else negotiable—such as Swiss franks, British pounds, or German marks. Then, when you do arrive in a country where dollars may be changed, you can change this money for them.

What is the best procedure in handling my money when I first arrive in a foreign country?

The first thing to do is change enough money to last a few days, according to your budget. The second and most important thing is to make yourself a conversion chart showing how much local money equals one dollar. Then, determine how much equals 50¢, 25¢, 10¢, 5¢, 1¢. For example, when you are in Italy, where 600 lire equals one dollar, then 300 lire equals 50¢, 150 lire equals 25¢, 60 lire equals 10¢, 30 lire equals 5¢, and 6 lire equals 1¢. This way, when you are shopping or paying for some service, you can simply consult your conversion chart to figure the equivalent in dollars and cents.

Conversion charts showing local money values around the world in dollars can be found in the individual map sections of this book.

What is the best way to have money sent to me from the United States?

There are many ways of handling this. If you are broke and stranded, go to the American Embassy. They will help you contact relatives or friends in the U.S. or other countries who might send you funds. The Embassy will send a collect cable or subtract the cost of the cable when funds arrive. Sometimes an embassy will not handle funds directly but will request that the funds be sent through commercial channels.

If you are not stranded and not in a hurry, simply write your bank an airmail letter telling them where to forward your funds. Your bank will notify the bank in the city you specify.

If you still have a few dollars on you but need more money in a hurry, you can send a telegram, and have your contact in the States cable the money to you in care of a local bank. Or you can telephone them to cable the money, and it should arrive within forty-eight hours.

It is a good idea to have the American Express handle it for you. Send a cable advising that your money be sent to you in care of American Express Company. The reason for this is that you will most likely pick up your funds in travelers checks; sending the money directly to American Express will eliminate other banks as middlemen and save time.

In most countries throughout the world, you are not allowed to receive American cash. It is illegal for any bank in India to issue American cash, and certain countries, for example, Greece, have a $300.00 limit. The rest may be issued in either local currency or travelers checks.

TIP: If you will be traveling for several months, arrange to receive money in several different cities along the way. You can either arrange this with your bank before you leave the States, or you can cable from one city while you are *en route* to the next to avoid having to wait for money anywhere. This way you carry less money with you at all times. You have less to lose, and you will not be tempted to exceed your budget.

Whatever amount of cash you keep on your person—$25.00

or $30.00 in one-dollar bills is recommended—will come in handy for quick transactions, i.e., airport tax, newspapers and snacks.

What is get-away money?

When I was leaving India, I arrived at the airport and gave the taxi driver my last rupee. Later, going through customs, I had to change a $10 travelers check (the smallest denomination) into Indian rupees in order to pay the airport tax 7R. ($1.00 U.S.). I then learned that in India as in many other Asian and Eastern European countries, it is against the law to change local currency back to U.S. dollars. Thus, I was left holding $9.00 worth of local currency which was of no value to me after I left.

You can avoid getting stuck with local currency in these last-minute transactions by using what I call "get-away money." This may be in two forms:

When you first arrive in a country, find out how much it will cost you to leave. Example: If you are leaving by airplane, add up all the last-minute expenses such as transportation to the airport, tipping and airport taxes. Put this amount away in local currency for your departure.

Another form of "get-away money" is your $1 U.S. bills. Instead of changing a $10 traveler's check, use these small bills as you need them.

NOTE: Try to use local currency whenever possible. Try to hold on to your U.S. dollars as long as possible. In most countries U.S. dollars are difficult to get once you have run out of them.

Where can I change money?

In the London-Paris-Rome circuit of western Europe, legal exchanges are located in the following places: airport, railway stations, Metropolitan banks in cities, or large tourist hotels, as well as some large tourist information centers and travel agencies, such as American Express. Once you leave western Europe for eastern Europe, the Middle East, Asia and parts of North Africa, you will find it easier to change money with shopkeepers or the man in the street. However, in some cases this is illegal (see "Black marketeering").

Where can I change money when the banks are closed?

Bank hours vary from country to country, but exchanges in

most airports and railway stations are open seven days a week and sometimes even twenty-four hours a day for the convenience of the tourist. If they are inconveniently located or closed, the large tourist hotels usually change money for guests only, but if you explain your need is urgent, they will usually cooperate. If they refuse, the hotel is usually full of other Americans who might help you by changing a few dollars for you.

THE BLACK MARKET

The black market, as it has been called for centuries, is the sale and distribution of goods and currency in violation of quotas, rationing and prices established by a government. Anyone who buys or sells such goods or currency through the black market is dealing illegally.

Black marketeers deal in secret. It is most successful in countries that cannot produce enough goods to supply the needs of the people or in countries with a low standard of living.

In the United States the black market is often called organized crime. Here the average citizen does not come into contact with organized crime, whose services include gambling, prostitution, abortion and "hot" merchandise (a truckload of cigarettes or whiskey, as yet untaxed, is hijacked and sold to the public).

In most foreign countries (exceptions are Australia, most of western Europe, and Japan) not only black marketeers but shopowners, peddlers, students and hotel clerks will frequently ask Americans if they have any money to exchange. Most foreigners want American greenbacks because they are probably the most stable currency in use in modern times.

In South America, the Middle East, Asia, and Russia there are two economies: the local economy and the American dollar economy. The reason is that in most countries all the goods needed are not produced within the country, so they're imported; imports must be paid for in negotiable currency. For example, if you were to purchase an item in a Parisian shop, you must pay for it in currency which is negotiable in France. A Parisian shopkeeper cannot spend German marks, Mexican pesos, or American dollars in France.

In India, there is a very low standard of living. In fact, most of the people there are poverty stricken. The black market is technically against the law but it's *morally supported* by the people and it's one of the only forms of merchandising that keeps the people alive. Take the black market away, and the lower classes would starve and revolt against the upper classes.

Because of this the peasants in India have set up a small economy within the national economy to keep themselves alive. I call this economy the "gray" market. It is as illegal as the black market, yet it has the moral support of the people.

An Indian tailor in New Delhi, for example, cannot use his money to buy goods abroad because the Indian rupee is worthless outside the borders of India; for all practical purposes it's worthless within the borders, too, because he cannot buy certain imported luxury items.

If the Indian tailor wanted to buy a sewing machine not made in India, he must go to America, Europe, or Hong Kong, where sewing machines are manufactured. He must pay for it in a negotiable currency. Nobody in his right mind would accept Indian rupees.

The tailor needs American dollars to get his sewing machine. How does he go about getting them? He wheels and deals with other Indian merchants to get his hands on American dollars.

He also wheels and deals with tourists. You come through New Delhi—touring, hitchhiking or on business—you go to the bank and get seven and one-half rupees for one dollar. The merchants would rather have you exchange your dollars with them, but it's illegal. To make it worth your while to break the law, they give you a bonus, giving you fifty per cent more than the bank. This is how the tailor gets his dollars for his sewing machine.

In many countries the black market is of advantage only to the under-privileged classes; of course, most of the wealthier classes control it. In Russia, where most people in the lower classes have sufficient clothing and food on their tables, the black market serves other purposes. Russians don't have things like nylon ski jackets, levis, cigarette lighters, sun glasses and other such items manufactured in the West.

Therefore, Russians use the black market to get American dollars to buy otherwise unobtainable items.

Black marketeers (in both Moscow and Leningrad) offered me as much as $30.00 for a pair of used Levis. Had I sold my Levis to them, they would have resold them for as much as $50.00. They were even willing to pay me in American dollars for my Levis.

In Rumania, students approached me to exchange money. The students said they needed the dollars to purchase electric guitars and American record albums for their underground rock band.

The black market also thrives in war-torn countries. The strain on the economy in a war-torn country forces the government to tax everything severely; therefore, untaxable merchandise is constantly being sold on the black market. There is normally a shortage of merchandise during a war. Because the outcome of a war is uncertain, currency of the countries involved is worthless outside of the respective countries.

For instance, if Israel wants to purchase arms, war materials, or general goods, she must pay for them in American dollars or British sterling. The same is true in Vietnam. Therefore, the black market is not discouraged in either country because it brings in much American and British currency. These countries also realize that if it is discouraged, the black market will turn and deal with their enemies.

In South Vietnam one dollar is worth 150 piastres; the black market there will give you 420 piastres for that same dollar. What's to stop a person for exchanging one dollar to 420 piastres through a marketeer, going to a bank and getting $3.50 in exchange for the piastres? It sounds easy. But in South Vietnam, as in any other country, when you legally exchange money at a bank, you get a receipt; the only way you can cash in the local currency for dollars is to present the receipt. This discourages people from changing money on the black market into large sums, going to a bank and doubling or tripling their money.

United States currency continues circulating throughout foreign countries without ever returning to American banks. Passing through India I picked up a two-dollar bill (now out of circulation); in Turkey I picked up a silver certificate. In

France, I picked up more silver certificates plus a 1928 five-dollar Federal note.

Black marketeers will buy and sell just about anything in order to make a dollar. Many young travelers who run short of money will sell unsigned travelers checks for as much as eighty percent of their face value, then report them lost or stolen and have them replaced. For example, if you have $100 worth of travelers checks and sell them for $80.00 cash, then report them stolen and get $100 returned, your profit is $80.00.

If caught, you will be prosecuted to the full extent of the local law, not to mention the charges pressed by the company issuing the travelers check.

Another illegal form of earning money is selling passports. American passports are worth up to $800 in Europe and up to $1,500 in Southeast Asia. If you don't mind a Communist, be he a North Vietnamese, Rumanian, Bulgarian or Russian, assuming your name and signature, go ahead and sell your passport. Chances are when you try to close the deal, you will not be able to collect the agreed price.

CON GAMES

MONEY RACKETS

One of the most popular con games plaguing tourists involves the swindling of large sums of money. Surprisingly enough, this crime is usually perpetrated by a fellow American who makes his living preying on American tourists. You may meet him at your hotel or in a popular tourist spot. After getting acquainted, he will tell you he has a friend who will give you a better rate of exchange for your money. He will try to impress you with the fact that he is not a black marketeer but just a friend who needs a lot of American dollars to send his kid to college or buy something. He won't be fussy; he will take travelers checks or greenbacks, and, to make the deal even more enticing, he will offer a much higher rate than the black market. Since most Americans are always looking for a bargain, they may find this offer hard to turn down. He will even let you go along to his friend's house or hotel, but you will never meet his friend. The swindler will ask you to wait outside while he takes your money in to make the deal. But he ducks out the back door, and you never see him or your money again.

Another swindle which Americans are currently falling victim to involves the exchange of black market money on the street. It works like this. You are ready to change money, when, all of a sudden, the black marketeer looks over your shoulder, gets or pretends to be scared and hollers "Police, police." At that point confusion arises, and everyone heads for cover (remember, black marketeering is illegal). In the confusion he grabs all the money and takes off.

This may also work another way. The black marketeer may have a friend working with him. Just as the exchange is about to take place, the friend taps you both on the shoulder, announces that he is the police and that you are under arrest. At this point the black marketeer pleads with the so-called cop to let you both go. After a bit of persuading, the cop consents but confiscates all the money. He splits the funds with his accomplice later.

CAMERAS AND RELATED PHOTOGRAPHIC EQUIPMENT

One of the biggest attractions in Europe and Asia for any value-minded American who loves to take pictures or the camera enthusiast who visits a country in order to pick up a bargain is photographic equipment. (Some of the most popular camera equipment is made in Germany and Japan. However, this equipment is not always cheapest in the country of manufacture. For example, Japanese cameras and lenses are less expensive in Hong Kong and Singapore. One of the biggest rackets plaguing American tourists involves the camera industry.)

Reputable camera shops, perhaps even displaying emblems of the larger camera manufacturers, may in fact, not be authorized dealers. After you have purchased an expensive camera and/or lenses at a remarkable savings, you will often find your first roll of film will not develop. Instead of precision lenses, you were sold equipment with cheap glass. In many cases, the people who purchase this equipment are hundreds or even thousands of miles away by the time he uses it. The camera shop that sold it to you counts on this. Very few people will fly back to Hong Kong or Singapore to return a lens.

IMPORTANT NOTE: Purchase cameras and equipment only from reputable, authorized dealers who give you a complete manufacturer's guarantee with the equipment. Then, should something be wrong, the guarantee will be honored in almost any country where an authorized dealer exists.

Equipment is available at such great savings that it is not worth the risk of getting stuck with inferior equipment just to save an extra dollar or two.

TIP: Always check expiration dates on film purchased abroad. (See chapter on Photographs.)

YOU OUGHT TO BE IN PICTURES

In the more popular tourist spots around the world well-dressed men and women may approach you with a camera in one hand and a receipt book in the other. They will offer to take your picture while you are standing in front of a famous monument, museum or just right there on the street. There will always be a fee, and they will give you a receipt for your money and promise to mail you the pictures. Don't fall for this. In most cases you will never see the pictures after you've paid for them. If the man with the camera is a reputable photographer, you will be able to pick up your photos at his studio the next day. If he does not agree to that, avoid him.

WANNA BUY A WATCH?

This expression "Wanna buy a watch?" can be heard anywhere there is a tourist from Times Square to Tokyo. Before I tell you how this con game works, let me tell you something about a watch.

A watch is like an automobile engine. It has individual moving parts. Should it break down, it can be taken apart, repaired and reassembled. The watch that will be offered to you will not be like that. Inside will be pressed or stamped workings; should they break down, they cannot be fixed, but must be thrown away. These watches, manufactured in the Middle East, Hong Kong and Singapore, will be offered by street vendors, black marketeers and even some tourist shops. They can be purchased from the manufacturer in the above mentioned locations for approximately $1.75 each or $2.00 apiece and about 15¢ more for the bands.

The way this con game works is as follows: In a majority of cases the peddler approaching you pretends the watch is either "hot" (stolen) or in some other way of shady origin. This entices the prospective customer to think he might get a really good bargain. In most cases these watches are imported from the manufacturer by a watch wholesaler and sold legally to the peddler who has a hawker's license.

Often the names on these watches will be those of popular brands, such as Omega, Timex, Bulova, and Rolex. Watches which cost over $100 or more will be offered to you for around $50. With a little effort you can buy it for $30. With a lot of effort you can buy it for $10, because chances are he paid under $5 for it. Don't let the popular brand name on the face of the watch impress you. If you purchased 1,000 at a time from the manufacturer, you could have your own name put on the face of the watch.

NOTE: NEVER PURCHASE ANYTHING EXCEPT TRINKETS FROM ANYONE ON THE STREET. BUY WATCHES FROM AUTHORIZED FACTORY REPRESENTATIVE DEALERS, AND BE SURE YOU RECEIVE THE GUARANTEE OR WARRANTY THAT MATCHES THAT WATCH YOU BUY. CHECK THE NUMBERS.

JEWELRY

Gems—Precious and Semi-Precious Stones

Almost every country is noted for a particular stone: India for the ruby, Burma for the star sapphire and Australia for the opal. Unless you are an experienced gemologist, however, don't buy from anyone but a reputable dealer. Even in the most backward peasant villages you may find trays full of used synthetic stones from high school rings.

Costume Jewelry

Costume jewelry and trinkets, for sale almost everywhere you go, make excellent souvenirs. In many instances, the design of the jewelry will symbolize some characteristic of the country. Always bargain with street peddlers selling these items. Materials and labor in most countries are very inexpensive. Costume jewelry which costs a dollar in America is usually made abroad and sells for 25¢ to 40¢. However, the price a tourist pays abroad is usually double that in America. Don't be afraid to bargain.

Clothing

In the bargain clothing department the wool has been pulled over many a tourist's eye. In most cases the clothes are no bargain. You get exactly what you pay for.

Some of the more popular clothing items which lure tourists to far off corners of the world are Spanish leathers, Afghan coats, and, of course, the world-famous $35 suits from Hong Kong.

Many of these items are offered to tourists at about half their price in America. Only they are not exactly the same items. They *look* the same. In some cases where importers' as well as department store standards are very high, merchandise which is offered to tourists is often counterfeit. Instead of double-stitched, synthetic thread in the seams you get cheap, single-stitched, cotton thread. In some cases there will be no lining. In some leather clothes the hides will be improperly tanned. Though some of the Afghan coats shipped to America are of high quality and pass U.S. Customs' standards, the coats sold to tourists in Afghanistan are often improperly tanned. I've even seen coats with pieces of flesh still hanging on the hides. If the coat gets wet, the odor never goes away. Many travelers find their coats confiscated by Customs officials upon return to America because they were improperly tanned.

In Hong Kong the world famous $35 suit racket is common. Often tailors will knock on your hotel room door uninvited and measure you for a new suit. Often tourists fall for this. Somehow these tailors always know when you are leaving. They will promise to have the suit finished before you leave, and in most cases they will. A day or two before your departure they will return with the suit you have bought, but it will need alterations. They will promise to return it before you leave. If they cannot, they will call and apologize for not having the suit ready and promise to mail it to you. But the same suit will be used again tomorrow on another sucker. Even if you go shopping for a suit, the same thing may happen. Never buy anything by mail.

There are some reputable tailor shops in Hong Kong, and they will turn out an excellent suit for $75 to $100 or more. But for this you don't have to go all the way to Hong Kong.

Art Galleries

Many Americans visit foreign countries with the hope of buying obscure art treasures for a few dollars. To fill this demand, people have begun manufacturing them. You might spot the exact painting with different signatures hanging in half a dozen galleries in different cities and hear the proprietor of each one tell the tourists that it is an original and only costs $300.

Real Estate Schemes

As I was walking down the street in Sydney, Australia, I was approached by a pretty young lady who asked if I wanted a free meal. The same thing happened to me in London and to a friend of mine in Paris. These were not prostitutes but canvassers drumming up business for real estate agencies, in of all places, Florida and Arizona. They offer to wine, dine and entertain you free of charge. After the feast is over, they show a film which demonstrates the benefits you can enjoy by investing in real estate. All they ask is a very small down payment and a few dollars a week. For this small sum you receive an all-expense-paid vacation from your home town in America to see your land; should you decide not to buy, your deposit will be refunded.

The philosophy behind this scheme is that you will be more receptive to the offer of a free vacation if you are presently paying to travel. This scheme snares many unsuspecting American tourists. Beware! You can savor the bait, but don't bite.

PIMPS

As dime novels tell us, a pimp is someone who will procure a prostitute for you. But modern travelers understand "pimp" to mean any person (male or female) who can perform any great service.

The modern-day pimp can procure almost anything for the tourist. He may be a black-market go-between for changing money and buying goods or a shopping guide who will lead you to the best bargains in town (usually to a shop owned by a friend of his who will give him a kickback). He may also act as a sight-seeing guide. If there is anyone who knows the city and all its intricacies, it will be a pimp. A good pimp is hard to beat. In fact, a guided tour by a pimp is often much more exciting than one by the local tourist board.

Pimps can be found almost anywhere. They usually hang out where the tourists are, sometimes in or around first-class hotels. Even cab drivers will double as pimps and offer to take you on guided tours, change money for you or show you the best places to buy souvenirs

The most common pimp, however, will be found on foot, not in a car. He will meet trains, planes or boats and offer to take you to the hotel which suits your budget. Once he has latched on to you, he will offer to help you in many ways. He can be a severe pain in the neck.

Many tourists are embarrassed to be seen with pimps. But to a traveler on a budget who wants to find the bargains and save money, they are a great asset. Caution must be taken with pimps as with anything else.

Many people who are not pimps meet boats, trains and airplanes and offer to take you to their hotel. They are canvassers for the local hotels who get a commission for each guest they bring. Sometimes they are middle or old-aged women who run pensions. They help you find a place to stay, but that's as far as their service goes.

SOUVENIRS

Souvenirs come in many different forms, but as far as I am concerned, the best souvenir is what the word literally means —a memory. Keeping a diary of your journey is the best way to refresh that memory. People who have bad memories or don't like to write can take pictures; as they say, one picture is worth a thousand words.

According to the dictionary, a souvenir is "something to remind one of a place, person or occasion; token of remembrance; keepsake." There is no end to what you can spend on a souvenir. You could even buy a car from each country. One American tourist I met bought some type of article of clothing in each country she visited. But I found that some of the best souvenirs are small insignificant things that I used en route.

The most common, inexpensive souvenir to represent each country is a coin collection. Many people find themselves with left-over coins which they cannot change back to American money, so they keep them as souvenirs. I found that the smallest bill of each country was even better. It is larger and easier to read than coins and also more decorative. When the bills are placed side by side underneath a glass top of a coffee table, they make a fine conversation piece.

FREE SOUVENIRS

Many travelers I met collected small tokens of each country. Beer coasters were most popular in Europe. Other free and unusual keepsakes are bus or train tickets, small stones found near national monuments, such as the Taj Mahal or the base of Mt. Everest, and some sand found near the Wailing Wall. (Never deface a monument.) One traveler even collected pigeon feathers which he found on the ground in each major city he visited.

INEXPENSIVE SOUVENIRS

Postcards representing scenes of the country you have seen.

Coca-Cola bottles with Coca-Cola printed on the bottle in a foreign language.

Beer mugs or empty wine bottles from each country.

The street map or tourist guide you got from the Tourist Information Center.

A small hatpin with the flag of the country.

Menus from restaurants (ask permission before taking).

Matchbooks bearing hotel names.

A small doll from each country.

Postage stamps from each country.

In many places the American tourist will be faced with fantastic bargains, and his greatest challenge will be trying to overcome the impulse to buy. Always consider whether you would race to the nearest store at home to purchase the item you are buying—even if it were offered at a reduced price. Many tourists arrive home and say to themselves, "Now why did I buy that? I don't need it." I have met many American travelers who had to cut their vacations and trips short because they spent their traveling money on one fantastic bargain.

A familiar phrase used by foreign merchants is "It would cost you twice as much in America. What a terrific saving!" Nine out of ten times the American tourist agrees with this reasoning and says to himself, "I could never get it anywhere else so cheaply."

AGREEING ON A PRICE

In most modern cities throughout Europe and Asia, department stores, tourist shops, and local establishments will usually have set prices such as in American stores. However, even in large cities you will still be able to bargain with street vendors and peddlers, and often, depending on the city, bargaining is also possible in the shops. For example, in Hong Kong and Singapore, although they are large thriving metropolises, most business is transacted by bargaining.

Throughout many of the developing countries in the Middle East and Asia there are usually three prices: the tourist price for people who do not bargain; the tourist price, which is substantially lower, for people who do bargain; and the local price, which is the price residents pay. Realizing this, when you are in these areas, you should do the following:

Find out what the labeled, or asking, price is. Then if you know someone you can trust, preferably a local inhabitant or a desk clerk or even the man on the street, find out what he would pay for it. Knowing the two extremes, the high and the low, you are better equipped to bargain with the shopkeeper and get the merchandise at a fair price.

Many people travel thousands of miles to buy something in a country where it is manufactured, figuring that the price will be cheaper there. This is not always the case. For example, Japan manufactures a watch named Seiko. The particular watch I own costs $110 here in America, $65 in Japan and at a duty free shop in Tokyo sells for $36. However, I purchased the same watch from a reputable, authorized Seiko dealer in Singapore. His original asking price was $35. I talked him down to $25. A good friend of mine who lives in Singapore returned to the same shop later and purchased the watch for me for $22. This illustrates three things:

1. Merchandise is not always cheaper in the country of manufacture.
2. The three-price system does exist.
3. You can save a great deal of money by bargaining.

DUTY-FREE SHOPS

Duty-free shops can be found in airports, on passenger ships, and airplanes. These shops afford travelers the opportunity of buying popular, brand-name merchandise at 25 to 75% less than it would cost in the country of the manufacturer. Many Americans will not pass up such bargains, and often purchase items they would not buy for the same price at home. These items must be declared at customs, but it is always a better feeling (and cheaper) to pay duty on a watch you bought for $75 in a duty-free shop than to pay duty on the same watch that costs $125 in a city shop.

I have found prices on merchandise in duty-free shops are jacked up because these shops are patronized by tourists. In some cases the price in town would be less. Always shop around.

Many people forget the purpose of their traveling. They spend all their time and money in tourist traps.

Remember: the best deal you made was when you decided to travel. Don't deal your time and money away.

CUSTOMS

Upon entering and exiting almost every country in the world, the traveler will come face to face with a customs agent. The purpose of his job is to check the flow of taxable merchandise, currency and undesirables. The thoroughness of customs checks will fluctuate from time to time depending on current events.

I found that customs officials generally search for firearms and other weapons which could be used in highjacking. But more often they were trying to curtail the flow of illicit drugs and illegal currency.

Most American travelers feel that their main customs concern will be re-entry to America. This is not always the case. Customs regulations vary depending on the country you are visiting. In most of Western Europe the strongest customs check points will be found upon arrival and departure from the Continent.

Throughout Eastern Europe, the Middle East, and Asia customs regulations are often more strictly enforced—if you are checked. In most cases it is merely a matter of chance if you are stopped and searched. Depending on the method used, sometimes as few as one out of five persons is spot-checked. However, occasionally entire planeloads of tourists have been intensely shakendown and personally searched.

Many tourists are under the impression that customs officials are only on the look-out for taxable items, so they can impose a duty. This will not always be the case. In most Eastern European countries and many countries throughout Asia, your money declaration seems to be of most importance and should be filled out with great care. Upon entering these countries, the tourist declares the amount of money in his possession. Upon leaving the country, he may be searched. Should he have almost the same or more than he entered with, the authorities may assume he was black marketeering and confiscate his money.

Many Communist countries are more interested in printed matter, such as newspapers, magazines and, most of all, private letters, than a suitcase full of taxable merchandise.

What can be done to expedite matters at customs?

Have your suitcase packed, so everything is easily accessible. Always try to check beforehand to see what you will be allowed to take into the country. Always cooperate with customs officials; never hide anything from them.

TIP: A good way to keep customs inspectors from inspecting your gear very thoroughly is to pack a roll of toilet paper directly on top of your belongings. When you open your suitcase or back pack, it will be the first thing they will see, and in most cases they will not move it.

Usually only your luggage will be checked. Personal searches are extremely rare and will only occur if the customs inspector suspects you of smuggling. Your appearance and attitude will largely determine how the inspector will treat you. If you are not smuggling and all your things are in order, then you have absolutely nothing to worry about.

The biggest concern for a majority of travelers will be returning and going through U.S. customs. The following information has been supplied by various agencies of the U.S. Customs Department and by may travelers. It should help you to become more familiar with U.S. Customs and help eradicate rumors.

CUSTOMS EXEMPTIONS

According to U.S. Customs, an American citizen returning from abroad is allowed a $100 exemption on taxable merchandise if he has been outside the United States at least 48 hours, and such exemptions have not been claimed within 30 days (no 48-hour absence required when arriving from Mexico and U.S. Virgin Islands).

An American traveler is allowed a $200 exemption when returning from Guam, American Samoa and the U.S. Virgin Islands.

Returning American citizens are allowed the following duty-free exemptions:

1 quart of alcoholic beverages for passengers over 21 years of age;

1 gallon of liquor if arriving from U.S. Virgin Islands, Guam, or American Samoa, provided that no more than 1 quart is purchased outside these areas;

100 cigars. There is no limit on cigarettes for personal use.

CUSTOMS INFORMATION

What is a customs declaration?

According to the U.S. Customs Department, "You must declare to the U.S. Customs, either orally or in writing, all articles acquired abroad and in your possession at the time of your return.

"The wearing or use of an article acquired abroad does not exempt it from duty and it must be declared at the price you paid for it. The customs officer will make an appropriate reduction in its value for wear and use."

Whether you declare orally or in writing, your statement also must include:

1. Items you have been requested to bring home for another person;
2. Any article you intend to sell or use in your business;
3. Alterations or repairs made to articles taken abroad;
4. Gifts presented to you while abroad, such as wedding or birthday presents, etc.

"A resident making an oral declaration may be required to prepare a written list if the customs inspector deems it necessary."

According to the U.S. Customs Department, "All articles acquired abroad must be declared to Customs in writing when:

"Their total fair retail value (including alterations and repairs) exceeds $100;

"More than 1 quart of alcoholic beverages or more than 100 cigars are included;

"Some of the items are not intended for your personal or household use, such as commercial samples, items for sale or use in your business, or articles you are bringing home for another person;

"A customs duty or internal revenue tax is collectible on any article in your possession."

When and how would I prepare a written declaration?

Usually customs declaration forms are available on ships and planes and should be prepared well in advance of your arrival. Declaration forms should be presented to immigration and customs officials upon arrival. Sales slips will be very helpful in preparing your declaration. Prices quoted on your declaration can be stated in U.S. currency or its equivalent in local currency in the country of origin.

Is knowing the value of imported articles important?

It is extremely important that you declare the actual price paid for each piece of merchandise purchased abroad. If you do not know the price, say so. Do not guess. Misinformation can result in delays and penalties.

If any article was a gift to you or you acquired it via trading, state its fair value in the country of its origin.

Customs inspectors in most cases are professional merchandisers and are familiar with every trick in the book. It is very difficult to pull the wool over their eyes. They see the same merchandise over and over again and can often tell the exact price and origin of any item even if you have changed the labels.

What is a family declaration?

U.S. Customs Department says, "The head of a family may make a joint declaration for all members residing in the same household and returning with him to the United States. A family of four may bring in articles free of duty valued up to $400 retail value on one declaration, even if the articles acquired by one member of the family exceeds his $100 exemption.

"Infants and children returning to the United States are entitled to the same exemption as adults (except for alcoholic beverages).

"Children born abroad, who have never resided in the United States, are not eligible for this exemption, but are eligible for exemptions as nonresident."

If I own a foreign-made article, may I take it abroad and return without paying duty?

If you own foreign-made items such as cameras, jewelry, clothing and watches and are planning to take them with you when you travel abroad, be sure to register them with U.S. Customs before you leave. Each time you return to this country, they will be subject to duty unless you have proof of prior possession.

You can obtain this proof by registering the article at your nearest customs office. This certificate will assure you free entry of these articles when you return through customs.

According to U.S. Customs, "Bills of sale or receipts for purchase, repair or cleaning will be considered reasonable proof of prior possession."

The following U.S. Customs rules apply to gifts:

"Gifts accompanying you are considered to be for your personal use and may be included within your exemption. This includes gifts given to you by others while abroad and those you intend to give to others after you return. Gifts intended for business or promotional purposes may not be included.

"Bona fide gifts of not more than $10 in fair retail value, when shipped, can be received by friends and relatives in the United States free from duty and tax, if the same person does not receive more than $10 in gift shipments in one day. If any article imported is subject to duty and tax, or if the total value of all articles exceeds $10, no article may be exempt from duty or tax.

"Write 'Gift Enclosed—Value Under $10' in large letters on the outside of the package. Alcoholic beverages and tobacco products are not included in this privilege, nor are alcoholic perfumes valued at more than $1. Gifts mailed to friends and relatives do not have to be declared by you on your return to the States."

Often packages containing gifts can be sent back to America at great reductions. Ask at the post office for a student or book rate. Pack your gifts safely in a box, and add an old shirt and/or a few magazines or books. On the label write: "Books, clothing and personal belongings."

PERSONAL BELONGINGS SENT HOME

Americans traveling abroad may find they have too much clothing and other personal belongings. Yet many are afraid to ship their excess belongings home in fear they may be taxed by customs. U.S. Customs regulations state: "Personal belongings taken abroad, such as worn clothing, etc., may be sent home by mail before you return and receive free entry provided they have not been altered or repaired while abroad. These packages should be marked 'American Goods Returned.' When a claim of United States origin is made, marking on the article to so indicate facilities customs processing."

May I return a vehicle purchased in America?

U.S. Customs states: "Automobiles, boats, planes, or other vehicles taken abroad for noncommercial use may be returned duty-free by proving to the customs officer they were taken out of the United States. This proof may be the State registration card for an automobile, the Department of Commerce certificate for an aircraft, a yacht license or motorboat identification certificate for a pleasure boat, or a customs' certificate of registration obtained before departure.

"Dutiable repairs or accessories acquired abroad for articles taken out of the United States must be declared on your return."

The following information is an exact quote from the U.S. Customs Information Booklet. It explains in simple language the regulations pertaining to the importation of motor vehicles, fruits, vegetables, plants, plant products, pets, antiques, firearms, gold, jewelry and coins.

MOTOR VEHICLES

The duty on foreign-made atuomobiles and trucks is as follows:

"Autos	*1971*	*1972*
	3½%	3%

"Trucks, each valued at $1,000 or more: 25 percent of appraised value."

"These rates apply to all countries, except:

1. Certain countries of the Sino-Soviet bloc
2. Canadian manufactured autos are admitted duty free."

How does Customs determine the value of a second-hand car?

Value of used automobiles imported into the U.S. is determined upon actual examination. "Since used automobiles reflect different degrees of wear and tear, there are no established allowances for use or depreciation."

The appraisement of a used car is based solely upon the production cost of a new car of identical year, make, mileage, and condition.

U.S. Customs states, "The selling price in the country of

exportation will be taken into consideration by the appraiser but may not coincide necessarily with Customs' appraised value. The prospective selling price in the United States has no bearing on the matter." (See Transportation—Auto for additional import costs.)

Excise tax

"A manufacturer's excise tax of 7 percent may be imposed on cars, new or used, imported into the United States for commercial purposes or by individuals for personal us.

"This tax is not collected by Customs but is paid directly to the Internal Revenue Service. Contact Internal Revenue Service, Washington, D.C. 20224, for further information."

May I sell my car after I import it?

Anyone bringing a foreign-made automobile into the United States may sell it only after he has paid customs duty plus any and all required taxes.

FRUITS, VEGETABLES, PLANTS, AND PLANT PRODUCTS

"The Department of Agriculture is responsible for preventing the entry of injurious pests and plant diseases into the United States. Fruits, vegetables, plants, cuttings, seeds, and unprocessed plant products are the hosts for these pests and diseases. Consequently these items either are prohibited from entering the country or require an import permit.

"The customs officer cannot ignore the Agriculture requirements—the risk of costly damage to our crops is too great.

"You can help by not bringing these articles into the country or by obtaining a permit in advance of importation. Applications for import permits or requests for information should be addressed to the Import and Permit Section, Plant Quarantine Division, 209 River Street, Hoboken, N.J. 07030.

"Remember, every single plant, plant product, fruit or vegetable must be declared to the customs officer and must be presented for inspection, no matter how free of pests it appears to be."

PETS

May a U.S. citizen import dogs, cats, birds and other wildlife?

"Only if the animals are free of evidence of communicable disease.

"All imported wildlife is subject to health, quarantine, agriculture and customs' requirements as well as federal, state and local laws and regulations."

What special arrangements for transportation are necessary?

Domestic and wildlife animals must be imported under humane conditions. U.S. Customs "regulations require that careful arrangements be made with the carrier for suitable cages, space, ventilation and protection from the elements. Cleaning, feeding, watering and other necessary services must be provided."

What markings should be on packages for shipping?

U.S. Customs advises, "Every imported package or container of pets must be plainly marked, labeled or tagged on the outside with the names and addresses of the shipper and consignee, along with an accurate invoice statement specifying the number of each species contained in the shipment."

What happens to pets and wildlife that are denied entry into America?

"They must be either exported or destroyed. While awaiting disposition, the pet will be detained in Customs' custody at the owner's expense at the port of arrival."

What is the Customs duty on pets?

"If they are imported for your personal use and are not intended for sale, they may be included in the amount of your customs exemption.

"If your purchases exceed the amount of your customs exemption, your pets may be imported at the rates of duty outlined below.

"The following rates will apply for the calendar years listed:

1. Live cats, dogs and monkeys: In 1971, 4 percent of their value; for 1972, 3½%;

2. live canaries, valued at over $5: For 1971, 6% of their value; and for 1972, 5%;

3. live birds, including canaries, valued at $5 or under: For 1971, 10¢; and for 1972, 8¢.

4. live birds, except canaries, valued at over $5: In 1971, 4½% of their value; and for 1972, 4%."

What about pure-bred animals for breeding purposes?

"Animals imported for breeding purposes are free of duty under certain conditions.

"A declaration is required to show that:

1. the importer is a citizen of the United States;
2. the animal is imported specially for breeding purposes; and
3. the animal is identical with the description in the certificate of pedigree presented.

"An application to the U.S. Department of Agriculture on AIQ Form 338 for a certificate of pure-breeding must be furnished before the animal is examined at the designated port of entry. For complete information write to the Chief, Animal Health Division, U.S. Agriculture Research Service, Hyattsville, Md. 20782."

The following special precautions exist when importing dogs or cats: "If a dog or cat comes from a locality having a high incidence of rabies, or arrives under conditions indicating that a special hazard of rabies is present, the animal will be subject to exclusion or to such additional requirements as are found necessary by the medical officer in charge and approved by the Public Health Service.

"*Dogs:* A certificate of vaccination for rabies usually is required for a dog, but there are exceptions if the animal arrives directly from Australia, Bahama Islands, Bermuda Islands, Denmark, Fiji, Ireland (Eire), Iceland, Jamaica, New Zealand, Norway, Sweden, or the United Kingdom of Great Britain and Northern Ireland. The vaccination must occur at least one month before arrival of the animal.

"*Cats:* If the animal is in good health at the time of arrival, a vaccination usually is not required."

What about importing psittacine birds (having to do with parrot family, such as parakeets)?

"Two psittacine birds per family may be imported without a permit if they are in good health, if they are not for sale or trade, and if you have not imported other psittacine birds during the preceding year. Owner must certify that the birds will be treated by or under the supervision of a licensed veterinarian for 45 days with chlortetra cycline or other medication approved by the Surgeon General of the Public Health Service."

For additional information on importing pets see the customs leaflet, "So You Want to Import a Pet," available at a customs office near you, or write to the Commissioner of

Customs, Washington, D.C. 20226. For more specific information on disease control write to Foreign Quarantine Program, U.S. Public Health Service, National Communicable Disease Center, Atlanta, Ga. 30333.

May I take my pet abroad?

You may find it hard to leave the family pet at home, but you will face many difficulties if you try to have him accompany you. Aside from the many discomforts your pet may encounter from prolonged hours of travel, there are many legal difficulties involved. For example: should you want to take your dog, cat or other domestic pet to Australia, the animal must first be sent to Great Britain, where he must spend 6 months in quarantine, and 6 months in residence. After the 12 months he must be sent by ship to Australia for an additional 2 months' quarantine.

The regulations for entrance of a pet to the continent of Europe are not as strict as Australia's. However, these regulations will vary from country to country. Before leaving the States, you should check with each country's embassy for specifics. In most cases for entrance to Western Europe (except Great Britain) you must show proof of valid rabies vaccination (not less than 1 month nor more than 1 year old) and a certificate of health from a veterinarian. Once your pet has been admitted to Europe, it is relatively easy to travel from one neighboring country to another with the same requirements with the exception of Great Britain. There a pet upon arrival must be placed in quarantine for six months.

ALWAYS CHECK REQUIREMENTS BEFORE YOU LEAVE AND BE SURE TO HAVE PROPER DOCUMENTS.

May I import merchandise from any country?

"The importation (as well as the purchase abroad) of all merchandise originating in North Korea, North Vietnam, or Cuba, and all goods containing Cuban components is prohibited without a Treasury license. The importation of articles originating in Southern Rhodesia also is prohibited. These licenses are strictly controlled and, for all practicable purposes, may be considered unavailable to tourists.

"Foreign Assets Control Regulations have been changed to permit entry of Chinese and Chinese-type merchandise by a returning resident. These goods must be for your personal use or as a gift, not for commercial use or resale. Certificates of origin are not required under this provision. Goods need not accompany you for entry; however, items shipped cannot be included in your duty-free, customs exemption."

ANTIQUES

According to U.S. Customs, "Antiques are free of duty if produced 100 years prior to their date of entry. Proof or evidence of antiquity must be furnished."

FIREARMS

What about import and export of firearms or ammunition?

"Firearms and ammunition are subject to restrictions and import permits approved by the Alcohol, Tobacco, and Firearms Division, Internal Revenue Service. Applications to import may only be made by or through a licensed importer, dealer, or manufacturer.

"Firearms, ammunition, or other devices prohibited by the National Firearms Act will not be admitted into the United States unless by specific authorization of Alcohol, Tobacco and Firearms Division.

"No import permit is required when it is proven that the firearms or ammunition were previously taken out of the United States by the person who is returning such firearms or ammunition. To facilitate the reentry of such firearms or ammunition, persons may have them registered before departing from the U.S. at any U.S. Customs office or Alcohol, Tobacco, and Firearms Division field office. However, not more than three nonautomatic firearms and 1000 cartridges therefor, will be registered for any one person. Quantities in excess of those indicated are subject to the export licensing requirements of the Department of State, Office of Munitions Control, Washington, D.C. 20520.

"Residents of the U.S. carrying firearms or ammunition with them to other countries should consult in advance the customs officials or the respective embassies of those countries as to their regulations.

"For further information, questions should be addressed to: Director, Alcohol, Tobacco, and Firearms Div. (CP:AT:BO), Internal Revenue Building, 1111 Constitution Ave., Washington, D.C. 20224."

GOLD, JEWELRY AND COINS

According to the Office of Domestic Gold and Silver Operations, "The Treasury Department gold regulations prohibit the importation of gold bullion or gold coins minted after 1933 except under license. Gold medals, other than special award medals, are prohibited entry. Gold-coin jewelry is restricted and may be imported only if it meets certain requirements. Gold-coin jewelry and gold coins taken out of the United States cannot be returned without special authorization."

For further information write to Director, Office of Domestic Gold and Silver Operations, Treasury Department, Washington, D.C. 20220.

AMERICAN EMBASSIES

What are American Embassies?

Embassies are the headquarters and official residences of our ambassadors to foreign nations. An embassy is the diplomatic channel of communication between two governments. Embassies in most cases are staffed by several hundred people, including counsellors, attaches, clerks, secretaries, and interpreters, among others.

One of the main functions of an embassy is to help Americans abroad. Embassies offer a wide variety of services, such as assistance with passport problems, information about other embassies, and a list of nearby English-speaking doctors and dentists. In many underdeveloped nations embassies may handle your mail. However, it is up to their discretion (See "Mail Sending and Receiving".)

Out-of-the-way embassies have cafeterias serving American food which are sometimes open to the public.

Operating budgets of embassies vary. Unfortunately allocation of federal funds is far below what it should be. Even though embassies are financially limited, they will assist you in contacting relatives and friends if you are in need of money. (See "Money")

I met a young man in Spain who had lost all his cash. The American Embassy in Madrid sent a cable for him. Until he received verification of a loan, the embassy issued him $1.50 a day in local currency for living expenses. When his loan came through, they deducted his daily allowance and gave him the balance of the loan.

I met another young man, an ex-G.I. who was on his way back to the United States via Southeast Asia and Europe. Stranded without money in Athens, he told me that our embassy had refused to help him. I advised him to be more persistent. Eventually he received State Department clearance, a ticket back to the United States, and $10.00 spending money. He was required to pay back the government within six months. These cases involved two lucky young Americans who were helped by concerned embassy officials. Although embassies have basic guidelines certain decisions are still left up to the staff of the individual embassy. Don't think you'll be as lucky. Remember it's up to you to stay out of trouble.

Rumor has it that any American stranded overseas simply has to go to an American Embassy, and he will be sent back home. This is not true. According to a State Department representative, "There is no specific law which covers repatriation of American citizens." If you are stranded overseas, you should notify the nearest American Embassy. The embassy will locate a relative or a friend in America for a stranded citizen. If that fails, the embassy will apply to the U.S. State Department for a repatriation loan. The State Department has a limited operating budget, which is more plentiful at the beginning of the year, for these cases and other demands. Therefore, you can receive help only at their discretion. If you receive a loan, your passport is valid for travel only back to the U.S. Once you return to the U.S. your passport is revoked until the loan has been repaid.

Each year hundreds of Americans, both young and old, are stranded overseas for various reasons, some of which are beyond their own control. For example, towards the end of summer 1971, hundreds of young Americans made news when they found their return charter flight tickets were worthless. They were stranded in Europe. The State Department at this point was penniless and therefore powerless to help them.

How far will my embassy go to aid me if I am in serious trouble?

Our embassies will act for you with local authorities. They will try to get a lawyer for you and will attempt to insure you a fair trial. Because there is no such thing as bail in many countries, our embassies often are unable to arrange for your release from jail.

IMPORTANT: Our embassies, operating within the legal framework of local authorities, will do all they can for you. It's up to you to stay out of trouble.

DRUGS AND INTERNATIONAL LAW

NOTE: Americans traveling abroad are subject to local laws and penalties. An American passport does not offer diplomatic immunity from punishment.

While traveling, an American may visit a country where the legal is illegal. In other words, something that is legal in America may be illegal in a country you are visiting, or vice versa.

Many Americans are not aware that our rules and regulations do not always apply in foreign countries. For example, in Spain, Portugal and Communist countries, there is absolutely no bending of the law. Should you be convicted of a crime, you will receive what the law prescribes.

Ask questions to avoid breaking laws. Upon arrival in a foreign country spend a few moments to clear up any doubts you may have about your stay in that country. Should you be arrested for any infringement of the law, no matter how slight, you should know your rights.

PROTECTION FACILITIES AFFORDED AMERICAN CITIZENS ARRESTED ABROAD*

"If an American is arrested abroad, the United States consular office will use all appropriate means to ensure that he has the opportunity to defend himself with the advice of legal counsel and receive a fair trial. If convicted of any offense committed in that country, the American is subject to the penalties provided by local law.

"A United States consular officer's activities in protecting arrested citizens are carried out in accordance with international law or the provisions of the consular treaty or convention, if any, in effect between the United States and the host state. International law, sometimes by agreement and sometimes by custom, prescribes the rights and functions of consular officers, and the obligations of authorities of the host

* Information supplied by U.S. State Department.

state in enabling consular officers to perform their duties. The Vienna Convention on Consular Relations of 1963, to which the United States and 44 other governments are parties, is the most authoritative multilateral agreement on consular privileges and functions. Treaties of friendship, commerce and navigation with some countries provide for certain fundamental rights. In the absence of a treaty or convention governing consular relations between the United States and a host country, activities of consular officers are carried out in accordance with generally accepted international practice. The provisions of the 1963 Vienna Convention generally reflect this practice.

"If the citizen requests that his situation not be reported to his next-of-kin, the Department respects his wishes unless he is a minor.

"In a case of extended detention, the consular officer visits the detained citizen periodically and reports to the Department any important developments, including outcome of the trial and any appeal. Periodic reports are also made about citizens sentenced to imprisonment. If relatives of detained citizens are unable to obtain information they desire from the citizen himself or his attorney, the consular officer will correspond directly with the relatives.

"The consular officer will forward personal letters to and from the arrested citizen if permitted to do so by prison regulations and if regular mail channels are not satisfactory. If the citizen's attorney is unable or unwilling to do so, the consular officer will assist in making supplementary purchases of food and clothing, scheduling appointments with doctors and dentists, obtaining permission for visits by friends and relatives, etc. If funds are needed for expenses of a detained citizen, the consular officer will accept funds as a trust fund deposit and dispense them as instructed by the citizen or the remitter. In such cases, a final accounting is prepared by the Foreign Service post.

(I feel that many consular officers are not familiar with this information. It is up to you to know your rights, in order to facilitate matters should you be arrested.)

"American consular officers are not provided with government funds for legal or other expenses of a detained citizen. They will, however, assist the citizen to obtain funds from private sources which may be available to him in the country of detention and in the United States.

"If a consular officer learns that the conditions of detention of an American citizen are hazardous to health or otherwise unacceptable, he will bring the matter to the attention of the appropriate authorities and request that the conditions be improved. A consular officer will not normally request preferential treatment for a detained American unless his physical or mental health requires it.

"With respect to trial, a consular officer seeks to ensure that an arrested citizen is given a prompt trial after having full knowledge of the charges against him and full opportunity to prepare his defense with legal counsel of his own choosing. While the consular officer is, of course, in no position to insist that an arrested citizen be given a jury trial or all the other safeguards provided for by the United States Constitution and legal system, he can and does seek to ensure that the trial, from the standpoint of substantive and procedural due process, accords with generally accepted legal standards prevailing in civilized countries. On occasion, these standards are higher than those which a foreign country may apply to its own nationals. Fortunately, national treatment is normally adequate.

"A consular officer may not formally intervene with a foreign government to protest what may appear to be an unfair procedure until the arrested citizen has exhausted all available remedies, such as appeal, to correct the error. However, if it appears to the consular officer that an unfair procedure may be prejudicing the case against the American citizen, he brings the matter to the attention of his mission for review and possible intervention.

"Although it is not possible in every case, a consular officer attempts to be present at the trial of an American citizen to ensure fair treatment. However, a consular officer will attend the trial in all major cases, and whenever possible if requested.

"Finally, if a citizen is convicted of the charges against him and all appeals have been exhausted, the consular officer may initiate an examination of the whole case to determine whether there has been a manifest denial of justice which would warrant a formal official protest to the foreign government and eventually, in some cases, the espousal of a claim against the government on behalf of the citizen. Such protests are made only after a case has been thoroughly reviewed by the United States Embassy and the Department of State.

"When a consular officer learns of the arrest abroad of an American citizen on the basis of local charges, he seeks to gain access to the citizen as soon as possible to inform him of his rights to legal counsel, provide him with a list of attorneys practicing in that area, and assist him to communicate with friends and others who would want to know of his plight and who may be able to assist financially or in other ways.

"When the place of arrest is at some distance from the consular officer, a personal visit by him is sometimes not immediately possible. The limited number of United States consular officers abroad, the large territories of some consular districts and the steady increase in the number of Americans abroad requiring consular services, add to the difficulty of making personal visits. However, if a consular officer is unable to visit an arrested citizen at once, he uses other means to contact the citizen and inform him of available assistance.

"Arrests of American citizens resulting in detention are reported to the Department of State by telegram if the matter is urgent. Reports include details of the arrest, charges, name and address of the attorney when one has been chosen, place of detention and the names and addresses of persons to be informed by the Department."

The largest number of arrests has been related to drugs. According to the State Department, "As of January, 1971, 700 Americans were under detention in foreign countries on charges of possession, use or trafficking in illicit drugs. This represents an increase of more than 70% over last year."

There are many other young Americans not included in this figure rotting in jails in remote areas.

A recent survey by the State Department reveals that in "a sample of about 1/3 of the cases in our card file, the ages of persons arrested for narcotics violations are from 18 to 49 years of age. The median age in the sample was 25.7 years, showing that by far the greatest number arrested are below 30 years of age."

Many of the young Americans I met who were involved with drugs did not leave America to become pushers. They had traveled around the world following false rumors and had gone broke. In order to live from day to day and get the fare home, they turned to dealing in drugs.

There are some young Americans who go abroad with the intention of dealing in drugs. However, many are unsuccessful in this highly illegal venture.

False rumors are rampant. People have heard that "many countries have legalized drugs." There has been a great deal of publicity about permissive drug policies in certain countries. Although some people in these countries advocate the restricted use of drugs for religious and moral reasons, technically drugs are illegal.

Many Americans have the impression that drug laws and their enforcement are more lenient in foreign countries. On the contrary, prosecution of offenders is being intensified as a result of an international drive to suppress drug trade. The penalties for violations in many foreign countries are very severe, including even the death penalty in some places. In some countries mere possession of narcotics or marijuana yields a jail term of 6 years plus a heavy fine. In other countries, sentences for possession or trafficking range from 1 to 3 years in a "detoxification asylum" (usually a mental hospital).

Trafficking or smoking marijuana can often incur the same penalty as possession or use of heroin.

In some places drug peddlers are also informers. After making a sale, the "peddler" will describe the buyer to police and customs officials. The buyer is then detained by officials, and when drugs are found in his possession, he is arrested. The seller does this for two reasons: he receives money when he sells the drugs, and he receives additional money in the form of a reward from the police or customs officials for acting as an informer. Many Americans have fallen victim to this practice.

The following information was supplied by the U.S. State Department:

1. TOTAL AMERICANS ARRESTED AND UNDER DETENTION ABROAD ON DRUG CHARGES

Arrests for the month of:		*Under detention for the year ending in September*	
September 1972	165	September 1972	966
September 1971	187	September 1971	797
September 1970	124	September 1970	613
September 1969	71	September 1969	242

2. TOP 20 COUNTRIES IN WHICH AMERICANS ARE UNDER DETENTION FOR NARCOTICS

Country	*Arrests for the month of 9/72*	*Total under detention for year ending 9/72*	*Country*	*Arrests for the month of 9/72*	*Total under detention for year ending 9/72*
Mexico	20	211	Morocco	4	24
Canada	38	106	Sweden	3	22
Germany	25	90	Lebanon	2	21
Israel	–	48	Netherlands	3	21
Spain	–	40	Australia	1	13
Greece	8	37	Bahamas	19	13
United Kingdom	5	31	Denmark	3	13
France	3	29	Italy	1	13
Japan	5	29	Pakistan	2	13
Colombia	1	26	Turkey	4	13

REPRESENTATIVE PENALTIES FOR POSSESSION AND TRAFFICKING IN NARCOTICS

(Pre-Trial confinement can be prolonged, in some cases up to 1 year. Some of this time may be spent in solitary confinement. Many countries have no provisions for bail for drug arrests.)

Australia — Penalties range from fines for simple possession of amphetamines and barbituates to large fines and up to 10 years' imprisonment for importation, manufacture or trafficking in narcotic drugs. There are requisite intermediate penalties for possession and use of LSD and other hallucinogens, as well as, for hashish and marijuana.

Bahamas — Possession: Americans have been sentenced from three months to one year. Most are fined $100 or more and expelled.

Canada — Possession small amount for use: - short jail sentence and expulsion. Possession trafficking amount: minimum seven years, maximum life.

Denmark — Possession: fine and detention up to two years.

France — Sale, purchase or use: prison term of three months to five years and fine of 3,600 to 36,000 francs. Customs court will also levy heavy fine. Expect minimum three to four months pre-trial confinement.

Germany — Possession for use: light jail sentence or fine. Possession for trafficking: maximum three years in prison and 500 DM fine.

Greece — Possession of small amounts: Prison term not less than two years. Possession trafficking amount: maximum 10 years and 10,000,000 drachma fine. Several Americans presently serving eight and ten year sentences.

Iran — Simple possession of marijuana, opium, heroin, or other illegal drugs in small quantities punishable by imprisonment for between 3-15 years. The illegal importation, manufacture or sale of opium, heroin, morphine or other opium derivative is punishable by death. The manufacture or import/export of hashish is punishable by 5-15 years imprisonment and fine of 500 rials per gram confiscated. There is no legal distinction between marijuana and hashish.

Israel — Large number Americans arrested every month for use or possession. Maximum sentence ten years and 5,000 Israeli pound fine. Those convicted of possession of small amount for personal use can expect heavy fine and possible expulsion.

Italy — Possession: Minimum three years 30,000 lire fine. Maximum eight years and 4,000,000 lire fine.

Jamaica — Possession: small amount for personal use: short prison sentence and fine. Bail seldom granted. Possession trafficking amounts: 18 months to three years at hard labor. Several Americans presently serving maximum term.

Japan — Possession small amount for personal use: one to two months pretrial detention; suspended sentence and expulsion. Possession trafficking amounts: maximum five years.

Korea — The illegal import/export or manufacture of prohibited narcotic substances or dangerous drugs is punishable by imprisonment for up to 10 years or a fine not to exceed 1,000,000 won. For possession and use of the same substances the sentence may range to 5 years and the fine to 300,000 won.

Mexico — Possession: Two to nine years and 1,000 to 10,000 peso fine. Possession by an addict is not a crime in Medico. Trafficking: three to ten years and 2,000 to 20,000 peso fine. Illegal import or export of drugs: 6 to 15 years and 3,000 to 30,000 peso fine. Persons arrested in Mexico can expect a minimum of six to 12 months pretrial confinement.

Morocco — Possession of any amount: Three months to five years and fine of 240,000 to 2,400,000 francs. Most hashish sold in Morocco is mixed with untaxed tobacco. Possession of untaxed tobacco always incurs a heavy fine in addition to that levied on hashish.

Netherlands — The illegal use of any narcotic substance or other dangerour drug is punishable by a fine up to $900 or from 1 day to 4 years imprisonment.

Philippines — Penalties range from minimum 6 months to maximum 6 years and fine for use of marijuana to capital punishment for offenders whose activities result in the death of a user. Maximum sentences are mandatory when the victim of the offense is a minor. Illegal importation of prohibited drugs is punishable by imprisonment from 14 years to life.

Spain — Possession less than 500 grams cannabis: fine and expulsion. Possession more than 500 grams cannabis or trafficking amount any other drug, or attempt or intention to traffic in any drug: minimum six years and one day, which may, at courts discretion, be reduced to a jail sentence, whose length depends upon circumstances of offense, and a heavy fine, based on valuation of drugs, amounting in one recent case to over $100,000. If fine not paid, alternative jail sentence may be four years or longer. Most Americans charged with trafficking in Spain have spent at least one year in pretrial detention.

Thailand — Attempted import or export of drugs: six months to ten years and fine not less than 3,000 baht. Possession, purchase or sale or opium; six months to 20 years and fine. Use of opium: maximum ten years. Use of cannabis is not illegal in Thailand, but attempted import or export is illegal.

Tunisia — Law prohibits consumption; possession, cultivation, storage, distribution, offer or sale of narcotic substances, including hashish and marijuana, and provides a minimum sentence of one year and fine of $20 with a maximum sentence of five years and $20,000 fine. The law excludes suspended sentences.

Turkey — Possession: Three to five years. Trafficking: ten years to life. Maximum sentence received by an American to date is eight years and six months.

U.K. — Possession, use trafficking: Maximum ten years and heavy fine. Possession of small amount for personal use usually punished by a light imprisonment and expulsion.

In April of 1970 when I passed through Afghanistan, there was a notice on the bulletin board of the American Embassy. It said, "Warning: The penalty in Iran for trafficking in drugs across the borders is death. 26 shot to date. 1 American on trial now. Don't be next." By November of 1970, 56 had been shot.

Drugs are legally sold and controlled by the government in Nepal and may be bought for personal use. However, it is illegal to resell drugs within the country or traffick in drugs across the border.

Prison conditions

Prison facilities in many countries are primitive, usually over-crowded, infested with rats and insects and inadequate toilet facilities. Food in most cases is substandard. One American who was recently released from jail in the Philippines told me that all he received was 5 eggs a day, cooked any way he wanted them.

In some countries you must pay for any additional food, and if your money is confiscated as evidence, you are out of luck.

Advice to drug users

Because of the availability of drugs, it is not worth while to jeopardize your freedom by carrying drugs across borders. Only purchase what you can consume. Cross the border completely clean, and purchase any additional drugs in the next country.

Only buy drugs from reputable sources. In most cases they will allow you to sample it before you purchase it.

In countries where drugs are morally legal yet technically illegal, remain as inconspicuous as possible.

Avoid black market areas, hotels or restaurants which are patronized by drug peddlers. These places are usually watched by police.

Should you be using any amphetamines or barbiturates under a doctor's care, make sure they are in a safe container (clearly labeled), and keep a copy of the doctor's prescription with you.

ACCOMMODATIONS

The first thing to do upon arriving anywhere is to find a place to stay, if only for the night. Once you have found lodging, you can go sightseeing with your mind at ease, knowing that you have a place to call home. Depending on your life style, you may require a first-class tourist hotel, pension, youth hostel or even campgrounds. Included here are descriptions of some of the more popular types of accommodations patronized by Americans.

What is a youth hostel?

A hostel is a supervised lodging place. Formerly hostels were patronized mostly by school aged youth. However, because of the lure of travel year-round, hostels have now opened their doors to travelers of all ages carrying the appropriate identification card proving that he is a member of the American Youth Hostel Association. According to the American Youth Hostel Association, there are over 4,200 hostels throughout the world where overnight accommodations range in price from 35¢ to $2.00.

AYH is one of 47 associations which comprise the International Youth Hostel Federation. Holders of valid AYH membership passes are entitled to stay in any of the Federation hostels throughout the world. If a traveler leaves America without this pass, he is still able to purchase an International Youth Hostel membership at any Federation hostel.

Where can I get a membership to the AYH, and how much does it cost?

Membership can be obtained by writing to American Youth Hostels, AYH INC., National Campus, Delaplane, Virginia 22025, or telephone (703) 521-3271. All membership passes are valid for one year from January 1 through December 31. However, if purchased in the fall, passes are valid until December 31 of the following year. Fees for passes are as follows:

Youth Pass—under 18 years—$5.00

Senior Youth Pass—18–20 years—$8.00

Adult Pass—21 years or over—$10.00

Family membership—$12.00 (Valid in U.S.A. and Canada only; includes children under 18 years of age).

Lifetime membership (individual)—$50.00.

Adult passes purchased abroad cost $6.00 and up, depending on the country.

What does a youth hostel look like?

A youth hostel can be a school, camp, church, student house, mountain lodge, community center, farm house, old castle, villa or even a retired sailing vessel. Youth hostels come in many shapes and forms, but members of the Federation are all governed by the same rules and regulations. Each youth hostel is run by house parents, or, as they are often called by travelers, wardens. It is their job to maintain the appearance and upkeep of the facilities and to make the travelers feel at home.

Hostels are patronized by people from many different countries, and in many cases the daily upkeep (sweeping floors, etc.) is maintained by the travelers themselves. Therefore, youth hostels give a traveler an excellent opportunity not only to live with people his own age from other countries but also to work side by side with them.

YOUTH HOSTEL CUSTOMS

According to the AYH, certain common-sense practices based on consideration for others are enforced in youth hostels, and house parents have the right to revoke passes for violations of the rules.

Many youth hostels have cafeterias which offer a choice of inexpensive meals. In some cases, where meals are not provided, kitchen facilities are, so hostelers can generally buy and cook their own food. In either case, it is a general rule that hostelers take turns cleaning up after meals.

Smoking is not permitted in bunk rooms.

Beer and other alcoholic beverages are not permitted except in some European countries, such as France, Italy, Spain and Portugal, where wine may accompany the meals.

The customary limit for a stay at a youth hostel is three to five days unless special arrangements have been made with house parents. However, if the hostel is not crowded, you will be allowed to stay longer.

Hostels usually lock their doors between 10:00 p.m. and midnight, and it is a general rule that travelers leave the premises by 9:00 or 9:30 in the morning. At this time the doors to the dorm rooms are locked. (At many larger hostels, lounges, lobbies and restaurants are open daily.)

The doors reopen again between 4:00 and 5:00 p.m. In Europe during the summer seasons there will usually be a long line of people waiting to check in at this time. It is advisable to make advance reservations and arrive early. You will find the larger youth hostels in Europe are completely booked with large student groups from other European countries. Even with reservations some individual travelers have been asked to leave to make room for these large groups.

If you are over 25 years of age, you may not use hostels in Bavaria (Southern Germany) or Switzerland, except with permission of house parents. In Luxembourg the maximum age is 35; in Morocco it is 30. In most countries priority is given to those under 30. Children under 14 years of age may not use hostels outside their own country unless accompanied by an adult relative of the same sex, and in some countries children under 10 may not be admitted. Accommodations for married couples are available in some countries.

Persons traveling by motorcycle, scooter or car are not permitted to use hostels in England, Wales and Australia. In Germany motor vehicles may not be parked on hostel grounds. Priority is often given to walkers and cyclists in Luxembourg, Morocco, Scotland, Canada, Malaysia and the U.S.A.

Are the other t pes of youth hostels available?

In many countries throughout Europe and Asia local governments as well as private individuals have established profit-making youth hostels for the convenience of travelers. These types of hostels do not abide by the same conditions as the Federation hostels. It is unsafe to leave your gear unguarded in these hostels.

The rules and regulations at Federation hostels seem strict for an adult. However, other than cleaning or domestic duties, the closing of the hostel from 9:00 a.m. to 4:00 p.m. encourages the traveler to get out and see more of the country that he is visiting rather than sit in some stuffy room.

For travelers on a budget, seeking a place with a clean bed, adequate food, good companionship and, most of all, a place to meet others, a well-run Federation hostel is your best bet.

For further information write to: American Youth Hostels Inc., National Headquarters, 20 West 17th Street, New York, N.Y. 10011

LIVING IN THE HOME OF A CITIZEN OF A FOREIGN COUNTRY

This is common throughout Europe, including some of the Eastern European countries. The local tourist information center can make such arrangements or direct you to the agency which handles these accommodations.

Many people think that living in the home of a local person would add to their cultural enjoyment of that country and would expose them to the "local people" and their way of life. However, if the home in which you stay is inhabited by people who do not speak English, you may find it difficult. You will find greater exposure to the people and their way of life if you stay in a small local hotel.

CAMP GROUNDS

Camping is an excellent way to get away from the routines of modern society, and camping facilities are as common in Western Europe as in the States. However, throughout countries of the Middle East and parts of Asia you will find that sleeping out is still a way of life, and camping facilities are rare.

Camping grounds throughout Europe are easy to find. Your tourist information center will supply you with the names and addresses of all the camp grounds in the area and a map with directions to reach these places. Roads are very well marked with signs leading to the camp grounds.

Many maps for finding locations of camping sites throughout Europe can be purchased here in the States. Many of these maps list locations and available facilities. One such book, *Europa Camping and Caravaning,* can be purchased by mail through American Youth Hostels, 20 West 17th St., New York, N.Y. 10011, or from Camp Grounds Unlimited, Blue Rapids, Kansas 66411.

Once you reach the camp grounds, you will usually find cars and trailers from all over the continent as well as other Americans. The fee for the use of a campsite ranges from 25¢ to $2.00 depending on the equipment and the vehicles accompanying you. Most campsites are situated in scenic spots, usually on rivers, lakes, or oceans, or in the mountains and forests. Facilities for camp grounds vary from country to country.

You will find a general store for the purchase of food and other necessities. Some of the more elaborate campsites have hot showers, restaurants and even swimming pools and sporting equipment. Some even arrange guided tours of neighboring towns and villages.

For campers who really like to get away from it all, a kind word to a farmer will often afford you a free campsite for the night. Do not abuse his kindness, leave his grounds as you found them.

Many countries have local laws governing camping, some of which are strictly enforced. For example, in Spain camping is forbidden within 150 feet of any road, or reservoir. It is always best when camping in a place other than a designated camping site to stop and ask the local police for permission.

Equipment

The type of camping equipment you will need will depend on your individual needs and your mode of travel. If you are hitchhiking with a back pack, it is best to keep your gear at a minimum. A sleeping bag, a small tent and some basic cooking utensils will suffice. With this type of equipment you can spend the night almost anywhere just by unrolling your sleeping bag. I have spent many a free and very comfortable night sleeping in the waiting rooms of railway stations, airports and parks.

NOTE: Since many camp grounds throughout Europe are open only to people with cars or tents, you should carry an all-weather poncho. Tie it between two trees or to the bumper of a car as a makeshift tent.

If you are camping with an automobile or trailer, you can include more elaborate gear, such as a large tent, an air-mattress with inflatable pillows, and a portable stove.

There is no need to purchase camping equipment in America and pay for excess baggage on the plane to Europe or Asia. In most places throughout the world, especially in Europe, camping equipment is less expensive than it is in America and can be purchased in any major city in Europe.

STUDENT ACCOMMODATIONS

Student accommodations are readily available during the summer months. Most schools and universities are closed, but their dormitories are open to visiting students. In addition, many local governments have set up special hotels to accommodate students.

The easiest way to find student accommodations is through the local student offices located in most major cities throughout Europe and Asia. Simply ask the tourist information center for the addresses of the student centers or the locations of the schools and universities in that area.

You can investigate certain accommodations before you leave America:

1. A fraternity or sorority from your school may have ties at a university in a foreign country.

2. Some of the larger student organizations have information on accommodations abroad. Many student organizations have set up hostels throughout the world.

3. An organization called SOFA will supply you with information on student tours and accommodations throughout Europe and parts of Asia. Write to SOFA, 1560 Broadway, New York, N.Y. 10036, or telephone (212) 586-2080.

PENSIONS

A pension is a small boarding house which takes in travelers. In some cases food is served.

Today pensions have a new look. Many hotels call themselves pensions because they have managed to maintain a homey atmosphere. Pensions are usually inexpensive—from $1.00 to $5.00 a night, sometimes including breakfast.

Some pensions have rules and regulations similar to those in youth hostels, but in most cases they are run like small hotels. Conveniences, conditions and regulations will vary from country to country.

How can I find a pension?

1. Through the tourist information center which will supply you with addresses and maps.

2. By word of mouth and recommendations from fellow travelers.

3. Often proprietors of pensions will meet trains, airplanes, boats and offer travelers transportation. However, once you arrive at a pension, you are not obligated to stay if you are not satisfied with the accommodations, and you do not have to reimburse the proprietor for transportation.

Pensions can be found just about everywhere, but a vast

majority of them are in the central part of town where everything is happening. In Europe, where everything moves by rail, a great number of pensions are located near the railway stations. Throughout Asia and Australia the bulk of pensions are set in the tourist sections of town. You can find pensions in villages, suburbs, and resort areas.

Pensions may be less expensive than youth hostels, student accommodations, or YMCA's. For example, in Sydney, Australia, the YMCA wanted $3.75 per night including breakfast, while a small chain of pension-type hostels called Goulds Hotels was charging $16.00 a week for bed and breakfast and clean, comfortable lodging in a good location. (See Australia).

Always agree on the price with the proprietor before you decide to stay. In almost every pension the proprietor will ask to copy information from your passport and may ask to hold it overnight. *Do not surrender your passport to the proprietor of a pension or any other hotel.* Let him copy the information and return your passport to you. In some cases you will then pay in advance for the time you intend to stay.

HOTELS

An American is never far from home when he travels. No matter how remote a country is, there will always be at least one Western-style hotel providing comfort and safety for the tourist. Many of these large hotels are owned and operated by American chains (Hilton, Intercontinental, etc).

However, some hotels bearing the name of American chains may actually be owned and operated by the local governments, for example, the Intercontinental, better known as the Bali Beach Hotel, in Indonesia. In such hotels the service may be somewhat different.

In addition to the American-type, first-class hotels, you will find local establishments which offer first-class accommodations with a local flare.

Even the most expensive hotels have their problems with thefts.

No matter how prestigious the hotel is, never leave valuables in your room. If you do not want to carry them, check them at the front desk. Make a detailed list of the items, and count out cash and/or travelers checks in front of the clerk. Have him sign a receipt stating the amount of the currency, list of the articles, date and his name.

Find out if tipping is allowed and how much or ask at the hotel. Don't feel obligated to tip. Only do so if you are satisfied with the service. The word TIPS means "To Insure Prompt Service" or the singular TIP, "To Insure Promptness." Don't pay for something you don't receive. This applies in restaurants, taxicabs and to porters.

Reservation Services

Tourist accommodations should be booked in advance by your local travel agency or an intercontinental reservation service, such as Sheridan (telephone, toll free, 800-325-3535) or American Express (telephone 800-AE-8-5000), and Hilton Hotels (telephone 212-594-4500). Reservation services are handy for tourists or the businessman on the move. You can book not only your hotel reservations according to your budget, but often car rentals plus airline transportation as well.

The same type of reservation service is offered by many airlines. Often airline and ship companies will offer package deals including transportation and accommodations for one price. Always check to see which hotels are included. If certain airlines favor one hotel or another, it might be because they are affiliated with that chain. For example, Pan American owns the Intercontinental Hotels, and TWA owns the Hilton Hotels.

Many tourist information centers operate a complete reservation service. Not only do they book youth hostels, student accommodations and pensions, but first, second, and third-class hotels. In most cases they will be very helpful in booking the hotel and location you prefer.

However, during peak travel seasons (such as July and August) entire cities may be booked to capacity, so try to make reservations well in advance.

Location

The location of a hotel is very important for accessiblity to transportation, sightseeing, etc. With the exception of resort hotels, large, first-class hotels are usually located in the nicer sections of town near or in the tourist areas.

No matter what your budget or expense account, you will find a hotel to fit your needs no matter where or how you travel, whether first-class, moderate tourist class or budget economy.

SALVATION ARMY

The Salvation Army does not just march in parades and ask for donations on street corners. It also runs a chain of inns throughout the world. These inns offer the traveler lodging and good meals at below-average cost. In many countries the Salvation Army Red Shield Inns are *the* place to stay. For example, in Calcutta travelers must take precautions against health hazards. The Salvation Army's Red Shield Inn is in a good location. There is a 24 hour guard at the gate and an enclosed courtyard for parking. Also, their water is boiled. All this and breakfast for 8½ rupees ($1.10 U.S.) a night.

RELIGIOUS ORGANIZATIONS

Many religious organizations have accommodations for travelers. The most popular are the YMCA's which exist almost everywhere. Rules and regulations vary from country to country as do the prices. They are usually fairly well located in the cities and, in most cases, clean and comfortable. Many serve meals.

In Asia, Sik Temples have been known to put up travelers for the night. It used to be the policy of these temples never to turn away a traveler, but unfortunately freeloaders have swamped some of them and worn out the welcome for future travelers. Also, many of them are in out-of-the-way places and difficult to find.

In Europe, some churches and convents put up travelers. They are usually for girls only. Inexpensive during the summer months, they are usually packed.

As a general rule, that dollar-a-night hotel, youth hostel, YMCA and even flop houses are safe places.

Most proprietors of these establishments realize most of their income is from foreign travelers. If word of thievery got around, they would lose their clientele. But no matter how safe an establishment may be, never relax your guard. Never leave valuables or documents in your gear or room, especially when sharing quarters.

I found that most often it's not the local inhabitants who steal from travelers but fellow Americans.

TRANSPORTATION

WALKING

All that is required is a good pair of shoes and determination.

Walking through the streets of foreign countries will give you the opportunity to get closer to the local inhabitants. Try to walk away from tourist areas. Take one path going and a different route coming back to add to your sightseeing. If you are unfamiliar with a certain part of town, it is best not to walk it alone or after dark.

HITCHHIKING

Hitchhiking or auto-stopping, as it is called in Europe, works basically the same way as in the States. There is, however, one basic difference. In some countries sticking your thumb at someone is considered an obscene gesture. Stand to the side of the road, and simply hold out an open hand. Better yet, hold up an easy-to-read sign naming your destination.

Your appearance is very important in procuring rides. The neater and cleaner you are, the better your chances of attracting a ride. Many gimmicks can be used, such as displaying the flags of various countries. However, for obvious political reasons this may sometimes hinder your chances of being picked up. It pays to know your territory.

Try to stand in front of your pack or luggage, or keep it out of sight. Cars in Europe are quite small, and a driver will think twice about picking up a hitchhiker with a lot of gear.

Avoid wearing sun glasses or keeping a hat pulled over your eyes. These will prevent you from making eye contact with prospective drivers.

When hitchhiking on a major highway, try to stand on the entrance ramp where traffic is slow enough to stop for you.

When your driver is nearing his destination, ask him politely if he will drop you off on the outskirts of town so that you can continue your journey. In most cases he will do this. You will find hitchhiking *through* major cities and towns extremely difficult. Taking a bus will save you time and trouble.

Make sure you have the appropriate foul-weather gear for emergencies, and see that your luggage or pack is well protected. It is a good idea to pack your belongings in plastic bags to protect them against moisture and dirt. A sturdy, comfortable pair of shoes is recommended.

AVOID HITCHHIKING AT NIGHT OR IN BAD WEATHER.

Girls should never hitchhike alone.

Boy/girl hitchhiking teams are popular for two reasons: (1) it is easier for a girl to get a ride, so she will do most of the hitchhiking while he stands on the side lines, and (2) he goes along to protect her.

Often strangers will meet at youth hostels or at other popular meeting places and team up for a journey.

Once inside the vehicle, whether it be car or truck, try to be as polite as possible. The driver may not speak English, but you can easily point out your destination on your map. (YOU SHOULD ALWAYS CARRY A GOOD ROAD MAP.)

If you are asked to share the driving on a long haul, do so only if you have a proper driver's license and you are familiar with the roads.

If you are asked by the driver to split gasoline expenses, do so only if you feel this is necessary to get to your destination.

KEEP AN EYE ON YOUR GEAR.

There is a very popular racket plaguing hitchhikers. After driving for a while, the driver may pull off the road near a shop and ask you to get him a Coke or a pack of cigarettes. While you are out of the car, he leaves with your luggage. It is a good idea to get a description of the car and the license number in case this should happen. It is an even better idea to have a hitchhiking companion, so only one of you leaves the gear at a time.

You will find additional information on hitchhiking in the map section of this book.

THUMBS UP AND GOOD LUCK!

Something new!! Government-sponsored hitchhiking. (See "Making it to Poland")

RICKSHAWS, TRISHAWS AND ANIMAL POWERED CARTS

A rickshaw is a two-wheeled carriage for one or two passengers and is usually pulled by one man.

A more modern form of rickshaw, very popular in Southeast Asia and Indonesia, is a trishaw which is a three-wheeled bicycle-powered rickshaw. The driver peddles the bicycle instead of walking.

The most common type of animal powered carts are horse-drawn vehicles. In more exotic places in Asia every form of animal transportation is used, such as elephants, ox carts and camel caravans.

Always make sure to agree on the price to your destination before you start. Make sure that the driver understands where you want to go, and make sure you understand what the fee is. He should be tipped the same as taxi cab driver.

BICYCLES

Throughout most of Europe and Asia the bicycle is a common means of transportation. Here in America we have automobile rental agencies; in Europe and Asia bicycles are rented. Bicycling is an excellent way to do your sightseeing. It is not only good exercise, but bicycles are inexpensive to rent, and you can cover much more ground in a shorter amount of time than you would by walking.

Organizations such as American Youth Hostels have devoted entire tours to cycling through Europe. Some youth hostels in Europe have rental facilities for their guests. Many tours include rental of bicycles.

Where can I rent a bicycle?

If you are staying in a large hotel, ask the desk clerk, or look in the yellow pages. Stop into a bicycle shop; or better yet, ask your local tourist information center.

You can arrange to bring your own bicycle to Europe, through the airline you are flying. Your bicycle can accompany you on the plane along with your baggage.

MOTORCYCLES AND MOTORSCOOTERS

Because they are extremely economical to operate and less expensive than cars to maintain, motorcycles and motorscooters are commonplace throughout Europe and even more common in Asia. In many tourists areas they can be rented by the day or week at various prices depending on the size and the manufacturer of the vehicle. For example, on the Island of Bali the rental for a 125 C.C. Honda was only $3.00 a day. I've met many people who fly to Europe for the summer, buy motorbikes, use them for their stay and then ship them home.

There are both advantages and disadvantages to traveling by motorbike. Some of the disadvantages are:

1. Chance of accident. Many countries have no speed limits, and motorbikes are vulnerable to accidents with fast-moving automobiles.
2. Roads, including main ones, may not be very good.
3. Gas and repairs can be expensive and, depending on the manufacturer, parts may be hard to get.
4. You will always be exposed to the elements.
5. Motorbikes are extremely tiring when you are trying to cover a large distance on bad roads.
6. You must limit your gear and traveling companions.
7. Upon entering a country your passport is stamped to show a motor vehicle has accompanied you. You may not leave the country unless that vehicle goes with you, or you will have to pay exorbitant duty. Should your motorbike break down in that country, you are stuck until repairs have been made.

Some of the advantages are:

1. If you buy a bike in Europe, you can use it as your means of transportation. After your trip you can ship it home and sell it in the States for what you paid for it in Europe, coming out with virtually free transportation for your whole trip. (See customs hints for duty on automobiles.)
2. You can leave the beaten tourist trail and venture into out-of-the-way places.

AUTOMOBILES

Surprisingly, America is not the only country which has paved paradise to open up a parking lot.

It is now possible with the recent opening of the Asian Highway to drive a well-paved road through Europe and Asia from London to Singapore (with the exception of crossing the Burmese border—See map section). Even a drive up the Malasian peninsular from Singapore to Bangkok looks much like a drive through the Catskill Mountains in New York.

You will find that the automobile is the best way to see a lot more in a short period of time and to reach out-of-the-way places.

For the tourist who likes to get away by himself, renting a car is the best way. Many internationally known American companies such as Hertz, Avis and National, as well as local car rental agencies maintain offices in the most convenient locations. They can be found in local phone directories, through tourist information centers, or the airline you are flying. Many airlines and steamship companies include car rentals in a package with their fares.

Prices for car rentals will vary from country to country. In most cases a daily fee plus a mileage chart is included. Always comparison shop. Some companies will throw in a few hundred miles free. Try to get the most economical car possible; gasoline is very expensive in many countries, often as much as $1.00 a gallon.

Some of the larger companies, such as Hertz, have rent-it-here—leave-it-there arrangements between most major cities in Europe and parts of Asia. Always consider the cost of the car ferries and road tolls along with the cost of the rental. Make sure you get the best road map possible for your journey. In most cases insurance is included with the rental fee, but make sure the insurance coverage is valid in each country you plan to visit.

Most car rental agencies will have long-term rental services for travelers spending a month or more abroad.

NOTE: Remember, a record of the automobile accompanying you—whether it is rented or privately owned—is made on your passport when you enter countries outside Western Europe. In some countries a bond is required, and the owner and/or driver of the vehicle may not leave the country unless he accounts for the location and disposition of that vehicle. If you rent-it-here and leave-it-there, make sure to get a receipt from the rental company when returning the car if the border authorities have noted on your passport that the vehicle accompanied you when you entered the country.

Buying an Automobile Overseas

This can be arranged in a number of ways. In the classified section of *The New York Sunday Times* under automobiles you will find a number of agencies which handle this type of transaction, i.e.:

Europe by Car, Inc.
630 Fifth Ave.
New York, N.Y. 10020
212-LT1-3040

Car Tours in Europe, Inc.
555 Fifth Ave.
New York, N.Y. 10017
212-697-5800

Auto Europe, Inc.
1270 Second Ave.
New York, N.Y.
212-535-4000

Volkswagen 5th Ave., Inc.
500 Lexington Ave.
New York, N.Y.
212-AL5-4060

Allowing for the cost of the car shipping, duty and excise tax you will save approximately $200 on the purchase, not to mention the convenience of having the car in Europe.

The best way to arrange an automobile tour in Europe is through the International American Automobile Association. IAAA will handle all arrangements at no additional cost.

Friends of mine who have brought cars back from Europe, say that joining this organization is a must, for should any problem arise, many doors are open to you. Also, membership in the IAAA will give you priority over non-members when entering crowded campgrounds. The IAAA will also help you acquire your international driver's license and camping carnet (ID booklet for camping). This is a must for campers. When checking into campgrounds, you leave your carnet in lieu of your passport.

The IAAA can also arrange international automobile insurance. Once you have bought this insurance, you will receive a green card which you will often find is more important than your passport when crossing borders.

No matter how you arrange for European delivery on an automobile, you will find there is a savings in the initial cost, not to mention the convenience it affords you while touring Europe.

Depending on the car you buy, expenses and savings will vary. The following is a detailed example of a vehicle purchased abroad by Mr. S. of New York. Mr. S. spent two months traveling throughout eight European countries and put 5,000 miles on his Volkswagen camper, which he bought at a total cost of $3,200. He picked it up in Germany, where he was charged an additional $375 to guarantee that he would not sell the vehicle in the country of manufacture. When the vehicle left Germany, this charge was returned to him. (This practice is common throughout many countries.)

When Mr. S. arranged for European delivery of his VW,

he was told it was available in only two colors, and the license plate's code number indicated he was an American. This announced to thieves that there might be a camera and other valuables in the car. Therefore, Mr. S. advises that one should be extremely careful when parking such a vehicle in a major city in Europe. He personally left his at the campgrounds which was relatively safe and used public transportation to tour cities.

Mr. S. said that shipping his Volkswagen camper from Germany to the U.S. would have cost approximately $150 but he shipped it from London at a cost of over $300. He said that normally shipping a vehicle from the country of manufacture is cheaper.

When the vehicle arrived in New York, he received a call from the shipping company. For a ten dollar fee they offered to act as his agent and see the car through customs, but Mr. S. advises you to do this yourself.

Mr. S. found that after initial cost, shipping and custom tax (based on the mileage and condition of the vehicle) were added, he had saved almost $500 on the purchase of his camper. (On a car the average savings is approximately $200.) Nevertheless, Mr. S. still had to face the usual state tax when registering the vehicle in America.

Buying a Used Car

Buying a used car in Europe will prove to be a less expensive initial outlay. Unless you are mechanically inclined, you may get stuck with a lemon.

Should the car break down on the road in a country other than where it was manufactured, repairs may prove to be costly. Depending on the length of time you are traveling, you may find that it is cheaper to rent a new car than to buy a used one and cope with the headaches.

Another deal offered by many companies guarantees you the resale value when you are finished using the new or used car you have purchased. In other words, the company you purchased it from will buy it back, depending on its condition at a prearranged price. For a one to two-month trip in Europe, with expenses split between three or four traveling companions, the cost will be only about $100 per person for transportation for the entire summer vacation.

Advantages and Disadvantages of Automobile Travel in Foreign Countries

Much to the disbelief of many Americans, traffic jams, rush hour and auto pollution can be found in every place around the world from Athens to Australia. Taking local transportation allows the traveler the opportunity of meeting different people and seeing their country firsthand. I am against owning or renting an automobile except in an emergency in a foreign country. Many times throughout my journey I met people whose vacation had been completely ruined because of problems with automobiles. Such problems included automobile accidents, mechanical breakdowns and political hassles.

Automobile Accidents—These speak for themselves. If the car is not damaged or completely destroyed, there is always the danger of personal injury. Driving on the other side of the street, lack of speed limits on many roads, poor road conditions, the high cost of repairs and gasoline, the initial layout for the cost of the vehicle and insurance, parking problems and traffic congestion can all add up to big disadvantages.

Political hassles with automobiles—In many countries the border officials note on your passport whether you have entered with an automobile. You may not leave the country without this automobile unless you account for it.

When passing through Turkey, I met two young Americans who were driving a used car from Europe towards India. Three quarters of the way across Turkey, the engine blew up. Since it was not worth fixing, they abandoned it. When they arrived at the border without the vehicle, they were detained until the vehicle was towed, at a cost to them of $125, to the customs agency at the border. Since the car was not worth fixing, it was then donated to the government.

An American couple driving through Russia in their new car had a breakdown. Since the USSR did not have trade relations with the country of manufacture, parts could not be shipped in to repair the vehicle. Instead the car had to be shipped out of the Soviet Union at a cost of $400 to the Americans.

Foreigners entering a country by automobile are often given a more thorough customs check at borders than those foreigners entering by means of public transportation.

Most Americans who travel by car through foreign lands

seem to think there is an advantage to this mode of transportation.

1. The most obvious advantage is, of course, the ability to leave the main tourist trail and reach the far-off places, such as small towns and villages in out-of-the-way areas.

2. Some travelers claim they save a lot of money using a car because they always have a place to sleep.

3. Another advantage is that splitting expenses among your traveling companions often makes automobile travel the least expensive of all means of transportation (barring mechanical break-downs and added expenses).

Automobile Insurance

Automobile insurance is required in almost every country in the world. The basic requirement is third-party liability insurance. The green card which is known as your auto passport must be shown at each border crossing and assures the customs officer that the vehicle is insured. Should you buy a used car which is not insured or enter a country which does not recognize the green card, you may be required to purchase that country's insurance at the border. In most cases insurance purchased at the border will range on the average from 50¢ to $1.00 per day for your stay in that country.

Also available and recommended is automobile marine insurance which covers loss or damage to your automobile on trans-Atlantic steamships or on various car ferries throughout Europe and Asia.

Insurance policies with a wide range of auto coverage are available here in the U.S. Contact your local AAA, or write to: American International Underwiters Corp., Head Office: 102 Maiden Land, New York, N.Y. 10005.

Shipping Arrangements for Automobiles

Shipping arrangements must be made by the owner of the vehicle or by an agent known as a customs house broker who will represent the owner of the vehicle. Customs brokers usually charge a fee for their services. U.S. Customs advises us that automobile undercarriages must be cleaned "to safeguard against pests, particularly the golden nematode, which thrives on the roots of Irish potatoes and tomatoes. The Department of Agriculture requires that the undercarriage of automobiles imported from overseas be free from foreign soil before they are permitted entry into the U.S. This may be accomplished by steam spray or through cleaning before embarking for the U.S." At the owner's expense.

Safety and Air Pollution Standards

New or used automobiles for foreign manufacture that you intend to import to the U.S. must conform to U.S. Federal Motor Vehicle safety standards if they were manufactured after December 31, 1967, with the exception of competition, show and test vehicles. Evidence of these safety standards must be attached to the car in the form of a manufacturer's certificate.

Air pollution standards: New motor vehicles or engines imported into the U.S. must comply with the standards of the Motor Vehicle Air Pollution Control Act. The only exceptions to these standards are vehicles and engines manufactured prior to March 30, 1966. For further information write to the Surgeon-General, Department of Health, Education and Welfare, Washington, D.C. 20201.

NOTE: Some European countries, in order to promote tourism, sell coupons to foreign visitors crossing their borders offering a discount on gasoline up to 30%.

TAXI CABS

Taxi transportation comes in many forms. The most basic is the kind we have in America, a metered, chauffered auto that may be hailed on the street.

When you get in, make sure that the meter is set for a new fare. Some cab drivers try to "take" tourists by driving around with the meter constantly running. The tourist who is unfamiliar with the local money usually does not notice.

Other cab drivers may "forget" to start the meter. When you arrive at your destination, they tell you that the meter does not work and charge you an arbitrary price.

If a cab is not metered, always agree on a price before you start. Make a few inquiries to get an idea of what is fair.

Some cab drivers will play dumb pretending they do not speak English and do not understand. They will take you for a ride, overcharge you, and you will probably have trouble getting change from them. If you know the price of the fare, have it in exact change. Hand it to the driver, and walk away.

If you don't like the taxi service, take a bus!

BUSSES

Local busses differ from country to country, but generally they are inexpensive, efficient, and a good way to see the sights.

In most eastern European countries the honor system is in force. There is no conductor. You simply deposit the fare if you feel like it. Surprisingly enough, the local citizens are honest—or are afraid of the large fines should they get caught.

In parts of Asia bus conductors are sometimes timid about asking a Westerner for the fare. They will wait for you to offer it.

Be sure to check schedules to see if there is a return bus. It is easy to get stranded in out-of-the-way places.

What is Europabus?

Europabus, created by the railways of Europe to supplement their extensive railroad systems, is a vast network of internal bus lines connecting many points of interest on the European tourist trail.

Europabus offers a pass which is much like a Eurailpass. This pass costs $99 and is valid from April 15 to October 15. It can be used on designated bus routes in Austria, Belgium, Czechoslovakia, France, Germany, Greece, Holland, Hungary, Italy, Luxembourg, Switzerland.

For additional information write to Europabus (Overseas) Inc., 630 Fifth Avenue, New York, N.Y. 10020.

In my opinion a Eurailpass is a better value than a Europabus pass.

RAILROADS

Despite the decline of rail travel throughout America, in many countries around the world it is of major importance. It has been said that Europe moves by railroads. In most European cities the train station is the hub of activity and is centrally located in the tourist area.

In the Middle East as in Southeast Asia, where hot weather prevails, rail travel seems to be most popular not only because it is less expensive but because in these climates it is often more comfortable. In Australia a modern, air-conditioned railroad cuts across a thousand miles of desert in less than three days; a bus or car would require three to five days to make the same trip.

Many countries try to encourage rail travel among tourists. Most Asian countries will offer student discounts upon request; thirteen Western European countries offer the Eurailpass and Great Britain offers a similar deal called Britrail Pass.

Eurailpass

A Eurailpass is a first-class train ticket good for unlimited mileage for the designated length of time, which is valid in Austria, Belgium, Denmark, France, West Germany (Berlin is not included), Holland, Italy, Luxembourg, Norway, Portugal, Spain, and Switzerland.

Once the traveler has paid the initial cost of the Eurailpass, he is then free to ride on any first-class train at no additional cost. With the exception of Spain, Portugal and parts of Italy, a traveler need not even make reservations. The initial cost of the Eurailpass is as follows:

21 days	$110 (U.S. money)
1 month	$140
2 months	$200
3 months	$230

Children 4 to 10 years—half fare.

The Eurailpass comes in a credit-card type of case along with a Eurail map of Europe showing all the major train routes.

THE EURAILPASS MUST BE ACCOMPANIED BY YOUR PASSPORT AT ALL TIMES.

The Eurailpass also entitles you to bus, boat and ferry travel at no additional cost. Examples: In Germany, a boat ride down the Rhine river between Dusseldorf and Frankfort; in France the Europabus line #241 from Paris to Nice; and numerous ferry boats throughout the Scandinavian area.

A EURAILPASS IS NOT AVAILABLE IN EUROPE. IT MUST BE PURCHASED THROUGH A TRAVEL AGENT OR NATIONAL EUROPEAN RAILROAD OFFICE IN THE UNITED STATES OR CANADA.

Upon purhase of your Eurailpass you will notice that your name and passport number have been printed on the face. There are two blank spaces, one for the date on which you start using your Eurailpass and the other for the date of expiration. Example: If you have a 60-day Eurailpass, and you start using it on July 1, it will be good until midnight of

August 30. These dates must be inserted by the station master or conductor upon embarking on your first journey. Should you decide not to use your Eurailpass, you can obtain a refund within one year of the date of purchase. However, after six months a ten percent service charge is levied.

If the Eurailpass is lost or stolen, no refund is available, and it cannot be replaced.

British Railroads

Although the Eurailpass is widely used throughout Western Europe, it is not available in Great Britain. Great Britain sells a Britrail Pass for $40 that is good for 15 days of unlimited travel throughout the British Isles on a second-class train. A one-month Britrail pass costs $70.00. Young people aged 15 to 22 can buy a Britrail youth pass for $35.00 good for 15 days of train travel.

Also available in Great Britain are Thrift Rail coupons which entitle you to 1,000 miles of second-class train transportation throughout Europe, Scotland and Wales for $40.00.

Britrail Pass, the youth pass and Thrift Rail coupons can only be purchased in North America before you depart. They are available through British Rail International, Inc., 270 Madison Ave., New York, N.Y. 10016, or British Rail International, Inc., 510 West Sixth St., Los Angeles, California 90014.

Types of Trains

Railroad facilities throughout Europe in most cases are clean and comfortable. In Asia everything from human cattle cars to ultramodern, streamlines, air-conditioned trains are available.

There are basically three classes of train travel. The standards for each class will vary from country to country. In most of Western Europe the difference between first and second class is minimal. The compartments in both cars are set up exactly the same: six seats in each compartment, three on each wall facing each other. The only difference between first and second class is the type of upholstery used on the seats, carpeting and other decorations. In first-class compartments the seats usually fold out so that the traveler may get a fairly comfortable night's sleep. This may also be the case in some second-class compartments. Sleeping compartments and couchettes cost extra.

Throughout the Middle East and parts of Asia, first and

second class in some ways might resemble their counterparts on European trains, but they will vary from country to country. In some of the countries of Asia a third-class train exists, which in some cases resembles a cattle car. There are usually about 50 or 60 seats and 300 people crowded into the car. This type of travel was established so that the peasants in these countries can afford some means of transportation. It is so inexpensive, in fact, that some of the more rugged travelers have made it from Istanbul to Calcutta for under $30.

Tips for Train Travel

Arrive early enough to get a seat. Even with a Eurailpass it's first come, first served (except in Spain and Portugal, where all travelers, including Eurailpass holders, must reserve in advance). Water on trains may not be potable, and if there is a dining car, it may be closed at night. It is advisable to bring a large bottle of water or soft drinks and a good supply of food aboard.

Always keep your tickets handy on a long train trip if you are crossing national boundries. Different conductors or customs inspectors will check your ticket and passport. If a railway ticket is lost, no refund is possible.

Don't throw away your ticket. In some places you must present it in order to leave the station platform.

A thrifty traveler will travel by night to save lodging expense. Most long-distance trains are scheduled so that you can leave late in the evening and arrive early the next morning.

Never leave your gear unguarded, even to go to the rest room.

For more specific information on rail travel see the map section of this book.

SHIPS

If you have the time, traveling by passenger ship can be a relaxing vacation in itself, but unless you like reading, shuffleboard or a close friend, after a few days of looking at water, what else is there? Considering that a trans-Atlantic voyage takes anywhere from five to twelve days depending on the ship, people traveling on a short two- or three-week vacation will not have much time to spend at their destination. Traveling by ship is also more expensive than air. The basic fare for a trans-Atlantic crossing is almost the same as the airfare, depending, of course, on the ship and the class of travel. But after a week on a ship, you will find little extras such as laundry, clothes and refreshments cause your expenses to mount.

Many people are under the impression that freighter travel is inexpensive. In fact, the fare can run anywhere from $300 to $400 or more from the East coast of the U.S. to Europe. Often departure dates are changed because of difficulties. Because freighters are limited to about ten to twenty passengers, bookings must be made at least four to eight months in advance.

In order to work on a ship, you must first acquire seaman's papers. According to seamen I've spoken to, high unemployment has greatly reduced the number of openings, and the most experienced seamen will have first option. For more information on freighter travel write to Harian Publications, Greenlawn, N.Y. 11740. Ask for their two books: *Today's Outstanding Buys in Freighter Travel*—($2.50) and *Freighter Days*—($1.50).

Passenger ships and car ferries around Europe and the Mediterranean run on regular schedules and are fairly reliable and inexpensive. Take night boats whenever possible when connecting with Scandinavia and North Africa.

AIR-TRAVEL

What airline is best?

When traveling to popular areas in Europe any will do. When going to out of the way places such as South and East Asia and the Middle East, Australia, etc. Pan Am is best. Pan Am maintains ticket offices in nearly every corner of the world and should a problem arise—a change of itinerary—they can serve you.

Why does Icelandic Airlines offer a lower fare to Europe than any other major airline?

Almost every international airline belongs to the International Air Transport Association (IATA). This organization more or less serving as the board of directors for all these airlines has established international rules and regulations to promote safety and convenience in air travel.

The fact that almost all international airlines belong to IATA is of great convenience to air travelers. When you purchase a ticket, you are purchasing air mileage. It does not necessarily make any difference which company sold you the ticket. In most cases your ticket can be transferred to any airline traveling that route. (Ticket may require endorsement by issuing company). This makes it possible for you to leave at a moment's notice and take the first available plane to your next stop or change your schedule to fit your plans.

Icelandic airlines does not belong to this organization and, therefore, does not have to abide by the organization's fixed price.

For this reason only it has captured its fair share of the tourist trade between America and Europe.

Try to fly the local airline into each country. The ground crews, the flight personnel and customs officials treat you better when you fly their national airline.

Round-the-World Tickets (See "Around the World Through Asia and Europe on $3.00 a Day")

Charter Flights

Always remember you get what you pay for. Many of these charter flights offer reduced fares. However, the flights may be on old, propeller-powered planes with cramped quarters. They may take as long as twenty hours to reach Europe as opposed to the seven-hour jet flight.

All kinds of organizations from church groups to college clubs offer charter flights. Excursions to Europe are the most popular. Recently plane loads of charter passengers made the news when they were stranded in Europe with worthless return tickets. This only proves that you cannot be too careful in choosing the right organization. Investigate the company before you hand over your cash. Find out what type of plane is being used and the flying time. It is worth a few extra dollars to fly with a more reputable company and assure yourself a safe return. It is common to find people in Europe selling return tickets on charter flights. These bargains may be tempting, but beware. Usually the appropriate passport and identification must accompany the ticket.

BEWARE: Many charter organizations demand money in advance for services they have no intention of rendering. They may demand that you pay for a round-trip fare but may give you only a one-way ticket and a voucher to pick up your return ticket on a specified date. *Never travel unless you have your return ticket in hand, and never pay for something you do not receive.*

In-transit accommodations—A traveler flying from point A to point C may have to change planes at point B. If the airline is forced to cancel the plane from point B to C because of mechanical difficulty, for example, the airline is then responsible for your room and board until another plane is available. Included are the following: transportation to and from the airport to the hotel, lodging and meals. Your accommodations will be determined by the airline representative. This will depend on the standard of living there. Usually the airline will place you in a first-class hotel. Any other personal expenses incurred, such as laundry and post cards, must be assumed by the traveler.

it waiting at local banks in strategic stops, so you won't exceed your budget.

There are many other money-saving hints and tips in each individual chapter of this book.

Mark Atlas attempts to keep abreast of the latest information of interest to travelers, but it is physically impossible for any one person annually to cover each of the fifty countries mentioned in MAKING IT ABROAD. Therefore, the author requests that the travelers themselves add to, comment on and help update the information for each edition. The attached post card is for your convenience. If you feel you have any vital information which will aid your fellow travelers, please write to the following address:

MAKING IT ABROAD
P.O. BOX 5847
GRAND CENTRAL STATION
NEW YORK, N.Y. 10017

AIR AND SEA DEPARTURE TAX

Afghanistan	$1.33
Australia	None
Austria	1.60
Belgium	2.00
Bulgaria	1.00
Burma	.42 (male only)
Cambodia	2.86
Ceylon	.42
Cyprus	1.20
Czechoslovakia	1.28
Denmark	2.00
Egypt	2.28
Finland	2.38
France	1.80 –Europe & North Africa .90 -France 2.70—elsewhere
Germany	None
Greece	1.34—air .50—1.50—sea
Hong Kong	1.65
India	2.00
Indonesia	1.60
Iran	3.34
Ireland	1.20
Israel	3.00
Italy	1.60—air 10., 12., 15. sea (depending on class)
Japan	None
Korea, South	1.00
Laos	.40
Malaysia	1.64
Morocco	1.57
Nepal	1.00
Netherlands	1.82
New Zealand	None
Norway	2.80
Pakistan	1.05
Poland	1.71
Portugal	1.40—Europe, N. Africa and other Portuguese airports 3.74—elsewhere
Romania	1.25
Singapore	3.29—if stay exceeds 5 days
Spain	.71
Sweden	3.96
Switzerland	2.33
Taiwan	1.50
Thailand	1.00
Turkey	1.00
United Kingdom	None
U.S.S.R.	1.67
Vietnam, South	.54
Yugoslavia	2.00

LUGGAGE, CLOTHING AND LAUNDRY

SUITCASES

Make sure they are sturdy, in good shape and that all locks and clasps work.

TIP: If a lock or clasp should break while you are on your trip, simply tie a string or belt around the outside of the suitcase.

Because of weight restrictions on airlines you should make sure your suitcase is lightweight. (See chart.)

The most popular type of suitcase is the fiberglass, or Samsonite type, which is lightweight and sturdy. The plaid, cloth-type luggage with zippers is also lightweight but can be easily ripped open.

Baggage handlers are not the most cautious people in the world. Therefore, choose your luggage for strength, not beauty.

A new attachment for suitcases which has become very popular in recent years is wheels. Two wheels are strapped onto one corner of the suitcase, and a handle is attached to the opposite corner. This allows the traveler the convenience of a suitcase and the mobility of a hitchhiker. Wheels also are very handy for long walks down railway platforms and while looking for accommodations in town. Use caution in handling suitcases with wheels, they may be easily broken.

BACK PACKS

There are many ways of carrying your belongings other than in the conventional suitcase. The duffel bag, commonly used by military personnel, offers the traveler ample room for his gear: however, it is awkward to carry.

After the suitcase, the most popular type of luggage is the back pack because it is so convenient to carry. It is most commonly used by people who are traveling on a budget, hitchhiking, camping and youth hosteling. Back packs are usually sold in stores that sell camping equipment and in sporting goods sections of large department stores.

When choosing a back pack, look for the following: (1) ample space for your belongings, (2) a lightweight, aluminum frame, (3) a waterproof outside covering, (4) padded shoulder straps.

Many packs come equipped with a strap that goes around your waist to hold the pack against your back. It is best not to fasten this strap while boarding or disembarking from boats, trains and automobiles. In an emergency you should be able to slip your pack off immediately.

If you are planning to stay in youth hostels, or camp out, it is a good idea to bring your own sleeping bag, preferably waterproof and warm. Some hostels charge for sheets if you do not have a sleeping bag. Be sure there is ample room on your back pack to attach your sleeping bag.

Whether you are using a back pack or suitcase, you will find that everyone's baggage is handled exactly the same.

TIP: Many suitcases look alike. To avoid mix-up and losses, mark your bags both inside and outside with your initials, or, better yet, use travel stickers, clearly labeled with your name and address.

Make sure to keep your baggage claim check in a safe

place. Should you lose this, it will be inconvenient and time-consuming to recover your luggage or file a claim for lost luggage.

If your baggage is damaged or lost in transit, notify the representative of the airline immediately. If your baggage is damaged, he will usually try to have it repaired or make a fast settlement. If your baggage is lost, he will do his best to find it.

According to the International Air Transport Association (IATA), which includes almost all international carriers, the international rate for maximum liability available on *checked* baggage is $7.50 per pound ($16.50 per kilo) up to 44 pounds in tourist class and 66 pounds in first class. (For *unchecked* items which you carry onto the plane the maximum liability is $330, according to the Warsaw Convention agreement.)

If you are charged for *excess* baggage (over the 44- or 66-pound limit), you will be given a receipt for payment for the additional weight at the airline's check-in counter. Don't lose it! To claim loss or damage to *excess* baggage, you must present this receipt to a representative of the airline; without it no adjustment will be made.

If your baggage has been temporarily lost or misdirected, it is the general practice of IATA carriers to allow up to $50 daily for your needs, such as a change of clothing and toilet articles, until your baggage is recovered.

BAGGAGE INSURANCE

Lost or stolen luggage is a great inconvenience. Insuring your baggage is inexpensive and wise if only for your own peace of mind. If your luggage should be lost or stolen and is insured, you will be reimbursed. However, settlement of your claim may take from a few weeks to a few months. A traveler may be forced to use money which could be spent for food, lodging or transportation to replace lost or stolen articles. Since in many countries the price of a toothbrush is the same as the price of a meal, this can be an expensive proposition.

Baggage insurance can be obtained in the following ways:

(1) Check to see if your household policy has a floater clause to cover your personal effects, such as camera and clothing, while traveling.

(2) If you do not already have such a policy, you can purchase baggage insurance from many companies such as Allstate.

(3) For less than 10¢ per $100.00 (up to $2500 maximum) some airlines, such as Pan Am, offer an excess evaluation policy for insuring especially valuable articles, such as photographic equipment, etc.

NOTE: Because of the high risk involved in traveling, baggage insurance, in most cases, will be sold in a package with health insurance.

In cases of loss or theft of your luggage it is extremely important that you notify the local authorities first; otherwise your insurance company will not be able to verify your claim.

BAGGAGE THIEVES

They often meet a plane arriving at the airport, pretend they are passengers, mingle with the arriving passengers, procede to the baggage claim area and abscond with someone's luggage.

A baggage thief may be sitting next to you on the plane. He will always use a common piece of luggage, preferably Samsonite or plaid canvas. When he arrives at his destination, we will pick up an identical suitcase belonging to another passenger while leaving his own which may be filled with telephone books or newspapers.

Your first concern upon arrival is claiming your luggage.

STORING LUGGAGE

Lockers are commonly found in bus and railroad stations and airports. You simply place your luggage in, insert the appropriate coin, and remove the key. If you lose it, see the station manager.

A baggage checking facility found throughout the world is the coat-room type. You simply hand your baggage over the counter, and it is stored on a shelf. However, since this is risky, it is advisable to use lockers whenever possible. Some coat rooms may charge you a few cents to tie string around your luggage and place a seal over the knot. This will guarantee that no one has tampered with your bags.

You will find these types of bag-checking facilities very convenient when you are not staying in a city overnight.

You simply check your bags, and you are free to do any additional sightseeing.

Hitchhikers or campers will find it safer to take only what they need for the night with them and check the rest of their gear in lockers.

PACKING

First of all, choose your suitcase. Always keep in mind that the more you decide to pack, the more suitcases you will need. The more suitcases you are burdened with, the less freedom and the more expenses (excess baggage charges on airlines, taxis, fees for porters, etc.) you will have. Also you will usually have to settle for the first accommodations you come across.

A wise traveler who has learned how and what to pack will carry only one suitcase. This will save him a great deal of money in many ways. Instead of taking expensive taxi cabs to and from railway stations and airports, he can take public transportation, such as busses and subways. And if he does not like the price the desk clerk has given him for a room, he can simply pick up his light load and walk down the street to another establishment without the help of a porter or a taxi.

By keeping your personal belongings at a minimum, you will save hours packing and unpacking. Instead, you can be out seeing the sights and enjoying the country.

Remember, your suitcase will not get lighter as you travel, but heavier. Since you will start accumulating trinkets, souvenirs and maps as you travel, you should pack your suitcase only three-quarters full, leaving space for your new-found treasures.

Many people traveling for the first time are under the impression that the world is going to be as it is in the movies, and they feel they must dress up. Actually, people dress very simply in most places. Unless you have been invited to diplomatic luncheons or afternoon tea with the Queen, there is no reason why you should not dress the same way you would to go to school or the office.

I do not think the author of any guide book has the right to tell a tourist what he should wear and should not wear. This is up to the individual himself. Most travelers will take with them what they feel necessary, if not for practical reasons, then for emotional security. I will, however, list some hints and tips to help you decide what to pack.

The first and most important thing is choosing your wardrobe according to the purpose of your journey. If you are

EXCESS BAGGAGE CHARGES

Normal Free Baggage Allowances

FIRST CLASS	30 kg.—66 lb.	CLASS "B"	30 kg.—66 lb.
TOURIST ECONOMY	20 kg.—44 lb.	SKYCOACH (UK CABOTAGE)	15 kg.—33 lb.

The charge for excess baggage in international travel (except between U.S.A. and Canada), is 1% of the normal adult, direct, first-class, one-way, through fare per kilo regardless of the class of service used. Special rates are available for golf and ski equipment.

The following table should be used for converting from pounds to kilograms for the purpose of computing excess baggage charges:

Lbs.	*Kilos*	*Lbs.*	*Kilos*	*Lbs.*	*Kilos*
1	.5	34	15.5	67	30.5
2	1.	35	16.	68	31.
3	1.5	36	16.5	69	31.5
4	2.	37	17.	70	32.
5	2.5	38	17.5	71	32.5
6	3.	39	18.	72	33.
7	3.5	40	18.5	73	33.5
8	4.	41	19.	74	34.
9	4.5	42	19.5	75	34.5
10	5.	43	20.	76	34.5
11	5.	44	20.	77	35.
12	5.5	45	20.5	78	35.5
13	6.	46	21.	79	36.
14	6.5	47	21.5	80	36.5
15	7.	48	22.	81	37.
16	7.5	49	22.5	82	37.5
17	8.	50	23.	83	38.
18	8.5	51	23.5	84	38.5
19	9.	52	24.	85	39.
20	9.5	53	24.5	86	39.5
21	10.	54	24.5	87	40.
22	10.	55	25.	88	40.5
23	10.5	56	25.5	89	41.
24	11.	57	26.	90	41.5
25	11.5	58	26.5	92	42.
26	12.	59	27.	93	42.5
27	12.5	60	27.5	94	43.
28	13.	61	28.	95	43.5
29	13.5	62	28.5	96	44.
30	14.	63	29.	97	44.
31	14.5	64	29.5	98	44.5
32	15.	65	29.5	99	45.
33	15.	66	30.	100	45.5

HELPFUL INFORMATION
CLOTHING SIZE CONVERSION TABLE
LADIES

DRESSES & COATS

American	10	12	14	16	18	20	40	42	44	46
French	38	40	42	44	46	48	50	52	54	56
English	32	34	36	38	40	42				

BLOUSES & SWEATERS

American	34	36	38	40	42	44
English	36	38	40	42	44	46
Continental*	42	44	46	48	50	52

HATS

American	21	21¼	21½	22	22½	23	23¼	23½	24	24¼
European**	53	54	55	56	57	58	59	60	61	62

SHOES

American	4	5	6	7	8	9	10
English	2	3	4	5	6	7	8
French	36	37	38	39	40	41	42
Italian	32	34	36	38	40	42	44

STOCKINGS

American	8	8½	9	9½	10	10½	11
European	20¼	20½	22¾	24	25¼	26½	27¾
(Size)	0	1	2	3	4	5	6

* excludes British Isles
** includes British Isles

CLOTHING SIZE CONVERSION TABLE
MEN

SUITS & COATS

American & English	36	38	40	42	44	46
Continental	46	48	50	52	54	56

SHIRTS

American	13	13½	14	14½	15	15½	16	16½	17	17½
European	33	34	35-36	37	38	39	40	41	42	43

HATS

American	6½	6⅝	6¾	6⅞	7	7⅛	7¼	7⅜	7½	7⅝
European	52	53	54	55	56	57	58	59	60	61

SHOES

American	6	6½	7-7½	8	8½	9-9½	10-10½	11-11½	12-12½	13
European	38	39	40	41	42	43	44	45	46	47

SOCKS

American	9	9½	10	10½	11	11½	12
European	23	24½	25½	26¾	28	29¼	30½

Sizes to Remember

____

____

____

traveling basically to sightsee and tour with little time for socializing, then leave jewelry, furs and other expensive items at home.

Know what the climate will be like when you reach your destination so that you may adjust your wardrobe accordingly.

Recommended detailed clothing lists can be obtained through a travel agent.

Take basically clothing made of synthetic materials that are wash-and-wear, drip-dry, stay-press and need no ironing. Then you can wash something in your hotel room at night which will be dry by the time you awake the next morning.

Wash-and-wear clothing not only saves you money on laundering, but lets you wear the same clothes several times. Therefore, you pack less. For example, instead of packing four or five changes of underwear, all you will need with wash-and-wear is two changes; while you wear one, you wash the other, saving valuable space in your suitcase.

Always make sure you pack breakable items safely. Plastic containers are lighter and safer than glass.

Carry a small make-up case, attache case or the very popular flight bag which can be carried onto planes and kept with you at all times while traveling. In it you can store valuables and other personal items and safeguard them against possible loss or theft and have immediate access to them.

After you have packed your suitcase, remove about one-half of what you packed, and you will still probably have more than you will need.

Carry your packed suitcase around the block. When you reach the first corner, I think you will change your mind about how much to bring.

IMPORTANT NOTE: Customs officials will often go through your gear whether it be a suitcase or a back pack, unpacking most of it. It is up to you to repack it. Therefore, having your gear well arranged will not only save time at customs inspection but also help you avoid embarrassing situations.

HITCHHIKERS OR BUDGET TRAVELERS

Your first concern is a good pair of walking shoes.

Use plastic bags to protect all your belongings inside your pack from dirt and moisture, and, of course, try to purchase a waterproof pack. Aside from keeping your gear dry, the next most important thing is keeping yourself dry. A waterproof poncho can easily be stored in one of the pockets of your pack. Also, light-weight nylon ski jackets with hoods are very popular. Of course, there is no end to what you can carry so long as it fits into your pack, but, like the tourist with the suitcase, try to leave room for things you may pick up along the way. Many budget travelers and hitchhikers try to get by on as little as possible, often traveling with only one pair of levis and a few personal items. This is indeed a challenging experience, but you should have at least one change of clothing in case you get caught in the rain.

Next to clothing, the most important thing in your pack should be your personal, or toilet, items including a small first-aid kit and a roll of toilet paper. A towel is the most often forgotten, yet most practical, item in your gear.

A small airline bag for your valuables and personal items is still a good idea even when you use a pack. It can be kept inside your pack or removed and carried with you when boarding airplanes or going on overnight excursions or camping. The bulk of your gear can be stored at a railway locker or left at the hotel, and the small bag will come in quite handily.

LAUNDRY

Most tourist hotels will have laundry facilities. Always ask the price first. Itemize what you send out. When your laundry is returned, recheck the list.

Do It Yourself—Throughout most of Western Europe conventional coin-operated laundromats much like those in America are available. In many cases there is an attendant who will look after your laundry once it is placed in the washer and often transfer it to a drier, remove it and fold it. If no fee is charged for this service, a small tip is expected. If you have the time, it is better to stay and do it yourself, if only to insure the safety of your belongings.

If you are traveling with friends, combine your laundry in one machine to save money.

Other types of laundries can be found throughout Asia and even in Europe which resemble the Chinese hand laundry here in America, where you simply drop off your laundry. If you are visiting rural areas in under-developed countries, the only laundry facility available may be a nearby stream or river. Surprisingly enough, I found my clothes came out cleaner this way than in the commercial laundry.

DRY CLEANING

Dry cleaning is available at most of the larger tourist hotels and elsewhere throughout most of Western Europe. However, in the Middle East, South and East Asia, dry cleaning shops exist only in larger cities. Wait until you reach a large city with the proper facilities to dryclean items.

SHOE REPAIR

This type of service will vary from country to country but can be found almost anywhere in the world at extremely reasonable prices. Always ask in advance how much the repairs will cost and when you should return to pick up your shoes.

PENSIONS AND INTERMEDIATE HOTELS

If there is no laundry or shoe repair in the hotel, the desk clerk or proprietor may recommend a local establishment or may even do the job himself in oder to pick up a few extra bucks. In either case, keep a list of the items you send out.

MAIL—SENDING AND RECEIVING

What is the best way to send letters to the United States?

Airmail is fastest. *Seamail* takes from three to eight weeks depending on location. If it's worth sending, it's worth spending a few extra cents to assure speedy delivery.

Most hotels will supply you with writing paper and envelopes at no extra cost.

TIP: It is not a good idea to carry envelopes and stamps in warm climates. The heat will make them stick together. Also stamps sell for different prices in each country; an Italian stamp will not get your letter out of Singapore.

Postcards are probably the most expensive form of letter. Not only do you have to pay for the stamp, but the card itself varies from 6¢ to 15¢, depending on which country you are in. Free postcards can be obtained from hotels and airlines.

Aerograms are cheapest of all and most commonly used by

travelers around the world. An aerogram is an airmail letter which folds into its envelope. In most cases, the stamp is already printed on the face of the aerogram.

Aerograms range in price from 8¢ to 10¢ in Asia, 18¢ to 22¢ in Europe. They cost 13¢ in the United States. There are none in Russia—the Russian government apparently tries to encourage citizens not to have pen pals in other countries.

Can mail be sent from any country in the world?

From most—but try to avoid countries with a strong black market and countries with a low standard of living where the price of a stamp buys a good meal. Often when you post a letter, before you even leave the post office, your stamp is peeled off and resold.

While in these countries, avoid sending mail from small towns. Only use major cities—capitals, if possible. When at a post office, ask the clerk to cancel the stamp on your letter, thus voiding it and making it of no use to anyone. Never send money or checks; such items can entice someone to steal.

Is it best to write to everyone at once?

If you write to all of your relatives and friends on one day, you will spend a large chunk of your ready cash; if you spread all those letters out over two weeks, it will be easier to pace yourself financially.

Is it safer to post my letters through the American Embassy?

No, all mail is ultimately processed through local post offices.

(Precaution should be taken in out-of-the-way places. In the London-Paris-Rome circuit, a traveler can drop a letter in a mail box and be reasonably sure it will reach its destination).

What other ways are there to communicate with the United States?

Telegram. Rates vary, depending on location. A telegram usually arrives at its destination only a few hours after it has been sent.

Lettergram. This is less expensive, but is not delivered until the following morning.

Telegrams and lettergrams can be sent from hotels and post offices. They must be paid for in advance—not sent collect.

The telephone is the most reliable way of getting a message across. If you need money, for example, it is the fastest way to get it. (See "Money.")

Where is the best place to make a long-distance phone call?

It is difficult to go to a pay phone in a foreign country and make a long-distance call. You will probably have trouble understanding the local operator if you do not speak her language proficiently and if she does not speak English fluently. If you are paying for the call, you might not have enough coins.

It is best to use the house phone in the lobby of a large tourist hotel. If there is no large hotel or if you have difficulty because you are not registered there, go to an American Embassy. They won't turn you away. They also will help you send telegrams. (See "American Embassy.")

Call collect whenever possible.

COMMUNICATIONS FROM STRATEGIC COUNTRIES

NOTE: **Prices quoted are from destination to New York and are subject to change.**

COUNTRY	*TELEPHONE RATES (First 3 min.) Day*	*Ngt/Sun*	*CABLES (Per Word)*	*AIR MAIL*	*NOON AT DESTINATION IS FOLLOWING IN N.Y.*
Afghanistan			71¢		3:30 a.m.
Australia	$12.00	$ 9.00	23¢	25¢	3:00 a.m. the following day.
Austria	St. $ 6.75 Ps. $12.00	$ 6.75 $12.00	41¢	20¢	6:00 a.m.
Czechoslovakia	St. $ 9.00 Ps. $12.00	$ 9.00 $12.00	28¢	11¢	6:00 a.m.
Denmark	St. $ 6.75 Ps. $12.00	$ 5.10 $ 9.00	35¢	12¢	6 hrs. later than U.S. (24 hour clock)
Finland	$ 6.80		37¢	11¢	5:00 a.m.
France	St. $ 6.75 Ps. $12.00	$ 6.75 $12.00	28¢	16¢	6:00 a.m.
Germany	St. $ 6.75 Ps. $12.00	$ 5.10 $ 9.00	26¢	13¢	6:00 a.m.
Greece	St. $ 6.75 Ps. $12.00	$ 6.75 $12.00	34¢	20¢	5:00 a.m.
Great Britain	St. $ 5.40 Ps. $ 9.60	$ 4.05 $ 7.20	18¢	18¢	6:00 a.m.
Hong Kong	St. $ 8.00 Ps. $12.00	$ 8.00 $12.00	30¢	9¢	16 hrs. later than U.S. Pacific Coast Time.
Hungary			26¢		
India			25¢		1:30 a.m.
Israel	St. $ 9.00 Ps. $12.00	$ 6.75 $ 9.00	30¢	25¢	5:00 a.m.
Japan	St. $ 9.00 Ps. $12.00	$ 6.75 $ 9.00	34¢	22¢	17 hrs. later than U.S. Pacific Coast Time.
Malaysia	$13.00		31¢	34¢	15½ hrs. later than U.S. Pacific Coast Time.
Norway	St. $ 6.75 Ps. $12.00	$ 5.10 $ 9.00	33¢	18¢	6:00 a.m.
Netherlands	St. $ 6.75 Ps. $12.00	$ 5.10 $ 9.00	22¢	17¢	6:00 a.m.

COUNTRY	*TELEPHONE RATES (First 3 min.) Day*	*Ngt/Sun*	*CABLES (Per Word)*	*AIR MAIL*	*NOON AT DESTINATION IS FOLLOWING IN N.Y.*
Pakistan			22¢	26¢	10 hrs. later than U.S. E.S.T.
Portugal	St. $ 6.75 Ps. $12.00	$ 5.10 $ 9.00	44¢	11¢	6:00 a.m.
Poland			26¢		5:00 a.m.
Rumania			42¢		5:00 a.m.
Spain	St. $ 6.75 Ps. $12.00	$ 5.10 $ 9.00	40¢	21¢	6:00 a.m.
Morocco			33¢	20¢	6:00 a.m.
Singapore	$13.00		31¢	34¢	15½ hrs. later than U.S. Pacific Standard Time.
Sweden	St. $ 6.75 Ps. $12.00	$ 5.10 $ 9.00	26¢	15¢	6:00 a.m.
Thailand	$19.00		39¢	40¢	12 hrs. later than U.S. (EST)
Turkey	$10.00		45¢	17¢	5:00 a.m.
Taiwan			50¢	20¢	
U.S.S.R.	$12.00		26¢ (Moscow) 34¢ (others)	15¢	4:00 a.m.
Yugoslavia			26¢		6:00 a.m.

RECEIVING MAIL

It is always nice to find a letter from home waiting for you in a foreign country. The biggest problem is for you and your mail to be in the same place at the same time. For a tourist on a two-week tour, it is not a very big concern. But for students and other travelers who are on the go for several months in out-of-the-way places, no communication from family and/or friends can be very depressing, and inconvenient if you are expecting important news or money.

Where is the best place to receive mail?

The general post office, Post Restante, is not the best place, contrary to popular belief. Most local clerks cannot read English; mail is often misplaced. General post offices sometimes charge a small fee for holding mail. But if you decide to use this system, have your mail addressed "John Doe, c/o General Post Office, City, Country."

American Embassies are safer than general post offices. Our embassies will forward your mail to your next address, sometimes for a small fee. Have your mail addressed "John Doe, c/o American Embassy, City, Country."

American Express offers its clients a mail service. Have your mail addressed "John Doe, c/o American Express, City, Country."

In most cases, American Express offices are more accessible than American Embassies. Almost all American Express clerks speak English. During summer months in Western Europe mail lines at American Express offices can be quite long, but they offer you an opportunity to meet your fellow travelers, exchange travel talk, and take advantage of other American Express services. (See "American Express.")

American Embassies, American Express and Post Restante will return unclaimed mail after 30 days.

What about sending small packages, boxes, or luggage to the United States?

If you have time to wait, send it by sea mail, but make sure it is well packed and insured.

In an emergency, take the parcel to a major airline with an air freight service. If it is valuable, insure it. Within twenty-four hours it will be back in the States, but air freight can be quite expensive.

What about receiving packages abroad?

Have relatives and friends send them air mail. Regardless of your address abroad you may have to claim your package at the Customs office at the port of entry, which may be a great inconvenience because of its location.

American Express will not accept packages, only letters. General post offices will send notices of package arrivals to American Express which, in turn, will notify you. Simply take the note to the post office and pick up your parcel.

What sources of international information are available abroad?

Go to embassies of countries you plan to visit (either at home or abroad). However, be aware that they tend to be diplomatic and will usually tell you things which present their country in a good light.

English language newspapers, such as the International Herald Tribune, can be found almost anywhere there are tourists. Other useful publications are *The New York Times,* various British newspapers, Time and Newsweek magazine.

If you cannot find these newspapers and magazines on the local newsstand, try the following:

Airport newsstands often have a wide selection of American newspapers and magazines.

American Embassies often have extra copies of the latest publications. (Depending on location, newspapers are usually a few days old.)

What is an American Library?

You will find one in nearly every capital of the world. Their main purpose is to expose local inhabitants to American history and culture. But they are also popular with American travelers looking for the latest issue of an American newspaper or magazine or just looking for a quiet place to spend an afternoon.

In most cases our libraries abroad are situated within our embassies. If not, any embassy representative or any tourist information center clerk will direct you to the proper location.

What is a newsletter?

This consists of a few mimeographed or printed pages of the latest headlines and news stories from America. This is often free for American tourists at the American Embassy, American Library, or other agencies of the U.S. Government overseas. The newsletter is more commonly found in the out-of-the-way places.

What is YANKS ABROAD?

YANKS ABROAD is a monthly publication for Americans who are living and working abroad. It informs them of their social, political and economic rights and advises them on such problems as voting in U.S. elections and paying taxes while abroad. Cost: $1.00 U.S. per issue; $11.00 U.S. per year. Write to YANKS ABROAD, 8 Kensington Mall, London W84AE, England.

AMERICAN EXPRESS COMPANY

What is it and how can it be of service?

American Express is the traveler's best friend. Many conflicting rumors about AE have originated abroad. One rumor in Europe has it that AE is owned by the Federal government. This is not true. It is understandable because, for example, in Britain the British Broadcasting Corporation is government-owned and, similarly, in India, India Airlines is government-owned. Companies with names like Pan American, United States Steel and American Motors lead foreigners to believe that they are government owned.

AE is in no way connected to, nor subsidized by, our Federal government. It is an independent firm whose primary function is servicing travelers.

AE was founded in 1841 by Henry Wells of the famed Wells-Fargo outfit. In the beginning, AE dealt mainly with cargo shipments.

The shipping business grew rapidly, soon extending to the other side of the Atlantic. When tourists and businessmen began venturing to Europe, a safer method of traveling with currency was instituted, eliminating the risks of carrying cash and also making letters of credit unnecessary. In 1891 the AE travelers cheque was born.

At the turn of the century it was already commonplace for American travelers in Europe to stop at AE offices for cheque services, mail and other information. In 1915, AE opened its first travel department in New York.

AE has since graduated from cargo transportation to human transportation and has also become involved in international banking, credit cards and reservation services.

AE maintains offices in nearly every country on Earth. Here are a few of the services offered:

AE will arrange your trip from start to finish, including transportation, hotels and sight-seeing. If you are already in a foreign country, you can easily arrange short trips through AE.

For reservation services, call (Toll free in the U.S.) 800-AE8-5000 for hotels, motor inns and car rentals around the world.

AE credit cards (often called money cards) are honored around the world in many hotels, restaurants and shops. These cards are available in most cases to persons with an annual income exceeding $8,500. Supplementary cards for the card member's immediate family are available but should be requested well in advance of any trip planned.

If you run out of money and are able to present a personal check or a bank check with your credit card at any AE office, you are eligible to receive up to $500 ($50.00 in local currency and $450.00 in travelers cheques.

If your card is lost or stolen, notify the nearest AE office immediately.

Travelers cheques are the safest form of money to carry. One per cent is charged when purchasing them, nothing when you cash them at AE. However, if you cash them elsewhere, local laws or custom may specify that a small charge be deducted for changing your money.

Be sure to record the number of each cheque on the form

provided when you purchase your cheques. Keep this form in a separate, safe place in case your booklet is lost or stolen. As an added precaution, mark down the cheque numbers and place of purchase on a separate sheet of paper, leaving it at home with a relative or friend.

In the event of loss or theft, go to the nearest AE office, fill out the appropriate report forms, and your cheques will be refunded without charge. Presentation of your cheque numbers will facilitate matters; otherwise the procedure could take a few days.

AE mail service is available to all of its clients, i.e., AE credit card holders, travelers cheque holders and members of its tours. Since you may be required to show an AE travelers cheque to collect your mail, it is a good idea to carry a $10.00 cheque with you.

Have your mail addressed to you, c/o AE, name of city and country. AE will hold it for you for 30 days, then return it to the sender. If you are willing to spend $2.00 to register a forwarding address with an AE office, your mail will be forwarded; additional postage costs must be paid upon receipt of mail.

During the summer months in Europe, AE offices often have long mail lines; therefore, it is advisable to arrive at an office as early in the a.m. as is possible.

NOTE: The addresses of AE offices throughout the world are listed in the map section of this book. If you would prefer a personal copy of these addresses, write to American Express Company, 65 Broadway, New York, N.Y.

THE LANGUAGE BARRIER

Which language is most widely spoken in the world?

Mandarin, the official language of Mainland Communist China, is spoken by more than 800 million people. Throughout the rest of the world the traveler will be most exposed to English, which is spoken in some of the most exotic places in the world; i.e., Pakistan, India, Malaysia, Singapore, and Hongkong.

English has become the international business language. In Japan, the world's third largest industrial power, English is a must for anyone going into business, so English schools have sprung up everywhere there.

It has been said that an American is never far from home when he travels. However, there are still quite a few communication problems to overcome. You may find yourself in a town where absolutely no one speaks English.

In a foreign country, where am I sure to find someone who speaks English?

The most obvious place is an American Embassy. If for some reason it is closed, try a tourist information center. If both are closed, you can be sure that any prestigious tourist hotel will have at least one employee who speaks English.

What languages are best to know?

You will find that in Western Europe most people are bilingual, mainly because the countries are very small and neighbors are exposed to one another.

In Europe, North Africa and the Middle East if you cannot communicate in English, try German or French; both are widely used in those areas.

In Asia, Japanese is very widely used. In Southeast Asia and Indochina, French is usually the second language.

In Australia, English is spoken. The accent of the rural (or outback) areas is difficult to comprehend at times.

If you are able to utilize high school French, German or Spanish, do so by all means: Language schools, like Berlitz, offer good, practical courses.

If you are going to spend a few weeks in a foreign country, it will be to your advantage to learn a few basic phrases in that country's language. If you are touring five or six countries over a period of a few weeks, you will most likely absorb basic phrases in each country. Do not try to cram. You will find it extremely frustrating if you try to learn a language within a short time. It will be more trouble than help and may ruin your vacation. If you find it difficult to pick up basic phrases, try to communicate in the "third language."

The "third language" means: you don't speak their language, they don't speak your language, but you both speak certain international words: you both use sign language, facial expressions and gestures. The third language requires a lot of patience and perseverance.

Many travelers get frustrated, lose their tempers, and shout. This doesn't accomplish anything. Besides, you're the one 12,000 miles from home having problems. LEARN TO BE PATIENT. Take your time in getting your message across.

The best approach is to simplify your questions and answers. When someone asks, "Where are you from?," simply answer "America." This will save a lot of unnecessary confusion yet answers the question in a polite way.

You will find the language barrier the most challenging part of your trip; overcoming it, the most rewarding part. After all, you are traveling to meet people and sample their way of life.

You will also find it rewarding to meet a foreigner who speaks English. He will probably be anxious to be of assistance and answer questions.

TOURIST INFORMATION CENTERS

What is a tourist information center?

The tourist information center is a traveler's most reliable and readily accessible source of information. These centers are set up by the national and local governments in every capital and major city around the world.

Are tourist information centers easy to reach?

They are usually situated in one of three places:

1) International airports; 2) central railway stations, and 3) in the center of business districts in every major city.

The airport centers are mainly for tourists. They provide hotel reservation service, car rentals, maps, transportation details and information about the area you are visiting.

Tourist information centers located in railway stations are completely separate from the general railroad information office. In Western Europe, the railway stations are situated in the center of town.

What type of information can be obtained at the tourist information center?

Most centers run a reservation service. They will help you find accommodations ranging from first class tourist hotels to inexpensive pensions, youth hostels, YMCA's and camp grounds. They will even place you in a citizen's home for the evening if you wish. There is usually a small fee charged for the reservation service, sometimes as little as 25¢. For best accommodations it is advisable to arrive early in the working day. During summer months youth hostels and pensions are filled to capacity. Because of this a traveler might end up paying twice as much as is necessary to spend.

Centers also will supply you with maps pinpointing certain areas of interest and details of mass transit systems. Upon request, you will receive travel brochures listing sights to see, and the addresses of every embassy in town.

The center will arrange guided bus tours.

You can obtain a list of available doctors, hospitals, and reputable merchants in town.

Centers normally will go all out to help travelers. That's what they're there for. The clerks speak English, are very polite and are human "yellow pages" full of information!

Even if you have arrived in town with advance reservations, centers are good places to get oriented. They are one of the most popular meeting places for travelers in town.

GUIDED SIGHTSEEING TOURS

In almost every major city in the world organized sightseeing tours are available. Excursions are usually conducted by agencies of the local government or by independent travel agencies, bus companies or American Express. Whether your tour has been pre-arranged by your travel agent or you are planning to wing it on your own, the following tips will be useful.

The average guided tour is usually one to four hours in length. Most tours do not allow the traveler sufficient time to satisfy his curiosity about the things he has traveled thousands of miles to see. It is a good idea to make a list of all the sights you plan to see in a particular city and then take the guided tour around town. This will familiarize you with the location of some of the more popular sights. During the tour, check off the places on your list which you would like to explore later in depth.

Whether you are returning to places your tour has skimmed over, seeing additional things the tour missed, or starting from scratch and doing it all on your own, I suggest that you follow my procedure for a do-it-yourself tour.

1. Go to the Tourist Information Center and get a map of the city. Have the clerk pin-point on your map the sights you wish to see.

2. Get a map of the local transportation system (subways and buses). Such transportation is cheap and enables you to mix with the local people. Unlike the neon-lit tourist who sees the city through an air-conditioned bus window, you will be able to sample the local way of life.

3. Ask the Tourist Information Center for brochures describing the sights you want to see.

If all the sights you want to see are situated in one central part of town, a walking tour might be best. Chart the most scenic route on your map, making sure that you stop at all the sights important to you.

After you have seen the more famous sights in town, you might want to visit some out-of-the-way places which are off the tourist trail.

FREE GUIDED TOURS

These are for the traveler on a budget. They are not actually free; someone has paid for them, but you are going to tag along and eavesdrop.

Suppose your do-it-yourself tour takes you to the Acropolis in Athens. Here many guided tours come and go each hour. Watch for one which has just arrived, and follow it. Make sure you stand in the back, and stay as inconspicuous as possible. Then just follow and listen to the English commentary.

For the more adventurous there is another way to get a free guided tour. (1) Simply wait at your sight for a tourist bus to arrive. (2) When the tourists are all almost off the bus, mingle with the crowd. (3) The guide pays for the entire group, and since the ticket taker never courts heads, you get in free.

For further information on sightseeing, see the individual map sections of this book.

GUIDED TOURS AND TEEN TOURS

GUIDED TOURS

Every organization from the YMCA to major airlines offers some type of guided tour ranging from long weekends to two-month excursions in almost every part of the world.

However, before you shell out your hard-earned cash, get all the facts in writing and read the small print. It is best to sit down with a reputable travel agent who is an expert on setting up tour packages throughout the world. Any small neighborhood travel agent should be able to set up your entire tour fairly easily.

But what happens when you are 5,000 miles from home? If a problem arises, your travel agent will not be there to help you. For this reason only, I recommend using an internationally known travel agent, such as American Express, Cooks Tours, etc., which have branch offices in almost every major city in the world. Then, if a problem does arise, assistance will be available.

Many travel agencies have specialists for each section of the world. Although the greatest bulk of traveling is done on the European continent, don't forget about South America, Africa, the Middle East, Asia and Australia. They are not only exotic, intriguing and inexpensive, but in many cases, out of the main stream of travel and unspoiled by tourists.

Once you make a decision and start your journey, it is very difficult to change your itinerary, so, plan your tour very carefully. It is your travel agent's job to arrange the kind of tour you want, but he can do this only if you give him some basic idea of where you want to go and how much you want to spend.

Guided Tour Tips

1. Investigate the reputation of the travel organization or agency.
2. Check references with people who have already gone on that tour.
3. Comparison shop with other organizations offering similar tours.
4. Find out what is included: meals—how many a day; accommodations—class of hotel, location; sightseeing tours and excursions within the country; transportation.
5. Find out if the price of the tour includes fees for visas and airport taxes. Usually it does not.

TEEN TOURS

From about November to late spring the last few pages in the magazine section of *The New York Sunday Times* are devoted to advertisements for guided tours of Europe, the Middle East, safaris to South America and Africa, cruises to the South Seas and other exotic places for young people. You will find in the Times the most competitive list available of organizations offering such tours. The only better source would be a relative or friend's recommendation.

As is the case in any business, there are reputable and not-so-reputable firms doing business. I am sure you will agree that your safety and well being are worth the few moments spent in choosing a dependable organization.

In Europe I met many young people traveling on various guided tours. Many of them complained that they had paid over $1000 for a six-week tour of Europe and were eating peanut butter and jelly sandwiches, sleeping in 60¢-a-night youth hotels and receiving almost none of the extras they had been promised.

Two 16-year-old girls had been turned loose upon their arrival in Europe and told only to report to a particular place for the flight home in six weeks. They were, by the way, on a guided tour with a well known organization which advertised "strict adult supervision throughout the entire trip."

So you see how important it is to choose a responsible, reputable organization. Not only will a fly-by-night organization take you for a lot of money, but what should be a memorable, educational experience could turn out to be a horrifying nightmare.

I have personally never taken a guided tour, but I have two brothers, one of whom was a camper and the other, a counsellor on two different teen tours. From their comments and those of many other teen tourists I met in my travels, I have compiled the following check list to help choose a tour.

1. When signing up for the tour, make sure you read the fine print.

2. Is a refund available if last-minute cancellation is necessary?

3. Is health and liability insurance included?

4. Get a day-by-day itinerary and a list of mail stops.

5. Check the sleeping accommodations. Make sure you get what you pay for. Many tour groups promise hotel accommodations which are actually youth hotels or school dorms.

(NOTE: Many organizations offer two basic types of tours to Europe: hotel tours and camping tours. Be aware of the difference in accommodations.)

6. How many meals do you receive a day? Since most tours include only 2 meals a day, you will need extra money for

food, adding to the cost of the trip.

7. Does the tour just pass through a country or really visit it? Are you merely dropped off and told to look around by yourself, or are guided tours provided?

8. What type of supervision is provided? Many tour companies advertise that their chaperons have been teaching for 20 years and are very experienced. People in their 50's cannot keep up with young kids who will be on the go both day and night. Chaperons should be over 21—but not *that* much over—and college graduates.

The average length of those summer teen tours is 4 to 6 weeks at a cost of approximately $800 to $1500. Two identical trips may advertise the same prices, but one of them may not include many of the extras, such as airport taxes, laundry, local transportation, meals and entertainment. This means you must supplement the trip.

I visited one of the more reputable teen tour agencies called American Trails. Dan Brent, Associate Director said of American Trails (which is a sister operation of Trails West) "Business is based on recommendations. A disreputable firm will tell you the same thing as a reputable place. We fulfill all our promises and run a tight ship. Curfews are enforced, and no drugs are allowed."

How do the kids feel about it? He replied, "We level with the kids. It is much better to set an example, and all our counsellors are young responsible college graduates, able to keep up with the kids and relate to them."

I asked Mr. Brent if he had any tips for parents who are trying to choose the right tour for their child. He recommended that you ask the tour organization to supply you with about 10 names of people who had been on the tour during the past two years. Any reputable firm will be glad to supply you with such a list he said. Contact these people and find out if all the promises are fulfilled. First talk to the parents to see if they were satisfied, and then talk to the children who went on the tour.

If you are planning to send your child on one of these tours, don't limit your interviewing to the telephone. Meet personally with the directors of the organization. Many organizations like American Trails visit the clients' home.

Brent said, "The difference between the $800 trip vs. the $1600 trip is usually in the extras and the meals."

Instead of giving your child a lot of cash to carry to pay for those things, it is wiser to pay for the more expensive trip and know that your child is eating regularly. According to Mr. Brent, American Trails is the only organization offering three meals a day.

PHOTOGRAPHY

Personal, passport-type photos should be carried along with your important papers. You will need photographs when applying for visas. (For number of photos required see Visas Information in the Map Sections.)

These photos, like your passport photos, should represent you as a clean-cut individual. Remember, your appearance may be the reason you are denied a visa. If you have long hair, wet it and pin it back, shave and put on a tie just for the photo. In most cases the clerk will hand your passport, photos and application to the embassy official who will not even look at you. He will base his decision on your photos and application.

CAMERAS

To avoid the heartbreak of spoiled photos, familiarize yourself with your camera. If you have not used the camera before, shoot a roll of film and have it developed before you leave. This way you can avoid mistakes on your trip.

Cameras with automatic lens-setters are not only time-saving but adjust to the proper exposure under varied lighting conditions. Movie cameras as well as still cameras are available with automatic settings.

If you are not sure how to operate your camera, any photo or camera dealer will usually be happy to help you. If photographs are an important part of your journey, you may want to carry a spare camera in case of accident, breakdown, loss or theft. Many travelers I have met also carried a small book with their cameras to keep track of each picture on each roll of film. Since a great deal of time often elapses before the film is developed, details and locations are easily forgotten, especially if you are taking a great many pictures.

Before leaving the States, register any *foreign*-made equipment you are taking with you at the Customs Offices at the port of exit to avoid having to pay duty on it upon your return. Make sure to take a copy of the registration along with you.

Camera equipment can be purchased in Hongkong, Singapore, Tokyo and Germany at extremely low prices. However, you should only buy from reputable, authorized dealers and get a complete warranty and guarantee with the equipment. (See Con Games.)

FILM

Film can be purchased in almost every major city throughout Europe, Asia, and Australia.

(NOTE: Check expiration date to see if film is still usable.)

It is a good idea to take a full supply with you when leaving the States, for in some countries film can be very expensive, if available at all. It is advisable to take a camera which used the standard, popular-size film, such as 35-mm, or the Brownie 720-size or some of the more popular cartridge types. Film for Polaroid cameras is difficult to find in many countries, since this camera is solely an American product. For a complete list of suppliers write to: Customer Service Department, Polaroid Corporation, Cambridge, Mass. 02139. For a list of Kodak film centers, suppliers and retailers throughout the world simply stop in at any Kodak Center here in the States and ask for a pamphlet called "Notes for the Photo Travelers Abroad," which also includes tips on cameras, film processing around the world.

PROCESSING

For short 2- or 3-week trips it is best to carry film with you and have it processed when you return home. Though it is possible to have black and white film processed in almost every major city of the world, developing color film may be risky. If you are impatient, have one roll developed as a sample. If you are satisfied with the results, continue. If you can wait, it is best to have your film developed in larger cities or mail it home.

MAILING FILM

Many people have their film processed by mail. This can be done from abroad as well, but travelers should be warned to mail only one roll at a time in the special containers supplied by film manufacturers, and make sure they are well labeled. It is not a good idea to send many rolls of film in a small package whether they have been exposed or not.

Many people take advantage of the ridiculously low price of film in certain countries to stock up for the future. However, when you send home a box of new or exposed film, you are risking possible damage by X-ray machines used by customs officials on packages entering a country through the mail. This can also happen at major airports. Because of tight security controls passengers may have to walk through an arch-way in which the X-ray searches for fire arms and other weapons.

MONEY SAVING TIPS

If weather conditions prevent taking photographs, you can usually buy sets of color or black and white slides of the main attractions of that country. Slides are sold in tourist shops, at large hotels and often at airports and railway stations. Also available are color postcards which are less expensive than photographs. It is a good idea, however, to purchase photographs, slides and postcards when you are ready to leave the country so that you may choose those that will represent sites you have seen during your visit.

When visiting countries in which, for political reasons, photographing is not encouraged by authorities, it is up to you to abide by the regulations or face possible confiscation of your film and camera or even possible charges and jail. The most commonly restricted areas are military installations and any scenes showing poverty or conditions that would give that country a bad image. However, a tourist is usually advised well in advance of entering restricted areas.

In countries where photo restrictions are enforced, keep a dummy roll of film in your camera and exposed rolls in your pockets, not in your luggage, when approaching borders or official places. Your luggage will be checked, but personal searches are rare.

Also check to see if local religious beliefs discourage picture taking. In many places people are afraid of cameras, and still others are just shy.

Don't be surprised if *after* you take a photo of a peasant in some far-off land, he approaches you and demands payment. Don't pay. (See "American Image.")

Someone may ask you to take his picture for a fee of "only" 50¢ or $1.00. If you do take a photo in this case, you should pay.

The camera bug whose purpose for travel is taking photographs should check customs rules relating to the importation of large quantities of film and equipment before he leaves the States or with embassies along the way.

Cameras and lenses will be big attractions in foreign countries and duty-free shops. You are allowed the first $100.00 of camera equipment duty-free; over that you must pay a duty of 12% on foreign cameras and 20% on lenses.

WORKING ABROAD

Many people are still under the impression that they can work their way around the world. However, in many countries unemployment is at an all-time high. It is difficult for local inhabitants to find a job, let alone an American who is just passing through.

Good business is built around its employees. The owner or manager of any business prefers to hire people who will stay, not drifters who are going to work for a few weeks or a month and then move on. It is very difficult to work your way around the world, unless you are planning to travel a few years and work a minimum of six months to a year in each place.

Beware of false rumors such as "an American high school dropout can teach English in Japan." (See chapter on Japan.)

The most difficult task in finding work is not finding someone who will hire you but getting a work permit or a work visa. What many people don't realize is that you must first find a job, leave the country in which you wish to work, apply for your work visa at one of its *foreign* embassies, and then return for your job. Work visas are very rarely issued to an alien while he is touring the country.

If you are fortunate enough to find work in a foreign country, you will find it extremely difficult to save money to move on to the next place. You will probably be paid on a local salary scale and earn just enough money to live on. It will take you approximately six months to a year to save enough money to get back to the United States.

Although no statistics are available, the majority of Americans I met who were working abroad were employed illegally without permits. If they were working, it was usually because they had technical skills which were needed.

Once you have left the States, you may find classified advertisements in newspapers. They will mostly be for men, truck drivers, and construction workers on projects on far-off, South Sea Islands. Also, in the South Pacific and Southeast Asia there are job openings in mining, construction and oil drilling expeditions. To apply for these jobs, you must either write to the head office, or, if you are in Southeast Asia, you may find many of these companies have offices in Singapore.

I've met many workers who told me that the salary for these jobs will vary. In most you sign on for 6 months to a year. You will receive a weekly or monthly salary and a living expense, should you be on location. For civilian workers in danger zones, such as construction workers in South Vietnam, the pay can be as high as $1200 a month.

Australia has unlimited job opportunities and in most cases work permits are not necessary. (See map section on Australia.)

If you are looking for work on the continent of Europe, plan ahead, and try to arrange for work before you arrive. If you are a teacher, a nurse, an engineer, or have some technical skill, it will not be difficult to find employment almost anywhere provided you overcome the local language barrier.

Various student organizations will help young people procure summer jobs. Contact American Student Information Service, 22 Avenoe La Liberte, Luxembourg City, Grand Duchy of Luxembourg, or Council on International Educational Exchange (CIEE), 777 United Nations Plaza, New York, N.Y. 10017, or send for the Overseas Employment Guide by writing to National Employment Service Institute, 1700 Pennsylvania Ave., Washington, D.C. 20006 (price $2.00).

There are various other types of temporary jobs throughout the world. These include working for the Olympic games, expositions, world fairs, tour agencies and charter companies. You can track these down by writing to the proper source. And, of course, don't forget the Peace Corps, which gives people, young and old, the opportunity to travel and receive a small amount of pay.

Once you have arrived in Europe or Asia, with a certain amount of hustling on your own you should be able to track down a job by following the local classified advertisements or by word of mouth. Only remember: without a work permit you are violating the law, and if you are caught, according to local laws you can be deported.

STUDYING ABROAD

Travel is the best education. Whether you study in a foreign country for just the summer or year-round, you will find your horizons will be broadened just by the experience of being a foreigner. If you stay in a country long enough to learn the language and the customs, your experience will be that much more rewarding.

Almost all the national tourist information services for each country represented at the United Nations in New York City will be able to supply you with information on exchange programs.

After you select the country where you wish to study, consult the corresponding map section of this book for the appropriate address of their national information service.

Your own college or university may also be able to supply you with information on courses and credits offered in foreign universities.

Chapman College offers a unique study program aboard a ship which tours the world, with academic credit. For information on World Campus Afloat contact Chapman College, Orange, California 92666.

Fulbright grants for graduate study abroad are available primarily to scholars holding Ph.D.'s or professional degrees, creative and performing artists and teachers. For information contact your campus representative or the Committee on International Exchange of Persons, 2101 Constitution Avenue, Washington, D.C. 20418, or the Institute of International Education, 809 United Nations Plaza, New York, N.Y. 10017.

Other arrangements for studying abroad can be made through the Council on International Educational Exchange (CIEE), 777 United Nations Plaza, New York, N.Y. 10017, or the Institute of International Education (IEE), 809 United Nations Plaza, New York, N.Y. 10017. Handbooks and brochures are available.

The New Guide to Study Abroad by Ganaty, Adams and Taylor, published by Harper and Row, is available at bookstores.

The New York Sunday Times has a section devoted to schools and educational institutions, including some abroad.

CHARTS

CONVERSION EQUIVALENTS

DISTANCE

English to Metric

1 Inch = 2.5 Centimeters (Cm)
1 Foot = .3048 Meter (M)
1 Yard = .9144 Meter (M)
1 Mile = 1.609 Kilometers
5 Miles = 8.045 Kilometers
10 Miles = 16.094 Kilometers
20 Miles = 32.187 Kilometers
30 Miles = 48.281 Kilometers
40 Miles = 64.375 Kilometers
50 Miles = 80.468 Kilometers
60 Miles = 96.562 Kilometers
70 Miles = 112.655 Kilometers
80 Miles = 128.750 Kilometers
90 Miles = 144.843 Kilometers
100 Miles = 160.936 Kilometers
Nautical Mile = 1852 Meters
(1 Statute Mile = 0.8689 Nautical Miles)

CAPACITY

English to Metric

1 Cubic Inch = 16.387 Cu. Cm.
1 Cubic Foot = 0.0283 Cu. Meter
1 Cubic Yard = 0.7645 Cu. Meter
1 Pint = 0.4732 Liter
1 Quart: 2 Pints = 0.9463 Liter
1 Gallon: 4 Qts. = 3.7853 Liters

Persons driving automobiles should make note of the following chart when purchasing gasoline.

1 English Gallon = 1.200 U.S. Gallons = 4.5460 Liters
1 U.S. Gallon = 0.833 English Gal. = 3.7854 Liters
1 Liter = 0.220 English Gal. = 0.2642 U.S. Gallon

WEIGHT

English to Metric

1 Grain = 0.065 Grams
1 Ounce = 28.35 Grams
1 Pound = 453.592 Grams
1 Short Ton = 907.18 Kilograms
1 Long Ton = 1,016.06 Kilograms

TEMPERATURE

Fahrenheit to Centigrade

+212°	=	+100°
+194°	=	+ 90°
+176°	=	+ 80°
+158°	=	+ 70°
+140°	=	+ 60°
+122°	=	+ 50°
+104°	=	+ 40°
+ 86°	=	+ 30°
+ 68°	=	+ 20°
+ 50°	=	+ 10°
+ 41°	=	+ 5°
+ 32°	=	0°
+ 23°	=	— 5°
+ 14°	=	— 10°
+ 5°	=	— 15°
0°	=	— 17.8°
— 4°	=	— 20°
— 13°	=	— 25°
— 22°	=	— 30°
— 31°	=	— 35°
— 40°	=	— 40°

TO COMPUTE FAHRENHEIT:

Multiply Centigrade by 1.8 and Add 32

TO COMPUTE CENTIGRADE:

Subtract 32 from Fahrenheit and Divide by 1.8

$$°F = (°C\,{}^{9}\!/_{5}) + 32$$

The following map sections of this book are designed to give vital, statistical information to enable the traveler to orient himself upon arrival at his destination. The listings under further information will make it possible to obtain sightseeing and additional information before starting your journey. Locations of tourist information centers are given whenever possible as is the recommended place to receive mail.

From time to time in strategic locations, mostly throughout Asia, I have mentioned the name of a hotel or restaurant which is a popular meeting place for young travelers.

Money charts are current as of this writing and have been quoted after the devaluation. However, all prices are subject to change.

At the end of the book you will find a post card in which you the traveler can add to, comment on and up-date information for future editions.

MAKING IT TO WESTERN EUROPE

As you can see, the map on page 128 has a double line. To the left of the line are the Western European Countries or, as I call them, the "London-Paris-Rome circuit," which seems to attract the bulk of American travelers.

Entering Western Europe is a simple matter.

VISA

None is required for a tourist stay of up to three months.

HEALTH REQUIREMENTS

Smallpox immunization is no longer required unless you are arriving from an infected area (Africa, South America or Asia). Always check first. No further vaccinations are needed to travel to Western Europe.

ARRIVAL AND DEPARTURE

The cheapest and most efficient way to get to and from Europe is by air. The three most popular ports of entry and departure used by travelers are London, Amsterdam and Luxembourg.

NOTE: When flying abroad you must pay a $3.00 airport tax leaving Kennedy airport.

Round-trip fares are as follows:

MAIN TRAVEL AREAS

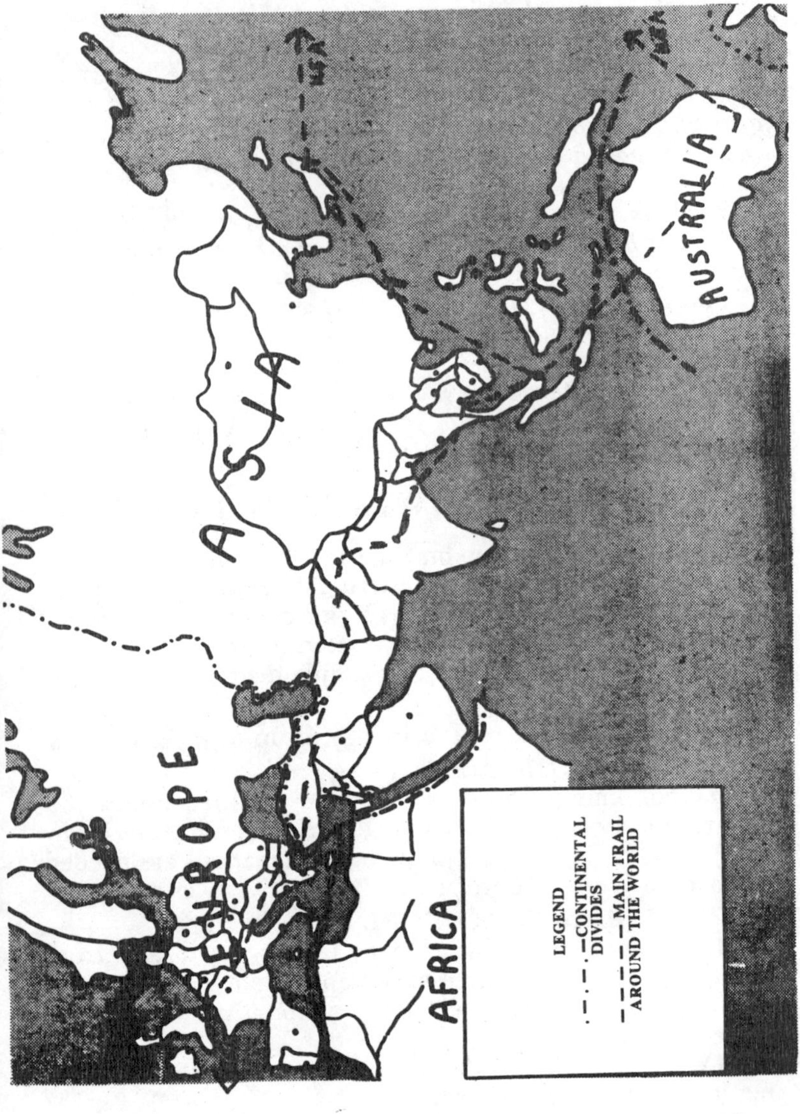

FINLAND
HELSINKI
SWEDEN
NORWAY
OSLO
STOCKHOLM
Moscow
U.S.S.R.
North Sea
COPENHAGEN
DENMARK
IRELAND
DUBLIN
ENGLAND
LONDON
NETHERLANDS
AMSTERDAM
BERLIN
EAST GERMANY
WARSAW
POLAND
BRUSSELS
BELGIUM
BONN
LUX.
PRAGUE
CZECHOSLAVAKIA
Atlantic Ocean
PARIS
WEST GERMANY
VIENNA
BUDAPEST
ROMANIA
FRANCE
SWITZERLAND
BERN
AUSTRIA
HUNGARY
Bucharest
BELGRADE
YUGOSLAVIA
BULGARIA
Sofia
ITALY
ROME
TIRANE
ALBANIA
GREECE
PORTUGAL
MADRID
SPAIN
LISBON
Athens
Mediterranean Sea

ECONOMY FARES From New York to

	LONDON	*AMSTERDAM*
April-May	$484	$504
June-July-Aug.	590	636
Sept.-Oct.	484	504
Nov.-March	430	452

On the following fares a $15.00 surcharge is levied when departing Friday and Saturday from New York and Saturday and Sunday from London.

ADULT FARES From New York to

	LONDON	*AMSTERDAM*
(14-21 day excursion)		
Sept.-May	$349	$382
June-July-Aug.	412	445
(22-45 day excursion)		
April-May	$190	$200
June-July-Aug.	210	220
Sept.-Oct.	190	200
Nov.-March	190	200

YOUTH FARES (12-26)—NO TIME LIMIT. RETURN TICKET GOOD FOR ONE YEAR FROM ISSUANCE.

April-May	$190	$200
June-July-Aug.	210	220
Sept.-Oct.	190	200
Nov.-March	190	200

ICELANDIC AIRLINES

ADULT FARES From New York to

	LUXEMBOURG
(22-45 day excursion)	
Sept.-Oct.	$205
Nov.-March	180
Apr.-May	205
June-July-Aug.	270

YOUTH FARES (under 26 years old) RETURN TICKET GOOD FOR ONE YEAR.

Basic	$165
PEAK SEASON:	
June 20-July 25 March 23-April 12 Dec. 15-Jan. 4	185

GETTING AROUND IN WESTERN EUROPE

AIR—All capital and most major cities are connected by air travel. One thing most people overlook is that an airport tax is charged whenever you leave a country via air. The tax can range from $1.00 to $4.00. (See chart page 95.)

HITCHHIKING—Hitchhiking in Europe will vary with the country. Technically, in some countries hitchhiking is illegal, but the law is rarely enforced because of the millions of young people—local Europeans as well as Americans—who hitchhike. It is common to arrive at an intersection and find half-a-dozen hitchhikers waiting ahead of you.

BOATS AND FERRIES—If you are arriving and departing from London and plan to visit other European countries, you should be warned that the cheapest ferry crossing the English Channel costs approximately $8.00 one way. To a traveler on a budget this is an unwelcome expense.

The following ferry schedules and prices will give you an idea of how to plan your trip:

	HOURS	*MIN. COST*
Between Great Britain & Belgium (Vice Versa)		
Dover (or Folkestone)-Ostend	**3½**	**$ 8**
Dover-Zubrugge	**4**	**8**
Felixstowe-Antwerp	**14**	**20**
Harwich-Ostend	**6**	**13**
Between Great Britain & France (Vice Versa)		
Dover (or Folkestone)-Boulogne	**1½**	**8**
Dover (or Folkestone)-Calais	**1½**	**8**
Dover-Dunkerque	**4**	**8**
Ramsgate-Calais	**40 min.**	**9**
Newhaven-Dieppe	**4**	**13**
Southampton-Cherbourg	**5**	**13**
Southampton-LeHavre	**7**	**13**
Between Great Britain & Spain/Portugal (Vice Versa)		
London-Madeira/Canary Islands	**4/6 days**	**100**
Southampton-Bilbao	**37**	**32**
Southampton-Lisborn (Casablanca)	**3 days**	**47**
Southampton-No. Spain & Canary Is.	**4/7 days**	**38/62**
Between Great Britain & Germany (Vice Versa)		
Harwich-Bremerhaven	**16**	**28**
Harwich-Hamburg	**20**	**28**
Between Great Britain & Holland (Vice Versa)		
Felixstowe-Rotterdam	**7**	**16**
Harwich-Hook of Holland	**7**	**13**
Hull-Rotterdam	**16**	**18**
Immingham-Amsterdam	**13**	**10/18**

	HOURS	MIN. COST
Between Great Britain & Ireland (Vice Versa)		
Ardrossan-Belfast	4	6
Fishguard-Rosslare	3	6
Heysham-Belfast	7	6
Heysham-Dun Laoghaire (Dublin)	8	6
Holyhead-Dun Laoghaire	3	6
Liverpool-Belfast	10	8
Liverpool-Dublin	7	7
Preston-Belfast	13	12
Preston-Larne	13	8
Stranraer-Larne	2	3
Swansea-Cork	9	8
Between Great Britain & Scandinavia (Vice Versa)		
NORWAY		
Harwich-Kristiansand	22	29
Newcastle-Kristiansand/Oslo	24/34	29
Newcastle-Stavanger/Bergen	19/24	29
SWEDEN		
Hull-Gothenburg	36	29
Immingham-Gothenburg	24	19
Tilbury (London)-Gothenburg	38	32
DENMARK		
Harwich-Esbjerg	18	29
Newcastle-Esbjerg	21	29
Between Germany & Scandinavia (Vice Versa)		
Hamburg-Bergen/Kristiansand	28/19	27/23
Isle of Sylt (Germany-Havneby, Denmark)	1	.50
Kiel-Oslo	19	15
Kiel-Gothenburg	12	14
Luebeck-Nynashamm/Helsinki	24/41	20/30
Ruttgarden-Rodby	1	4
Travemuende-Copenhagen/Halsingborg	8/10	12/14
Travemuende-Copenhagen/Helsinki	9/43	20/30
Travemuende-Gedser	3	5
Travemuende-Malmoe	8	12
Travemuende-Ronne (Bornholm)	6	8
Travemuende-Trelleborg	7	13
Warnemuende (E. Germany)-Gedser	2	4
Major Inter-Scandinavian Services		
Aarhus, Den/Horten, Norway-Oslo, Norway	16	11
Arendal, Norway-Hirtshals, Denmark	4	8
Copenhagen, Denmark-Malmoe, Sweden	1½	1
Copenhagen, Denmark-Oslo, Norway	16	13
Dragor, Denmark-Limhamm, Sweden	1	.50
Frederikshavn, Denmark-Gothenburg, Sweden	4	3
Frederikshavn, Denmark-Larvik, Norway	9	8
Frederikshavn, Denmark-Oslo, Norway	10	10
Grenaa, Denmark-Varberg, Sweden	5	5
Helsingor, Denmark-Helsinborg, Sweden	½	.50
Stockholm (via Kapellskar)-Naantali/Helsinki, Fin.	14	3

	HOURS	MIN. COST
Hirtshals, Denmark-Kristiansand, Norway	4	7
Norrtalje, Sweden-Turku, Finland	9	7
Sundsvall, Sweden-Vassa, Finland	10	7
Stockholm, Sweden-Turku, Finland	11	10
Umea, Sweden-Vassa, Finland	5	7
Ystad, Sweden—Bornholm, Sweden	1	3
Helsinki, Finland—Stockholm, Sweden	19	14
Between France & Mediterranean		
Marseilles-Corsica	11	8
Marseilles-Palma Mallorca/Ibiza	13	11
Nice-Corsica	7	6
Toulon-Corsica	9	8
NORTH AFRICA (Vice Versa)		
Marseilles-Algiers	21	30
Marseilles-Oran	27	30
Marseilles-Tangier/Casablanca	57	70
Marseilles-Tunis	23	30
Between France, Greece, Israel, Lebanon, Spain (Vice Versa)		
Marseilles-Piraeus, Greece	4 days	N.A.
Marseilles-Haifa, Israel	5 days	110
Marseilles-Beirut, Lebanon	6 days	50 (deck) 85 (cabin)
Marseilles-Alicante, Spain	20	25
Marseilles-Malaga, Spain	41	50
Between France and Ireland (Vice Versa)		
Le Havre-Rosslare, Ireland	22	23
Between Greece, Israel, Turkey (Vice Versa)		
Piraeus-Haifa	3 days	40
Piraeus-Istanbul	23	14
Between Holland, Sweden, Norway, Morocco, Madeira, Canary Islands		
Amsterdam-Gothenburg, Sweden	24	22
Amsterdam-Stavanger/Bergen, Norway	22/28	28
Rotterdam-Casablanca, Funachai, Tenerife, Las Palmas	1 week	100
Between Italy, Malta, Sardinia, Spain, Tunisia, Turkey, Corsica (Vice Versa)		
Sicily, Syracuse-Malta	9	12
Naples or Civitavecchia-Cagliari/Olbia (Sardinia)	14/7	15
Genoa-Porto Torres/Olbia/Cagliari (Sardinia)	12	15
Genoa-Barcelona (Spain)	21	14
Naples/Palermo-Tunis (Tunisia)	23/10	22/15
Genoa/Naples-Istanbul (Turkey)	4/5 days	37/34
Venice/Brindisi-Izmir (Turkey)	65/39	46/31
Genoa/Naples-Istanbul/Izmir (Turkey)	N.A.	75/96
(Trieste)-Venice-Brindisi—Istanbul/Izmir (Turkey)	4 days	75/96
Genoa-Bastia (Corsica)	7	12
Genoa-Mallorca	25	20
Genoa-Alicante/Malaga	40/43	30/35
Genoa-Tunisia	25	30
Morocco (See Map #158)		

	HOURS	MIN. COST
Between Italy & Greece (Vice Versa)		
Ancona/Brindisi-Piraeus/Limassol	43	20
Ancona-Patras	36	25
Brindisi-Corfu/Patras	11/19	8/15
Venice-Corfu/Piraeus	48	44
Venice-Rhodes	85	60
Between Italy, Israel (Vice Versa)		
Brindisi-(Greece-Turkey) Haifa-	N.A.	40
Genoa (Marseilles) Naples-(Cyprus) Haifa	7 days	85
(Trieste)-Venice-Bari-(Cyprus) Haifa	5 days	85
Venice-(Greece)-(Cyprus) Haifa	5 days	85
Between Italy & Yugoslavia (Vice Versa)		
Ancona-Dubrovnik	12	8
Ancona-Split	8	7
Ancona-Zadar	7	4
Bari-Dubrovnik	7	5
Pescara-Split	9	5
Rimini-Pula	4	7
Venice-Dubrovnik/Kotor	36/60	18
Venice-Trieste	5	4
Rijeka-Dubrovnik	N.A.	8

MAKING IT TO THE BRITISH ISLES

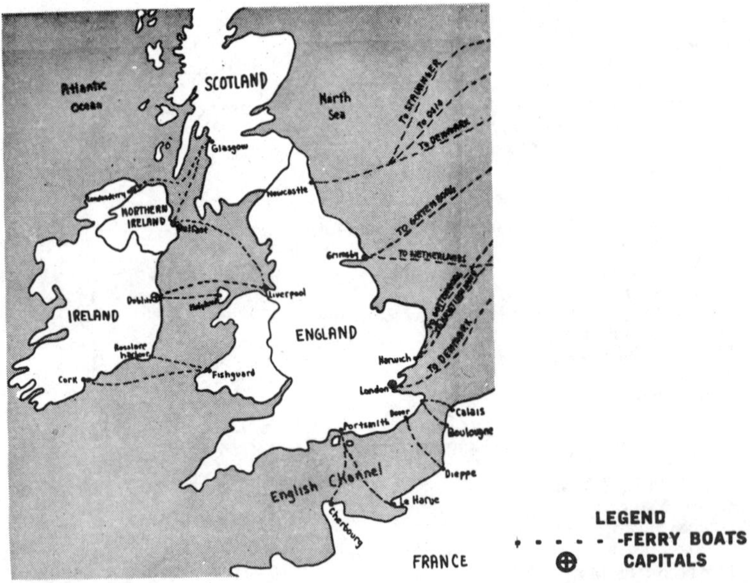

MAKING IT TO GREAT BRITAIN

ENGLAND

For many tourists England will be the first or last stop. One thing most people overlook is crossing the English Channel which will cost a minimum of $8.00 each way. British money can be used in Ireland and Scotland, but the reverse is not true.

MONEY CHART

MONEY CHART

GREAT BRITAIN

MONETARY UNIT: Pound
1 Pound = $2.40
100 New Pence = 1 Pound
Code: £

Amount of Local Currency You May Enter With	*Amount of Local Currency You May Leave With*	*Coins*	*Notes*	*Conversion Chart $1.00 US ='s*	*Black Market Rates*
No limit	£25	½ New Penny	1 Pound	US £	None
		1 New Penny	5 Pounds	$2.40 = 1 Pound	
		2 New Pence	10 Pounds	1.20 = 50 Pence	
		6 Pence (2½ New Pence)	20 Pounds	.60 = 25 Pence	
		5 New Pence		.24 = 10 Pence	
		10 New Pence		.12 = 5 Pence	
		50 New Pence			

LONDON

Picadilly circus is the Times Square of London. (5 on map) From Picadilly you can take the subway (underground) almost anywhere in the city. The cost for subway and bus tickets depends on the distance, and they can be expensive. To save money, buy a student transportation pass valid on all red busses and the underground. The pass, which includes a sightseeing trip around London, costs £3.80 (approximately $10.00 U.S.) for 7 days and £2.90 (approximately $7.50 U.S.) for 4 days. Passes are sold at the London Transit Inquiry Offices which are located in the major underground stations, such as Picadilly, Oxford Circus and Trafalgar Square

ACCOMMODATIONS

Accommodations in London are often hard to find during the summer season. To accommodate the overflow of travelers, an International Youth Camp has been set up. This camp houses over 500 people in large tents equipped with bunk beds. Facilities include showers and toiles, and inexpensive meals are provided. The cost per night is 35 p (approximately 75¢ U.S.), plus 8 p for bedding (or you can use your own sleep-ing bag). This may seem inexpensive, but to get there from central London, you must take the train to East Action. Including the train fare to and from central London, the cost per night at the campground and one meal, you will be spending about a pound a night (Approximately $2.50 U.S.). For almost that price you can probably find an inexpensive bed-and-breakfast hotel or a youth hostel in town.

YOUTH HOSTELS

The head youth hostel office in London is located at 29 John Adams Street (3 on map) off Villiers Street near Charing Cross Underground Station. It is there you can get information on youth hostels throughout the rest of Great Britain.

The three most popular youth hostels in London are the following:

King George VI Memorial Hostel
Holland House
Kensington, London
Tel: 937-0748

Underground:
Kensington High Street
or Holland Park

The office of the hostel remains open between 10 a.m. and 5 p.m. for members to check in.

38, Bolton Gardens
Earls Court
London SW50AQ
Tel: 373-7083

Underground: Earls Court
(Earls Court Road Exit)

84 Highgate West Hill
Highgate
London N6 6LU
Tel: 340-1831

Underground: Archway

(This hostel is closed on Thrusday nights from October to April).

Throughout London you will find bed-and-breakfast hotels where for a pound ($2.50 U.S.) and up a night you will get a room and breakfast. One such hotel is Hillary House (#9 on map) located 54 Upper Berkeley Street only a two-block walk from the Marble Arch Underground Station. Hillary House is among the better bed-and-breakfast hotels I found in London. Peter, the proprietor, offers an all-you-can-eat breakfast.

RECOMMENDED PLACE TO RECEIVE MAIL

American Express International, 6 Haymarket Street, London S.W., 1. (#4 on map) Arrive early; the lines are long. If you don't have an American Express credit card or travelers cheque you will have to pay 20 p (Approximately 50¢ U.S.) just to check to see if you have any mail.

The General Post Office (King Edwards Street Branch near Trafalgar Square) has a Post Restante which is open twenty-four hours a day seven days a week.

THINGS TO DO

After you have done all your sightseeing, take a trip on Sunday to Hyde Park's Speaker's Corner (#8 on map). It is there that you will find anyone with anything to say getting up on a soap box and speaking his piece.

TIP: Bring your own matches. Book matches are not free.

FURTHER INFORMATION

British Travel and Holiday Association, 680 Fifth Ave., N.Y., N.Y. 10019.

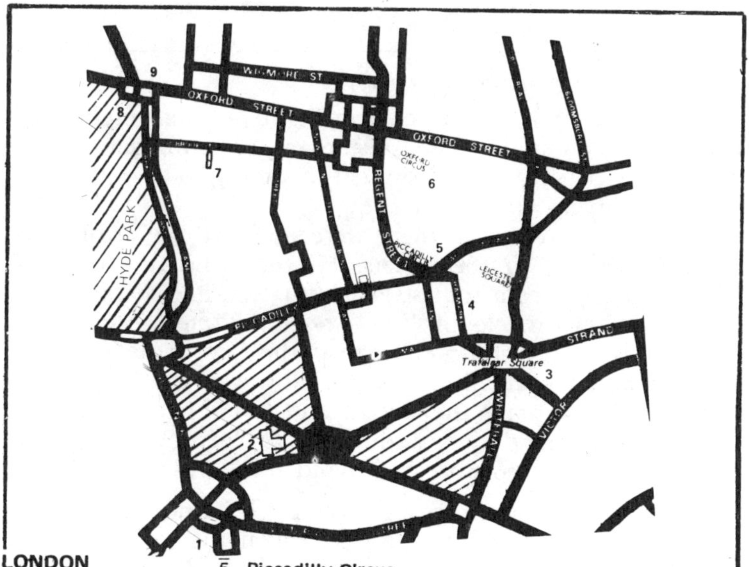

LONDON

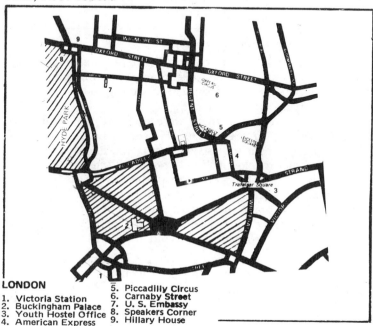

1. Victoria Station
2. Buckingham Palace
3. Youth Hostel Office
4. American Express
5. Piccadilly Circus
6. Carnaby Street
7. U. S. Embassy
8. Speakers Corner
9. Hillary House

MAKING IT TO AMSTERDAM

TOURIST INFORMATION CENTER AND RESERVATION SERVICE

Located directly in front of the central railway station.

MONEY CHART

NETHERLANDS

MONETARY UNIT: Guilder
3.244 Guilders = $1.00
100 Cents = 1 Guilder
Code: Hfl

Amount of Local Currency You May Enter With	*Amount of Local Currency You May Leave With*	*Coins*	*Notes*	*Conversion Chart $1.00 US ='s*	*Black Market Rates*
No limit	No limit	1 Cent	2½ Guilder	US Hfl	None
		5 Cents	5 Guilder	$1.00 = 3.244	
		10 Cents	10 Guilder	.50 = 1.622	
		25 Cents	25 Guilder	.25 = .811	
		1 Guilder	100 Guilder	.10 = .324	
		2½ Guilder	1000 Guilder	.05 = .162	
		10 Guilder			

SLEEPING IN THE STREETS

Because the majority of charter flights, student flights and commercial flights land in Amsterdam, accommodations are rare and expensive. Establishments claiming to be youth hostels have sprung up all over.

Until a few years ago there were no local city ordinances against sleeping in the streets. However, because of complaints (mostly from tourists) the situation has changed. According to an article in *The London Times,* August 24, 1970, it is now technically against the law to sleep in the open in and around Dam Square. However, the large number of violators make the law difficult to enforce. If you cannot find accommodations and decide to sleep out, remain as inconspicuous as possible and avoid public places.

The past two summer seasons of 1971 and 1972 saw a decreasing number of people sleeping in the streets mainly because of the establishment of Vondel Park Sleep-In (#11 on map). Vondel Park is easily reached via trams #1, 2 or 16 from the central railway station. Once there you will find a beautifully lanscaped park with a lake where it is absolutely free to camp out. (No tents or camp fires are allowed.) Facilities at the park include washrooms, toilets, luggage lockers, a counseling service and showers (for approximately 15¢ U.S.)

For those who like to sleep indoors a number of inexpensive youth hostel-type hotels are available:

Hotel Schreierstoren (#5 on map) located at 10 Geldersekade Centrum, only a few blocks from the central railway station, offers 450 of the cleanest beds in town. Ample facilities include hot showers and a pleasant atmosphere. The hotel is very strictly run, and no drugs are allowed.

Price: 7 guilders for the first night, 6 guilders for the second night plus 2 guilders with breakfast.

H88, (#7 on map), located at 88 Herengracht, also offers youth hostel-type accommodations. It is not as nice as the Hotel Schreierstoren, but it will do if you need a place to stay.

Price: 7½ guilders, 2 guilder deposit for sheets.

Directly across the street is the Hotel Post (#6 on map), located at Herengracht 101. More of a hotel than a youth hostel, Hotel Post has a lounge with a juke box, pinball machine, color TV and all the tea and coffee you can drink.

Price: 11 guilders without breakfast.

MEETING PLACES AND THINGS TO DO

Kosmos - located at Prins Hendrekkade 142, (#9 on map) a few blocks' walk from the central railway station. It is open Monday, Wednesday, Thursday and Friday 6:00 p.m. to midnight and includes a co-ed sauna. Kosmos offers a meditation center, movies, band, yoga and a video workshop. Membership for 3 months: 5 guilders. Admission: 2 guilders. Drugs allowed - bring your own.

Paradiso - (#12 on map) has a rock band and workshop and allows soft drugs bring your own. Take tram #2 from the central railway station. Membership: 2.50 guilders, Admission 2 guilders. Open 8:00 p.m. to 1:00 a.m., Wednesday, Thursday and Friday; 8:00 p.m. to 4:00 a.m. Saturdays.

Tour the *Heineken Brewery*. Take trams #1 and 2 from the central railway station or you can walk from Vondel Park. There is a place to leave your gear during the tour. Arrive early around 7:00 or 8:00 a.m. Two hundred tickets are given out about 9:00 a.m. The tour starts about 10:00 to 10:30 a.m. and you can drink for free till 11:45 a.m.

Anna Frank's House, now a museum, is a worthwhile tour. Price: 1.50 guilders.

Canal Ride - Board across from the central railway station. This tour of Amsterdam showing popular sights takes approximately 1 hour and costs 3.50 guilders.

The local police frown upon misicians playing in the streets. Instruments are often confiscated and are hard to get back. A popular place to buy or sell good used autos or VW campers is Auto Swart located at Langestraat 8, Tel: 230154.

RECOMMENDED PLACE TO RECEIVE MAIL

Amsterdam: c/o American Express International, Damrak 66, P.O. Box 762, Tel: 62042/6.

FURTHER INFORMATION

Netherlands National Tourist Office, 605 Fifth Avenue, New York, N.Y. 10017.

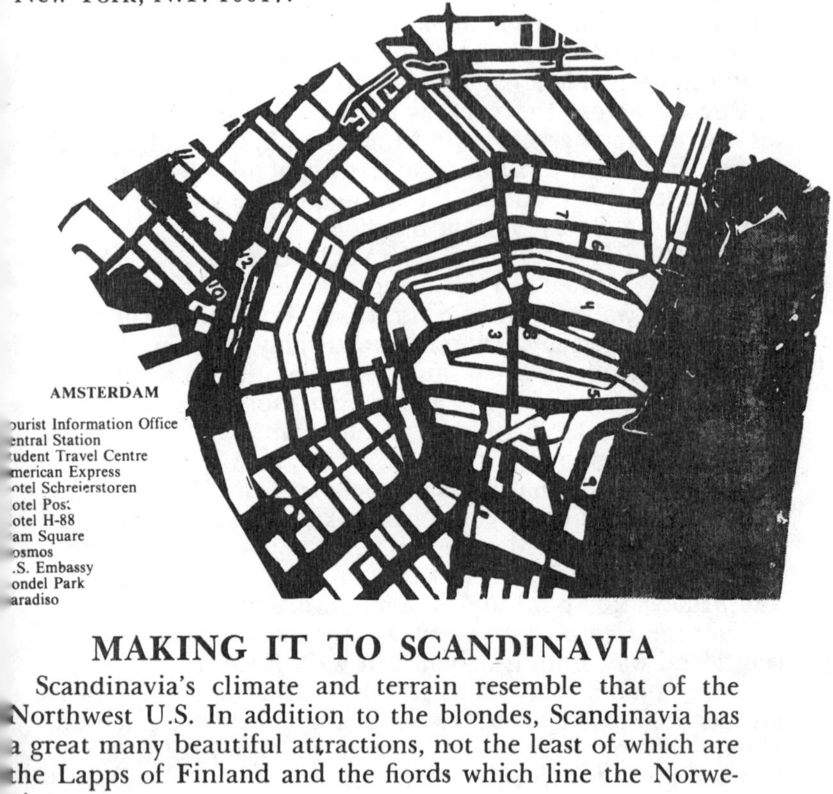

MAKING IT TO SCANDINAVIA

Scandinavia's climate and terrain resemble that of the Northwest U.S. In addition to the blondes, Scandinavia has a great many beautiful attractions, not the least of which are the Lapps of Finland and the fiords which line the Norwegian coast.

However, budget-minded travelers should be warned that Scandinavia enjoys one of the highest standards of living in the world. Because of this visitors will find these countries extremely expensive. For example, the cheapest accommodation in Stockholm is a youth hostel which is a permanently docked, refurbished sailing vessel which costs $2.75 a night. And with its five night limit per person per season, travelers wishing to stay longer must seek more expensive accommodations.

Although the country side is beautiful, the capital cities seem to host the majority of travelers. Consequently youth hostels and student accommodations are often booked to capacity throughout the summer.

TRANSPORTATION

All major cities are connected by air travel. Roads are better than adequate, but with the exception of Finland, hitchhiking is probably the worst in the world in Scandinavia. It is not uncommon to wait six or eight hours for a ride in Sweden.

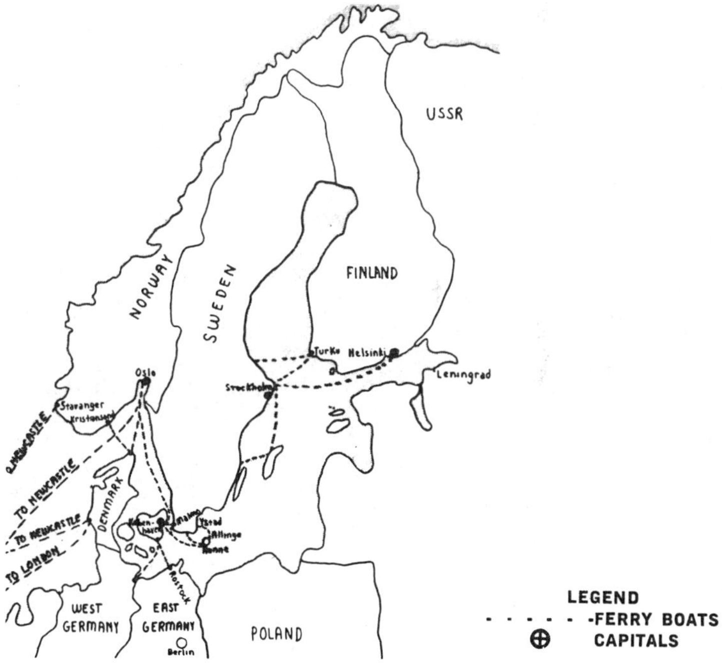

SCANDINAVIA

Fast and efficient rail service is available in each country. Eurailpass, which can also be used on certain designated ferry boats, is honored except in Finland. Transportation discounts for students are not offered in Finland during the summer months.

RUMOR

The stories that the sexual revolution originated and is rampant in Scandinavia are somewhat exaggerated. When you arrive, instead of two blondes in every bed, you will find an over abundance of porno shops mostly in Copenhagen which sell everything from magazines and films to sexual gadgets. You will even find vending machines featuring sexual novelties on the streets in certain areas.

Although the merchandise may be tempting, you must be careful passing through U.S. customs. You may find your new-found trinkets confiscated.

MAKING IT TO NORWAY

TOURIST INFORMATION CENTER AND RESERVATION SERVICE

Located in central railway station in Oslo.

MONEY CHART

NORWAY

MONETARY UNIT: Krone
4.76 Kroner = $1.00
100 Ore = 1 Krone
Code: Nkr

Amount of Local Currency You May Enter With	*Amount of Local Currency You May Leave With*	*Coins*	*Notes*	*Conversion Chart $1.00 US =’s*	*Black Market Rates*
Nkr 1000	Nkr 350	10 Ore	10 Kroner	US Nkr	None
		25 Ore	50 Kroner	$1.00 = 4.76	
		50 Ore	100 Kroner	.50 = 2.38	
		1 Krone	500 Kroner	.25 = 1.19	
		5 Krone	1000 Kroner	.10 = .476	
		10 Krone		.05 = .238	
		25 Krone			

RECOMMENDED PLACE TO RECEIVE MAIL

American Express, c/o Winge & Co., Travel Bureau, Ltd. (R), Karl Johans Gate 33, P. O. Box 1705, Oslo, Norway. Tel: 20.50.50.

FURTHER INFORMATION

Norwegian National Travel Office, 505 Fifth Avenue, New York, N.Y. 10017.

MAKING IT TO DENMARK

TOURIST INFORMATION CENTER AND RESERVATION SERVICE

Located adjacent to central railway station in Copenhagen.
Money Chart

MONEY CHART

DENMARK

MONETARY UNIT: Krone
6.98 Kroner = \$1.00
100 Ore = 1 Krone
Code: Kr

Amount of Local Currency You May Enter With	*Amount of Local Currency You May Leave With*	*Coins*	*Notes*	*Conversion Chart \$1.00 US ='s*	*Black Market Rates*
No limit	Kr 2000	1 Ore	10 Kroner	US Kr	None
		2 Ore	50 Kroner	\$1.00 = 6.98	
		5 Ore	100 Kroner	.50 = 3.49	
		10 Ore	500 Kroner	.25 = 1.75	
		25 Ore		.10 = .70	
		1 Krone		.05 = .35	
		2 Kroner			
		5 Kroner			
		10 Kroner			

ARRIVAL AND DEPARTURE

Many travelers arriving by land have complained that they were asked to show proof of intention to depart from Denmark in the form of air, boat or rail tickets or money before they were allowed to enter.

RECOMMENDED PLACE TO RECEIVE MAIL

c/o American Express Company A/S, Dagmarhus, H. C. Andersens Blvd. 12-DK 1598, Copenhagen, Denmark. Tel: 122301.

FURTHER INFORMATION

Danish National Travel Office, 505 Fifth Avenue, New York, N.Y. 10017.

MAKING IT TO SWEDEN

TOURIST INFORMATION CENTER AND RESERVATION SERVICE

Located in Central Railway Station in Stockholm.

MONEY CHART

SWEDEN

MONETARY UNIT: Krona
4.82 Kronor = $1.00
100 Ore = 1 Krona
Code: Skr

Amount of Local Currency You May Enter With	*Amount of Local Currency You May Leave With*	*Coins*	*Notes*	*Conversion Chart $1.00 US ='s*	*Black Market Rates*
Skr 6000	Skr 6000	1 Ore	5 Kronor	US Skr	None
		2 Ore	10 Kronor	$1.00 = 4.82	
		5 Ore	50 Kronor	.50 = 2.41	
		10 Ore	100 Kronor	.25 = 1.21	
		25 Ore	1000 Kronor	.10 = .48	
		50 Ore		.05 = .24	
		1 Krona			
		2 Kronor			
		5 Kronor			

RECOMMENDED PLACE TO RECEIVE MAIL

c/o American Express, Resespecialisterna Resebureau AB (Travel Specialists of Sweden) (R), P.O. Box 5112, Burger Jarlsgatan 32, Stockholm 5, Sweden. Tel: 11 87 05 and 23 34 20.

FURTHER INFORMATION

Swedish National Travel Office, 505 Fifth Avenue, New York, N.Y. 10017.

MAKING IT TO FINLAND

Helsinki, Finland is an excellent stopping off point for a short journey into the Soviet Union. From Helsinki it is possible to take a ship or train to Leningrad. Arrangements can be made in Helsinki, but since they take one to two weeks it is best to plan this side trip prior to your departure from the U.S

TOURIST INFORMATION CENTER AND RESERVATION SERVICE

Located in the central railway station in Helsinki, and on the corner of Norra Esplanadgaten and Union Sgatan.

Across the street from the tourist office you can get tram #3T which encircles the entire city. An English speaking voice guides your tour with information at every stop.

MONEY CHART

FINLAND

MONETARY UNIT: Markka
4.10 Markkaa = $1.00
100 Pennis = 1 Markka
Code: Mk

Amount of Local Currency You May Enter With	*Amount of Local Currency You May Leave With*	*Coins*	*Notes*	*Conversion Chart $1.00 US ='s*	*Black Market Rates*
No limit	Mk 3000	1 Penni	1 Markka	US Mk	None
		5 Pennis	5 Markkaa	$1.00 = 4.10	
		10 Pennis	10 Markkaa	.50 = 2.05	
		50 Pennis	50 Markkaa	.25 = 1.03	
		1 Markka	100 Markkaa	.10 = .41	
		10 Markkaa		.05 = .21	

RECOMMENDED PLACE TO RECEIVE MAIL

c/o American Express, Travek Travel Bureau, Ltd. (R), Etelaranta 16, Helsinki, Finland. Tel: 61.631.

FURTHER INFORMATION

Finnish National Travel Office, 505 Fifth Avenue, New York, N.Y. 10017.

MAKING IT TO FRANCE

PARIS

Because Paris is centrally located, it is a good place to meet other travelers bound for England, Spain and other parts of Europe.

Everything is happening in the Left Bank in the student area directly across the bridge from Notre Dame Cathedral. There you will find inexpensive pension-type hotels, restaurants and a great many of Paris' 179 movie theatres.

In each of the past three summers I have met at least one young traveler who was arrested for jaywalking in Paris. This summer of 1972 one young American was taken away in a paddy wagon, spent three days in jail and had to pay a 50 franc fine. For jaywalking????...

MONEY CHART

FRANCE

MONETARY UNIT: Franc
5.115 Francs = $1.00
100 Centimes = 1 Franc
Code: Ffr

Amount of Local Currency You May Enter With	*Amount of Local Currency You May Leave With*	*Coins*	*Notes*	*Conversion Chart $1.00 US ='s*	*Black Market Rates*
No limit	No limit	1 Centime	5 Francs	US Ffr	None
		5 Centimes	10 Francs	$1.00 = 5.115	
		10 Centimes	50 Francs	.50 = 2.558	
		20 Centimes	100 Francs	.25 = 1.279	
		½ Franc	500 Francs	.10 = .512	
		1 Franc		.05 = .256	
		5 Francs			
		10 Francs			

RECOMMENDED PLACE TO RECEIVE MAIL

Paris: American Express International, 2 Rue Auber (directly behind the Opera House) Tel: Opera 42.90. During the summer lines are long; try to arrive early in the morning.

SOUTHERN FRANCE (NICE, CANNES AND MONACO)

Don't expect to be let into some of the casinos unless you are properly dressed, if even just to look around. You will also find that it is against the law to sleep on the world famous Riviera Beaches. Instead of soft white sand as one might expect, the beach in some places consists basically of stones.

FURTHER INFORMATION

French Government Tourist Office, 610 Fifth Ave., New York, N.Y. 10020. Tel: (212) 757-1125.

MAKING IT TO LUXEMBOURG

Luxembourg has become one of the three major arrival and departure routes between the U.S. and Europe mainly because Icelandic airlines lands there.

It's a good idea to arrive via Icelandic early in the a.m. and continue your journey to another country in Europe. The reason for this is that because of the thousands of travelers coming and going through Luxembourg the youth hostel is almost always booked as is other inexpensive accommodations.

The tourist information center is located next to the central railway station.

MONEY CHART

LUXEMBOURG & BELGIUM

MONETARY UNIT: Franc
44.81 Francs = $1.00
100 Centimes = 1 Franc
Code: Bfc

Amount of Local Currency You May Enter With	*Amount of Local Currency You May Leave With*	*Coins*	*Notes*	*Conversion Chart $1.00 US ='s*	*Black Market Rates*
No limit	No limit	25 Centimes 50 Centimes 1 Franc 5 Francs 10 Francs 50 Francs 100 Francs	20 Francs (Luxembourg) 10 Francs 50 Francs 100 Francs 500 Francs 1000 Francs 5000 Francs	US Bfc $1.00 = 44.81 .50 = 22.41 .25 = 11.20 .10 = 4.48 .05 = 2.24	None

RECOMMENDED PLACE TO RECEIVE MAIL

General Post Office.

FURTHER INFORMATION

Luxembourg Economic and Tourist Department, 200 East 42nd Street, New York, N.Y.

MAKING IT TO SWITZERLAND

Although Switzerland is one of the smallest European countries it has some of the most beautiful unspoiled scenery. Throughout the country you will find a great many lakes. Ferry boats connect small towns on most lakes. Fares can be as high as $5.00 to take a trip around or even across some of the large lakes. Eurailpasses are honored on most.

The Swiss Alpine R.R. system pushes in and out of mountain tops while you look at cities thousands of feet below. However, with all this to offer, it is almost impossible to find a youth hostel, student lodging, or other inexpensive accommodations during the summer months.

Tourist information office is located in the central railway stations in larger cities.

MONEY CHART

SWITZERLAND

MONETARY UNIT: Francs
100 Centimes = 1 Franc
3.85 Francs = $1.00
Code: Sf

Amount of Local Currency You May Enter With	*Amount of Local Currency You May Leave With*	*Coins*	*Notes*	*Conversion Chart $1.00 US ='s*	*Black Market Rates*
No limit	No limit	1 Centime 5 Centime 10 Centime 20 Centime 50 Centime 1 Franc 2 Franc 5 Franc	10 Francs 20 Francs 50 Francs 100 Francs 500 Francs 1000 Francs	US Sf $1.00 = 3.85 .50 = 1.92 Centimes .25 = 96 .10 = 38 .05 = 19	None

RECOMMENDED PLACE TO RECEIVE MAIL

Geneva: American Express International, 7 Rue du Mont Blanc, Case Postale 243, Tel: 32.65.80.

FURTHER INFORMATION

Swiss National Tourist Office, 608 Fifth Avenue, New York, N.Y. 10016.

MAKING IT TO BELGIUM

RECOMMENDED PLACE TO RECEIVE MAIL

Brussels: American Express International, 22-24 Place Rogier, Tel. 19.01.90.

Money (*see Luxembourg*)

FURTHER INFORMATION

Belgian Tourist Bureau, 589 Fifth Avenue, New York, N.Y. 10017.

MAKING IT TO WEST GERMANY

Many travelers overlook the following. Directly outside the town of Fussen (in the Bravarian Alps) is located a castle built by crazy Ludwig, the King of Bravaria. The castle resembles the one guarding the entrance to Disneyland. It is on top of a mountain and it takes an hour to make the climb. The tour cost $1.00 U.S.

There is a youth hostel in Fussen a short walk from the central railway station.

Not far from Fussen is Munich. A ten minute train ride from Munich takes you to Dachau, the site of a Nazi concentration camp in World War II which has now been converted into a museum.

Tourist Information Center

Generally located in or around central railway stations throughout West Germany.

MONEY CHART WEST GERMANY

MONETARY UNIT: Deutsche Mark
3.22 Marks = $1.00
100 Pfennig = 1 Mark
Code: Dm

Amount of Local Currency You May Enter With	*Amount of Local Currency You May Leave With*	*Coins*	*Notes*	*Conversion Chart $1.00 US ='s*	*Black Market Rates*
No limit	No limit	1 Pfennig 2 Pfennig 5 Pfennig 10 Pfennig 50 Pfennig Deutsche Mark 1 2 5 10	Deutsche Mark 5 10 50 100 500 1000	US Dm $1.00 = 3.22 .50 = 1.61 .25 = .81 .10 = .32 .05 = .16	None

RECOMMENDED PLACE TO RECEIVE MAIL

When in the following major cities in Germany, use American Express Offices: Duesseldorf, Frankfurt, Hamburg, Heidelberg, Munich, Stuttgart, Strasbourg.

FURTHER INFORMATION

German Tourist Information Office, 500 Fifth Avenue, New York, N.Y. 10036. Tel: (212) OX 5-1952.

MAKING IT TO VIENNA

The Opera House (#2) is the center of things. The tourist information center (#1) is in an underground arcade opposite the Opera House. American Express (#5), American Embassy (#6), Spanish Riding School (#4), OK Cafeteria (#3), are all with a few blocks walking distance of the Opera House.

Avoid large youth hostels. They are often booked up with large groups. Smaller ones are your best bet. Ask the tourist information center for directions to Don Boscos Youth Hostels (men only). This is located in a nine-story church tower, walk up with six to eight bunks on each level. Another unusual youth hostel is located underneath Esterhazy Park at 1 Schadekgasse (Tel: 57-91-31). This youth hostel was an underground shelter used by the Nazis during WW II. At this hostel breakfast is mandatory for a price of 36¢. Single rooms for $1.00 and doubles for $1.80.

Vienna is an excellent place to obtain visas for Eastern European countries especially the U.S.S.R. It's central location makes access to these countries easy. Consult the local tourist information center for location of these embassies.

MONEY CHART

AUSTRIA

MONETARY UNIT: Schilling
23.30 Schillings = $1.00
100 Groschen = 1 Schilling
Code: As

Amount of Local Currency You May Enter With	*Amount of Local Currency You May Leave With*	*Coins*	*Notes*	*Conversion Chart $1.00 US ='s*	*Black Market Rates*
No limit	No limit	1 Groschen	Schillings	US As	None
		2 Groschen	20	$1.00 = 23.30	
		5 Groschen	50	.50 = 11.65	
		10 Groschen	100	.25 = 5.83	
		50 Groschen	500	.10 = 2.33	
		1 Schilling	1000	.05 = 1.17	
		5 Schilling			
		10 Schilling			
		25 Schilling			
		50 Schilling			

ARRIVAL

The ride from Schwechat airport to Vienna by bus costs 20 schillings (76¢ U.S.). The taxi fare is 180 schillings (approximately $6.96 U.S.) plus 10% tip. Airport tax is 40 schillings or $1.54 U.S.

FOOD

Some of the most popular Austrian dishes that should not be missed are Wiener Schnitzel, Goulash, various strudels and pastries. Excellent restaurants serving varied international menus can be found throughout Austria.

For the budget-minded traveler other facilities are available. For example, in Vienna there is the O.K. cafeteria conveniently located in the center of town opposite the Opera House at 61 Karntnerstrasse. Other chains are the W. O.K.'s and the Billaterias. All these restaurants serve a variety of meals for under $1.00.

SIGHTSEEING

Operas, ballets and concerts are some of the biggest attractions of Vienna. People must often wait months for tickets but standing room is available at the door for each performance for approximately 60¢ U.S. Jackets and ties may also be required. If you are without, often ushers will rent them to you for 20 to 30¢ for the evening.

The Spanish Riding School is usually not in session in the summer months in Vienna. It is possible when it is in session to visit practice sessions weekdays from 10:00 a.m. to noon for about 2 schillings (40¢ U.S.) and from 12:00 to 1:00 p.m. to tour the stables. Performances are held on Sundays only and tickets must be reserved in advance. Standing room is available but it is advisable to be one of the first in line.

RECOMMENDED PLACE TO RECEIVE MAIL

Vienna: American Express International; Kaerntnerstrasse 21/23. Tel: 52 05 44.

FURTHER INFORMATION

Austrian State Tourist Department, 545 Fifth Avenue, New York, N.Y. 10022. Tel: (212) 697-0651.

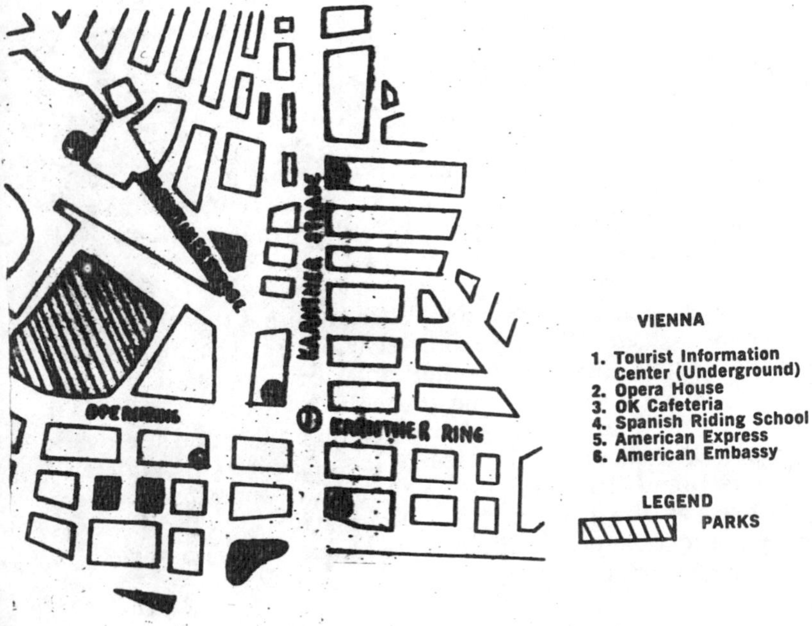

MAKING IT TO ITALY

Housing some of the worlds greatest art, religious and historical treasures from many periods, Italy lures its fair share of tourists. A great majority of travelers head for Rome. However, I have found that it is best to establish headquarters in Florence. Its central location and inexpensive accommodations, most of which are located around the central railway station, make it an excellent home base. From Florence you can head west to Pizza, south to Rome and Naples, east to Venice and north to Milan. Youth hostels and pensions are booked up solidly throughout the summer months. It is wise to arrive early in the day. In some areas banks and many shops close between 1:00 and 4:00 p.m. for siesta.

TOURIST INFORMATION CENTERS

Generally located in or around the central railway stations throughout Italy.

MONEY CHART

ITALY

MONETARY UNIT: Lire
590 Lire = $1.00
Code: Lit.

Amount of Local Currency You May Enter With	*Amount of Local Currency You May Leave With*	*Coins*	*Notes*	*Conversion Chart $1.00 US =’s*	*Black Market Rates*
No limit	Lit 100,000	1 Lire	500 Lire	US Lit	None
		2 Lire	1,000 Lire	$1.00 = 590	
		5 Lire	5,000 Lire	.50 = 295	
		10 Lire	10,000 Lire	.25 = 147	
		50 Lire	100,000 Lire	.10 = 59	
		100 Lire		.05 = 29	

THE VATICAN

Mini skirts, bare shoulders and low necklines are forbidden. Dress conservatively if you want to see what you came for.

RECOMMENDED PLACE TO RECEIVE MAIL

American Express offices are located throughout most major cities in Italy. The one most commonly used by travelers is located in Rome.

FURTHER INFORMATION

Italian Government Travel Office, 626 Fifth Avenue, New York, N.Y. 10020.

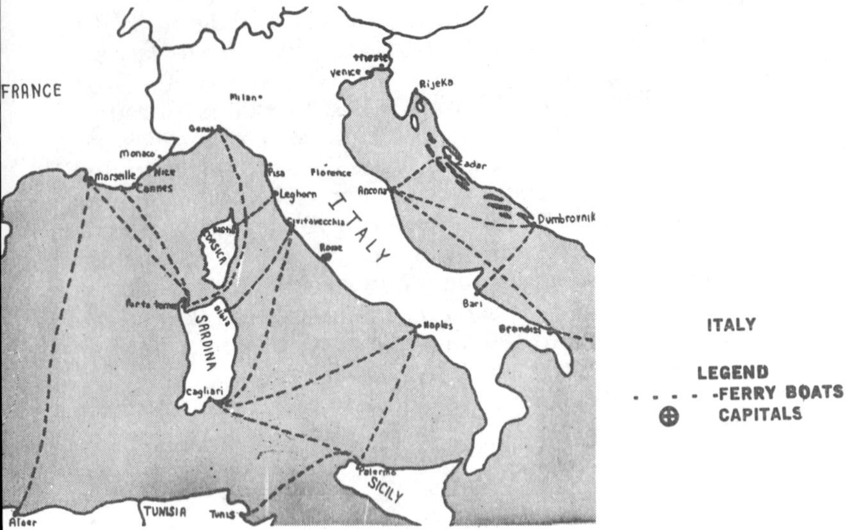

MAKING IT TO ATHENS (GREECE)

VISA

No visa is required.

MONEY CHART

GREECE

MONETARY UNIT: Drachme
30 Drachmai = $1.00
100 Lepta = 1 Drachme
Code: Dr

Amount of Local Currency You May Enter With	*Amount of Local Currency You May Leave With*	*Coins*	*Notes*	*Conversion Chart $1.00 US ='s*		*Black Market Rates*
Dr 750	Dr 750	5 Lepta	Drachmai	US	Dr	33 Dr = $1.00
		10 Lepta	50	$1.00 =	30.	
		20 Lepta	100	.50 =	15.00	
		50 Lepta	500	.25 =	7.50	
		1 Drachme	1000	.10 =	3.00	
		2 Drachmai		.05 =	1.50	
		5 Drachmai				
		10 Drachmai				
		20 Drachmai				
		30 Drachmai				

TRANSPORTATION

AIR—Athens is serviced by most major airlines and is accessible from almost every major city.

LAND—Good roads connect Athens with Western Europe. *Recommended Route:*

Trieste, Italy to Rijeka, Yugoslavia. Rijeka to Belgrade, Yugoslavia, to Thessaloniki, Greece, and south to Athens. This route, a two-to-three day journey, can be used if you are driving or hitchhiking.

Regularly scheduled ferry services connects Brindisi, Italy with Piraeus, Greece. Fare: approximately $21.00 U.S. (See ferry schedules on page #131) From Piraeus busses and trains will take you to nearby Athens. Train costs 45 dracma (approximately $1.50 U.S.) bus costs 85 dracma (approximately $3.00 U.S.).

ATHENS

In Athens you will find almost everything you need located near Syntagma Square (Constitution Square). From Syntagma Square, bus #16 goes to the Acropolis, admission 50¢—FREE on Sundays.

Besides the Government Information Center in Constitution Square there is also an organization called Tourist Police. Located about a block from the American Express office at Constitution Square, they will give you information, maps and will even help you find a place to stay. If you have any complaints, they are there to help you.

RECOMMENDED PLACE TO RECEIVE MAIL

American Express located at (Hellas) Travel and Shipping A.E., Syntagma Square, Cor. Hermes Street, P.O. Box 671, Tel: 224-190.

ACCOMMODATIONS

There are three youth hostels in Athens. Hostel #2 is the most popular. To get there, take bus #10 from Syntagma Square to the end of the line, and walk across Leoforos Alexandras St. Hostel #2 is recommended for the following reasons: It is a good place to exchange travel information. You will meet travelers who have just arrived from places you might be heading for, and there is a bulletin board with transportation information to Istanbul and India or back to Europe and boat information to the islands of Crete and Rhodes. Hostel #2 also offers clean accommodations and a choice of excellent food. The cafe is open all day until midnight

CRETE AND RHODES

It is best to check first. Boat fare to Crete is approximately $16.00 round-trip. During the summer months of July and August the islands may be so crowded with visitors that it is hard to find a quiet beach to camp. Also, it is possible that parts of or even an entire Greek island may be closed to tourists for archeological reasons.

TIP: Avoid engaging in political discussions. Politics is a touchy subject in Greece, and anyone who takes an active part could face prosecution.

FURTHER INFORMATION

Greek National Tourist Organization, 601 Fifth Ave., New York, N.Y. 10017.

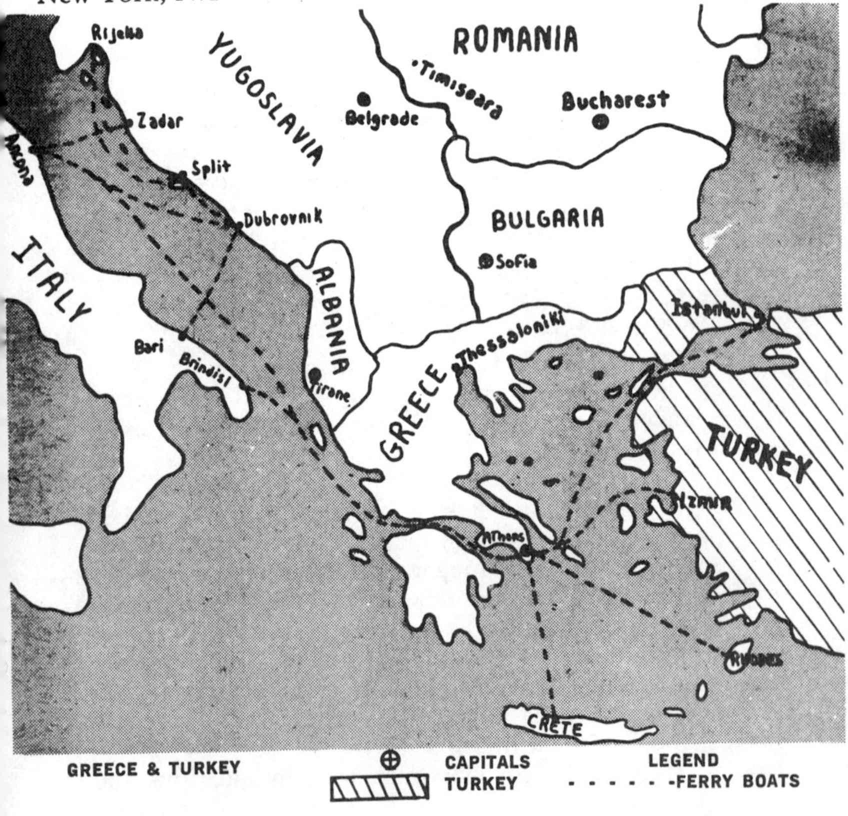

GREECE & TURKEY

MAKING IT TO SPAIN AND PORTUGAL

The population of Spain is 36 million people, but in 1970 26 million visited it for many reasons. First, Spain's low standard of living lures many budget minded travelers. The slow pace, unique life styles, and inexpensive livings make this area popular. Another attraction is the climate. The warm year round temperatures attract Europeans and Americans escaping cold winters. Thirdly, many travelers *en route* to the Balearic Islands, Morocco, France and Portugal must pass through Spain.

Spain and Portugal have many similarities besides economic conditions. Because they are both governed by dictators, young travelers should avoid getting into trouble, for there is absolutely no bending of the law.

On the cultural side bullfighting is a big attraction in both countries, however, in Portugal they do not kill the bull.

The siesta is a time honored custom in Spain and Portugal. Don't plan on accomplishing anything important between 1:00 and 4:00 p.m. Most restaurants and shops will be closed.

MONEY CHARTS—SPAIN & PORTUGAL

SPAIN

MONETARY UNIT: Peseta
64.47 Pesetas = $1.00
100 Centimos = 1 Peseta
Code: Pst

Amount of Local Currency You May Enter With	*Amount of Local Currency You May Leave With*	*Coins*	*Notes*	*Conversion Chart $1.00 US ='s*		*Black Market Rates*
				US	Pst	
Pst 5000	Pst 3000	10 Centimos	100 Peseta	$1.00 =	64.47	67 Pst $1.00
		50 Centimos	500 Peseta	.50 =	32.24	
		1 Peseta	1000 Peseta	.25 =	16.12	
		2½ Peseta		.10 =	6.45	
		5 Peseta		.05 =	3.22	
		25 Peseta				
		50 Peseta				
		100 Peseta				

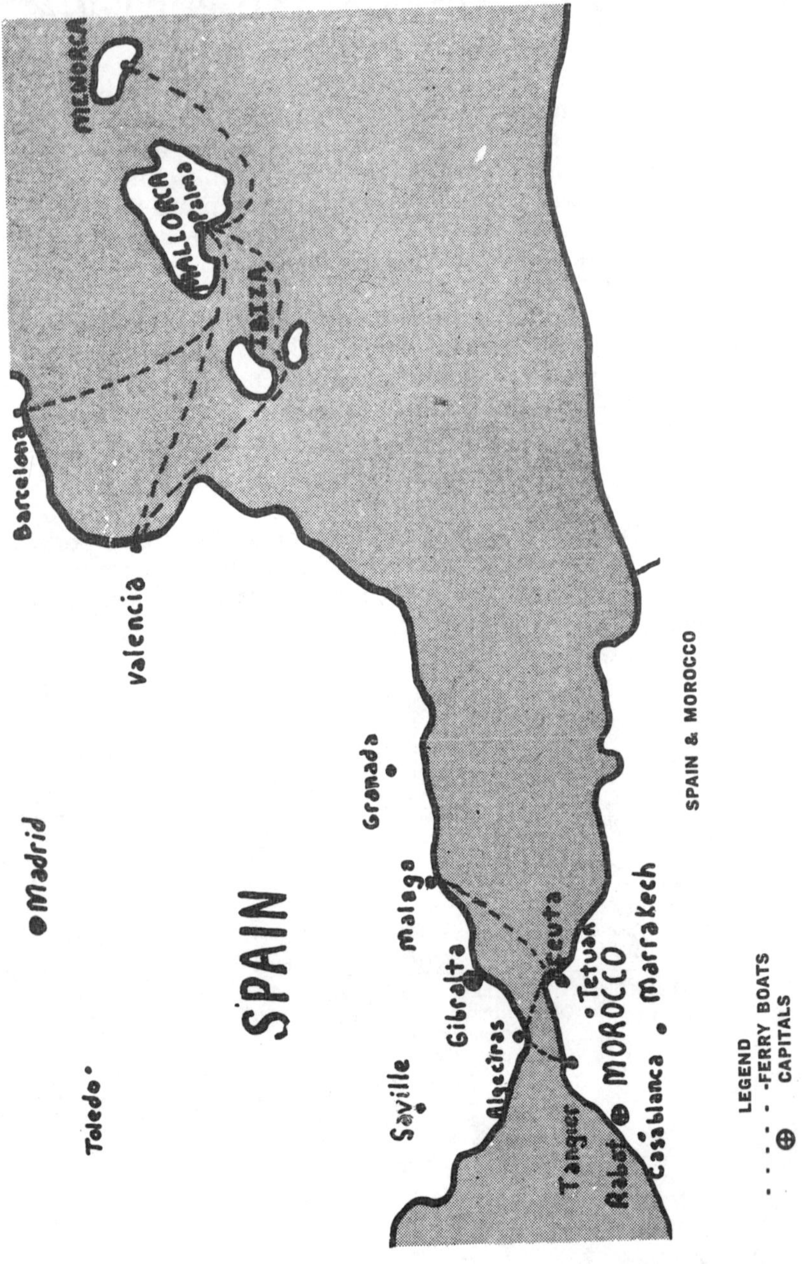
MENORCA
MALLORCA
Palma
IBIZA
Barcelona
Valencia
Madrid
Toledo
SPAIN
Granada
Malaga
Seville
Gibralta
Algeciras
Ceuta
Tetuan
MOROCCO
Tangier
Rabat
Casablanca
Marrakech
LEGEND
- - - -FERRY BOATS
⊕ CAPITALS
SPAIN & MOROCCO

PORTUGAL

MONETARY UNIT: Escudo
27.25 Escudos = $1.00
100 Centavos = 1 Escudo
Code: Esc

Amount of Local Currency You May Enter With	*Amount of Local Currency You May Leave With*	*Coins*	*Notes*	*Conversion Chart $1.00 US =’s*	*Black Market Rates*
No limit	No limit	10 Centavos	20 Escudos	US Esc	None
		20 Centavos	50 Escudos	$1.00 = 27.25	
		50 Centavos	100 Escudos	.50 = 13.63	
		1 Escudo	500 Escudos	.25 = 6.81	
		2½ Escudo	1000 Escudos	.10 = 2.73	
		5 Escudo		.05 = 1.36	

RECOMMENDED PLACE TO RECEIVE MAIL IN PORTUGAL:

Lisbon: c/o American Express, Star Travel Service (R) Avenida Sidonio Pais 4A, P.O. Box 2662. Tel: 53.89.71.

IN SPAIN:

Madrid: American Express Company of Spain, Plaza de las Cortes No. 2, Tel: 2-22-11-80.

Barcelona: c/o American Express, Viajes Taber, S.A. (R), C. Balmes 200-5th Floor. Tel: 2882806.

FURTHER INFORMATION

PORTUGAL: Portuguese Government Tourist Information Bureau, 570 Fifth Ave., New York, N.Y. 10017.

SPAIN: Spanish National Tourist Office, 589 Fifth Avenue, New York, N.Y. 10017.

MAKING IT TO THE BALEARIC ISLANDS

Majorca, Ibiza and Minorca are the largest of the Balearic Islands situated in the Mediterranean off the southern coast of Spain. Because they have a warm climate nearly year round they have become the destination of many European-bound travelers seeking an island paradise.

ARRIVAL

The islands are connected by jets to most points in Europe. However, the least expensive way to reach the islands is by ship. The ships leave daily from Valencia and Barcelona, usually run overnight, therefore you save a night's rent. You can travel fourth, or deck class for approximately $1.00 U.S. or two can get a small cabin for $2.50 apiece.

Once in the island, you will find that most of the cities are over-run with tourists. Avoid Palma the capital of Majorca, which is usually booked up solid. The youth hostels and student accommodations are usually booked for the entire summer season. Once you have escaped from the tourist sections of the islands, you will find unspoiled beaches, cliffs and numerous coves. To get even further away from it all, take a trip to some of the smaller islands.

Since the islands are a possession of Spain, they use the same currency. Prices are comparable with that of Spain except in the large tourist areas.

RECOMMENDED PLACE TO RECEIVE MAIL

Palma: c/o American Express, Viajes Iberia, S.A. (R), Generalisimo Franco #48, Tel: 22 67 43.

MAKING IT TO MOROCCO

VISA

A visa for Morócco is not required for a stay of up to three months.

ARRIVAL

Each year many young Americans make their way through Europe *en route* to Morocco. But the suppress-the-hippie policy is at its strongest here. Anyone remotely resembling a hippie will be turned away from the boat from Algeciaras, Spain, to Tangier, Morocco. (See Map.) However, there are alternate ways of gaining entry to Morocco.

Two ferry boats, one from Algeciras, the other from Malaga, make runs to Ceuta, the Spanish province of North Africa bordering Morocco. The price is less than $2.00. It is often easier to enter Morocco by bus from Ceuta to Tangier, depending on the attitude of the customs officer at the Moroccan border. If you are turned away, black marketeers in Ceuta will offer to escort you through farms across the border for about $5.00. Such entry is illegal, and if caught, you face a minimum of thirty days in jail. As stated before, the best way to enter any country with the least hassell is by airplane. (Most people with long hair whom I met in Morocco had arrived by plane.)

Planes leave Spain from Malaga for Tangier every Tuesday, Thursday, Saturday and Sunday at 9:05 a.m. The cost is $11.30 U.S. one way and $22.60 U.S. return.

Regularly scheduled busses leave Tangier for the capital, Rabat, and travel south to Casablanca and Marrakesh.

MONEY CHART

MOROCCO

MONETARY UNIT: **Dirham**
4.67 Dirham = $1.00
100 Morocco Francs = 1 Dirham
Code: Drh

Amount of Local Currency You May Enter With	*Amount of Local Currency You May Leave With*	*Coins*	*Notes*	*Conversion Chart $1.00 US ='s*		*Black Market Rates*
				US	Drh	
None	None	1 Franc	5 Dirhams	$1.00 =	4.67	1 Drh = $.15
		5 Franc	10 Dirhams	.50 =	2.34	
		10 Franc	50 Dirhams	.25 =	1.17	
		20 Franc	100 Dirhams	.10 =	.47	
		50 Franc		.05 =	.23	
		100 Franc				
		1 Dirham				
		5 Dirham				

RUMOR

Rumor has it that you can buy almost anything in the Kasbah (which means old market) but today with the influx of tourists almost everything is made in Japan.

RECOMMENDED PLACE TO RECEIVE MAIL

Rabat: c/o American Express, I.T.O. Atwater Bureau (R), Rabat Hilton Hotel.

MAKING IT TO THE MIDDLE EAST AND ISRAEL

See Map (*Making it to India*)

Because of the war both sides have been severely hurt economically. Therefore, both sides welcome the tourist dollar. It is possible for tourists to see Jerusalem and Israel and within the same day see the pyramids of Egypt. This is very easily done. Israel will issue a loose visa upon request (a card which is removed from your passport when you leave).

This will leave you with no record in your passport and therefore, you will not be prevented from entering Soviet Satellite or Arab countries. Let us say you have just visited Israel and would like to go to Egypt. You fly or take a boat to the island of Cyprus, which is an intermediate neutral point. There you change planes or ships and continue on to Egypt. With a student discount it is cheaper to fly. The fare from Cyprus to Tel Aviv by boat is $16.00. The student flight costs $12.00. It is not possible to enter Israel by land, for you cannot cross the borders. Boats leave Italy, Athens and Istanbul for Hiafa, Israel. (See ferry schedules.) Planes connect Israel or Egypt with almost all of Western Europe and the U.S.

Both sides know you're either coming or going from the other, but as long as you are a tourist nothing is said. It is wiser, however, not to engage in any political discussions. American travelers should avoid Iraq, Syria and Jordan. We are not welcome there.

MAKING IT TO TEL-AVIV

Because of the war economy, prices for accommodations are generally high. The youth hostel in Tel-Aviv costs $2.00 a night and is usually overcrowded. I recommend staying at Hotel Josef located at 15 Bugrashov Street and corner of Ben Yehuda St. Tel: 225955. For $2.00 per night (the same as the youth hostel) Hotel Josef includes (and all you can eat) breakfast. Hotel Josef's location is excellent. Situated two blocks from the beach, two blocks from the Dan Hotel, which is located on Herbet Samuel Street. There you will also find the American Embassy and the kabutz offices where you will go if you care to be placed on a kabutz, and to receive mail you'll find the American Express office located at Meditrad Ltd. (R), 16 Ben Yehuda Road, P.O. Box 4312, Tel: 58130/9. On Allenby Road bus #4 will take you to the central bus station where regularly scheduled busses leave for Jerusalem. However, for approximately the same price ($1.00) you can share a taxicab to Jerusalem. Israel is a small country and the entire trip takes between one and one and one-half hours.

Hitchhiking in Israel is easy, however, it is not uncommon to see 100 or more hitchhikers waiting for a ride. Military personnel are picked up first.

Once in Jerusalem you will find almost every religious organization represented, many of which offer accommodations for between $1.00 and $2.00.

MONEY CHART

ISRAEL

MONETARY UNIT: Pound
4.2 Pounds = $1.00
100 Agorot = 1 Pound
Code: IP

Amount of Local Currency You May Enter With	*Amount of Local Currency You May Leave With*	*Coins*	*Notes*	*Conversion Chart $1.00 US ='s*	*Black Market Rates*
IP 100	IP 100	1 Agora	5 Pounds	US IP	4.5 IP = $1.00
		5 Agorot	10 Pounds	$1.00 = 4.20	
		10 Agorot	50 Pounds	.50 = 2.10	
		25 Agorot	100 Pounds	.25 = 1.05	
		½ Pound		.10 = .42	
		1 Pound		.05 = .21	
		5 Pounds			
		10 Pounds			

KABUTZ

A kabutz is a community of people living and working together. Kabutz's may take the form of a small community. Besides food and lodging many kabutz's have movie theatres and swimming pools. The work done on a kabutz will vary. Generally they are agriculturally oriented, including dairy herds, orchards and growing vegetables. Some may even specialize in textiles or manufacturing. When you sign on as a working member of a kabutz your needs are taken care of including medical needs and in some cases a monthly salary.

To go to a kabutz is not a simple matter. You must first go to Tel-Aviv where two or three organizations representing kabutz's are located. It is there you'll decide which type of kabutz suits you best. You will receive the appropriate papers and then proceed to the kabutz.

TOURIST INFORMATION CENTER

Located on the corner of Ben Yehuda and Mendele Street, Tel-Aviv.

FURTHER INFORMATION

Israel Government Tourist Office, 574 Fifth Ave., New York, N.Y. 10036.

MAKING IT TO CYPRUS

TOURIST INFORMATION CENTER

VISA—Not required.

Located at the airport, 26 Evagoras Ave.

MONEY CHART

CYPRUS

MONETARY UNIT: Pounds
1 Pound = $2.60
1000 Mils = 1 Pound
Code: CP

Amount of Local Currency You May Enter With	*Amount of Local Currency You May Leave With*	*Coins*	*Notes*	*Conversion Chart $1.00 US ='s*		*Black Market Rates*
				US	CP	
No limit	CP 10	1 Mil	250 Piastre	$1.00 =	.3846	Negotiable
		3 Mil	(Mils)	.50 =	.1923	
		5 Mil	500 Piastre	.25 =	.0962	
		25 Mil	(Mils)	.10 =	.0385	
		50 Mil	1 Pound	.05 =	.0192	
		100 Mil	5 Pounds			
		500 Mil				

FURTHER INFORMATION

Cyprus Mission to the U.N., 165 East 72nd St., New York, N.Y. Tel: 212-986-3360.

MAKING IT TO EGYPT

VISA

Acquired upon arrival. Valid for one month, can be extended.

NOTE: Entry to Egypt not possible if traveler has Israeli visa stamp on passport.

MONEY CHART

EGYPT

MONETARY UNIT: Pounds
1 Pound = $2.30
100 piastres = 1 pound
Code: L.E.

Amount of Local Currency You May Enter With	*Amount of Local Currency You May Leave With*	*Coins*	*Notes*	*Conversion Chart $1.00 US =’s*	*Black Market Rates*
None	None	1 Millimes 5 Millimes 10 Millimes 20 Millimes 5 Piastres 10 Piastres 20 Piastres 25 Piastres 50 Piastres	5 Piastres 10 Piastres 25 Piastres 50 Piastres 1 Pound 5 Pounds 10 Pounds	US Piastre $1.00 = 45 .50 = 25 .25 = 12 .10 = 5 .05 = 2½	Negotiable $1.50 US = 1 Pound

TOURIST INFORMATION CENTER
Located at 5 Adly Street, Cairo.
FURTHER INFORMATION
United Arab Republic Tourist Office, 630 Fifth Avenue, New York, N.Y. Tel: 212-C16-6960.

MAKING IT TO EASTERN EUROPE AND THE SOVIET UNION

(Countries to the right of the double line on page #128)

When an American visits an Eastern European country (or, as they are called, the Eastern Bloc; Soviet Satellites; Iron Curtain, Communist or Socialist countries), he will confront certain situations at borders and customs check-points unique to this area.

Customs officers are more interested in printed matter than in a suitcase full of taxable merchandise, and newspapers, magazines and personal letters may be confiscated. Never deliver mail to or from anyone in these countries.

Upon entering a country, you will be required to declare the kind and amount of currency you are carrying including travelers checks. When you leave, you will have to make another currency declaration. Obviously you should have less than when you arrived. Should border officials discover you have almost the same or even more money than you arrived with, they will assume you have been dealing on the black market. They may confiscate your funds, and there may be serious consequences.

Unlike the black marketeers of Asia who deal for necessities as well as currency, most Eastern European black marketeers seem to be interested in luxury items such as sunglasses, cigarette lighters, levis, nylon ski jackets and other Western-made synthetics and colorful clothing which are not sold in these countries.

NOTE: Be careful. Black marketeers may be government plants who will arrest tourists attempting to deal illegally.

TOKEN MONEY

A daily token fee is charged except in Romania, Bulgaria and the U.S.S.R. The fee fluctuates and may reach as high as $9.00 in Poland, $5.00 in Hungary and Czechoslovakia and $1.50 in East Berlin (per day).

For example, upon purchasing your entry visa for East Berlin, you are required to buy 5 marks' worth of East Germany money (approximately $1.50 U.S.). Since you cannot legally take this money out of the country for a souvenir, you must spend it there.

In Hungary, Czechoslovakia and Poland the system works as follows: Using Hungary for an example, let's say you wish to stay seven days. The visa costs $5.00. Token money at $5.00 a day will cost you $35.00 for the week—paid in advance. You receive a voucher which is then converted into local Hungarian money upon your arrival. It cannot be converted back to U.S. or any other currency and must be spent in Hungary. Should you need more than $5.00 a day, you may purchase additional Hungarian money for which you will receive a receipt. With this receipt any left-over Hungarian money (other than token money) can be converted back to American money.

The reason for token money in these countries is the lucrative black market. The $35.00 you paid the government for your seven-day visit could be illegally changed with dealers on the street for $70.00 worth of Hungarian money. Thus token money guarantees that the government will collect badly needed American dollars and that they will not be ciphoned down to the people.

Should you decide to stay longer in one of these countries, in most cases you need only a good reason (tourist) and to pay the additional token money for each day you intend to stay.

MAKING IT TO THE UNION OF SOVIET SOCIALIST REPUBLIC (U.S.S.R.)

VISA

It is easier than most travelers think to enter the Soviet Union. First you must go to Intourist (the Russian Tourist Agency) or any other travel agency affiliated with Intourist. Tell them the exact dates and the various places you want to visit in the USSR. Intourist will cable Moscow for reservations. When Moscow confirms them you must pay in advance for your hotel and for your transportation to and from the U.S.S.R. Arrangements for a visit to your next stop must be made in advance. You must pay for everything in American dollars and leave your passport with Intourist. They will secure your visa in approximately a week.

The Russian visa is not stamped in your possport. It consists basically of a three-page booklet with your photos affixed to it. Do not lose it. This booklet is printed in Russian so that the border guards or customs officials will have no problem in identifying you. Upon your arrival they will remove one page. Upon departure the remainder of the booklet will be removed. To the Russian customs officials it is more important than your passport.

Throughout the U.S.S.R. you will find the following conditions prevail:

Once you have arranged your entire journey, reservations or your itinerary cannot be changed. You must enter the U.S.S.R. on a prearranged date, check into the designated hotel (however, no one checks to see that you are there all the time), and you must leave on the designated date. If any problems should arise with your accommodations, you will find that very little can be done. For example, when I was in a hotel in Moscow, an American couple was having problems with a lumpy bed. In most Western hotels the desk clerk

MONEY CHART

U.S.S.R.

MONETARY UNIT: Roubles
1 Rouble = $1.22
100 Kopecks = 1 Rouble
Code: Rbl

Amount of Local Currency You May Enter With	*Amount of Local Currency You May Leave With*	*Coins*	*Notes*	*Conversion Chart $1.00 US ='s*	*Black Market Rates*
None	None	1 Kopeck	1 Rouble	US Rbl	4 Rbl = $1.00
		3 Kopeck	3 Rouble	$1.22 = 1 Rbl	
		10 Kopeck	5 Rouble	.61 = 50 Kop	
		15 Kopeck	10 Rouble	.30 = 25 Kop	
		20 Kopeck	25 Rouble	.15 = 12 Kop	
		50 Kopeck	50 Rouble	.07 = 6 Kop	
		1 Rouble	100 Rouble		

would have offered to talk to the manager and try to do something about it. The reply from the desk clerk in Moscow was, "Sorry, there is nothing I can do about it. That is your room."

You will also find that it is wise to bring extra funds even though you have everything prearranged and prepaid. For example, the tourist agency which arranged my tour in Vienna, sold me a train ticket from Berlin through Poland to Moscow. I arrived at the Polish/Russian border with a ticket for sitting through to Moscow. An Intourist representative advised me that I must purchase a sleeping ticket at an additional cost of $7.00. If I did not want to pay for this ticket, I would not be allowed to enter, and all my prepaid and prearranged reservations would be forfeited.

You will find when making reservations that although the advertised second-class rates of $12.00 a night are listed, they are usually not available to Americans. The least expensive rate for Americans is $20.00 a night (first-class). However, the accommodation fee covers guided transportation to and from your hotel, vouchers for meals and sightseeing.

An Intourist guide will meet you at your port of entry whether it be the railway station or airport, check you in at your hotel, and tell you where the Intourist Office is located should any problems arise. Once checked into your hotel, you are on your own.

Although you are paying $20.00 a night for so-called first-class accommodations, it is wise to bring soap, towels, a flat sink stopper and even toilet paper.

The guided tours are usually conducted in the morning. However, you are free to roam the cities as you wish taking the subways, going in and out of stores and shops and visiting the suburbs.

Many Americans like to go on guided group tours of Russia which include all meals and lodging. A tourist agency can make all arrangements for you. Some tours include hotels, car rentals and transportation in a package.

It is also possible to drive your own vehicle through Russia and out, but you must still arrange everything through Intourist and arrive at designated places at certain times. You should be warned that gas stations in the Soviet Union are few and far between and when you do finally find one, you will usually have to wait in line.

TIP: Because accommodations are expensive, it is a good idea to take night transportation. For example, spend the day in Moscow. Take a night train to Leningrad arriving in the morning, and spend the entire day in Leningrad, thereby getting two extra days in Russia while saving $20.00 on a night's accommodations.

RECOMMENDED DO-IT-YOURSELF TRIP TO THE U.S.S.R. FOR SUMMERTIME TRAVELERS

If you really want to make your trip to Europe different take the following side trip to the U.S.S.R.

Arrange for your visa in either Vienna or another Western European city with an Intourist Office. Remember: you must wait a week to ten days in that city because your passport will be in the hands of this agency. Arrange the entire trip via train starting from either Vienna or from Germany through Berlin to Warsaw, Poland, and on to Moscow. Stay a couple of days in Moscow; then take a night train to Leningrad. After visiting Leningrad for a couple of days, leave the U.S.S.R. via night train bound for Helsinki, Finland. If you prefer, you can travel from Helsinki to Berlin or Vienna via the U.S.S.R. The entire trip via rail from either Berlin or Vienna to Helsinki will take eight days and will cost approximately $80.00 for rail fare and $80.00 for four nights' accommodations at $20.00 each. Total cost: approximately $160.00 U.S.

RECOMMENDED PLACE TO RECEIVE MAIL

Allow at least ten days for sending mail to and from the Soviet Union. If you must receive mail there, use American Express International, Hotel Metropole, Suite 384, Sverdlov Place, #2/4 Moscow. Tel: 256-384.

FURTHER INFORMATION

Intourist Office, 45 East 49th Street, New York, N.Y. 10017. Tel: (212) 752-3030.

TRANS-SIBERIAN EXPRESS

It's been said that this is the shortest way around the world and the least expensive way to go from Europe to East Asia (Japan, Hong Kong etc.). As with any trip to Russia arrangements must be made through Intourist. The entire trip from Moscow heading east to Nakhodka (North of Japan), takes approximately 11 days and costs in the neighborhood of $350. The train stops twice along the way and the scenery tends to get boring. Travelers contemplating taking this route should check on weather conditions and occasional flare-ups on the Russian-Chinese border. Due to the above, trains are often canceled.

MAKING IT TO BERLIN

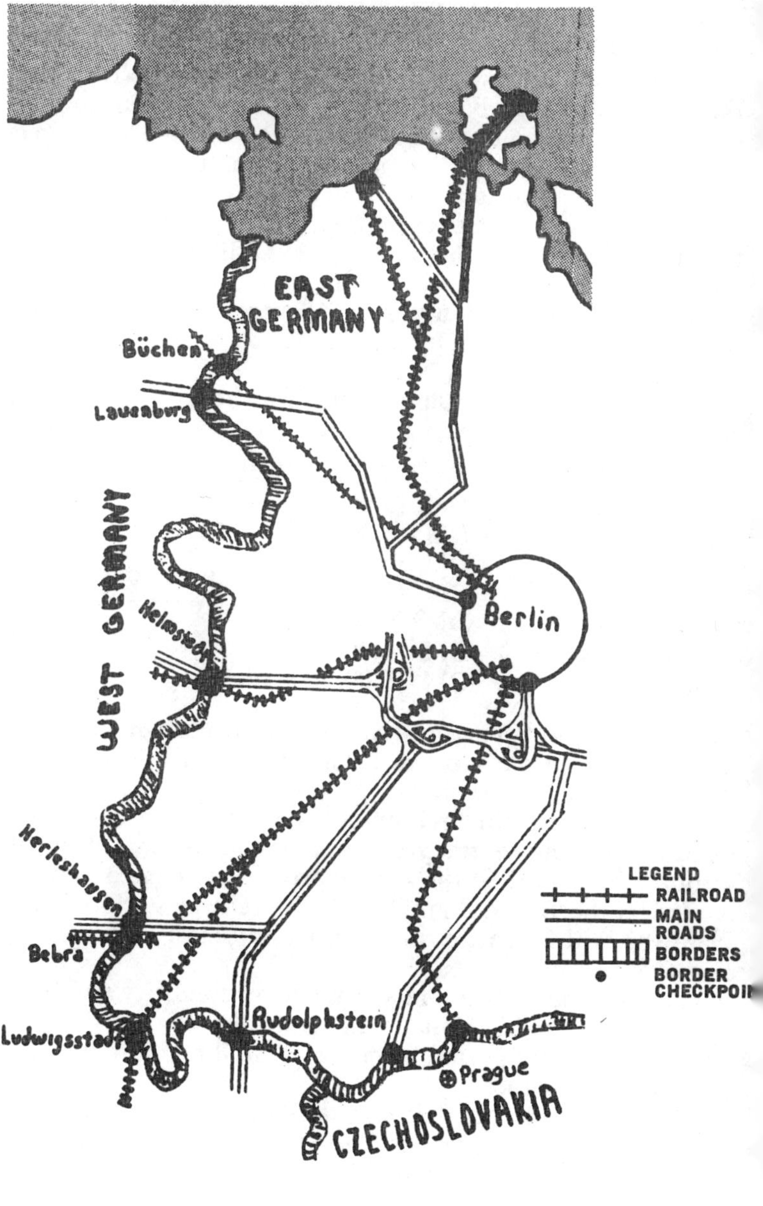

MAKING IT TO BERLIN

Berlin is connected by air with almost every major city in Europe. Excellent roads and regularly scheduled trains connect West Germany with Berlin. The cheapest train to Berlin costs approximately $13.00 U.S. one way. To pass through the East German zone to Berlin, you will need the following:

(1) A valid passport—The passport is stamped on the train or at the checkpoint to make it valid for transit to the Eastern zone. The cost is 4 marks for the one-way trip. All checkpoints are open both day and night. Additional documents are required if you are traveling by car:

(1) vehicle registration papers, (2) green international insurance card, (3) vehicle identification plate with initial indicating nationality.

Make sure you have sufficient fuel for the trip through the Eastern zone before entering.

ROAD TOLLS—FROM BERLIN TO:

Ludwigsstad	DM 15.00	
Helmstedt	DM 5.00	
Rudolphstein	DM 15.00	Only traffic leaving Berlin pays.
Buchen	DM 15.00	
Lauenburg	DM 15.00	
Herleshausen	DM 15.00	
Bebra	DM 15.00	

As a rule, foreigners must also purchase temporary liability insurance in addition to paying the road tolls and visa charges.

In Berlin, you will find almost everything you need clustered around the central railway station. It is located in the section of town called the Zoo, appropriately named because it borders the Berlin Zoo. Outside the railway station in the Plaza you will find a tourist information center with reservation service.

You will find Berlin a modern, Westernized city with subways. Because it is an island in itself, almost everything in Berlin must be imported from the West. Therefore, services are extremely high.

To cross the Berlin wall into the Eastern sector, go to the Allies' checkpoint known as Checkpoint Charlie. There you can get a tourist visa costing 5 marks (approximately $1.50

U.S.) good for the day. You are obligated to change another 5 marks into East German money which you are not allowed to take out of the Eastern zone.

RECOMMENDED PLACE TO RECEIVE MAIL

Berlin: American Express Company m.b.H., 11 Kurfuerstendamm, Tel. 881 43 33.

FURTHER INFORMATION

German Tourist Information Office, 500 Fifth Avenue, New York, N.Y. 10036.

MAKING IT TO EAST GERMANY

NOTE: U.S. Government is not represented in East Germany. For latest information always check with the nearest American Embassy before departing.

The procedure for visiting East Germany is similar to that of visiting Russia. (See Making It To Russia.) All arrangements must be made in advance and all transportation and accommodation prepaid. This is all done through designated travel agencies throughout the U.S. and cannot be done while in Europe.

Allow 4 to 6 weeks to obtain a tourist visa; no fee, no photos. Should you be visiting relatives in East Germany your visa will involve additional red-tape (primarily paperwork) and 4 photos. I have been told that in the near future a visa fee of $10.00 will be levied.

MONEY CHART

EAST GERMANY

MONETARY UNIT: East Mark
4.M = $1.00
100 Pfennig = 1 Mark
Code: DMEast

Amount of Local Currency You May Enter With	*Amount of Local Currency You May Leave With*	*Coins*	*Notes*	*Conversion Chart $1.00 US =’s*	*Black Market Rates*
None	None	1 Pfennig 5 Pfennig 10 Pfennig 50 Pfennig 1 Mark	5 Mark 10 Mark 20 Mark 50 Mark 100 Mark	US M $1.00 = 4 .50 = 2 .25 = 1 Pfg. .10 = 40 .05 = 20	Negotiable

FURTHER INFORMATION

Hansa-Lloyd Travel Bureau, Inc., 221 E. 86th Street, New York, N.Y. 10028. Tel: (212) SA 2-3092.

MAKING IT TO POLAND

VISA

A transit visa valid for up to seventy-two hours and one crossing costs $4.50 ($5.00 for two crossings). You need two photos. A transit visa is required for passing through Poland from Germany to the U.S.S.R. or vice versa. However, a transit visa will not be issued unless you have a visa for your destination.

A tourist visa costs $5.50. Arrangements can be handled through your local travel agent or Orbis (Polish Travel Bureau)

A copy of your voucher for prepaid service covering hotels and meals for your entire stay must accompany your visa application.

An American citizen of Polish background visiting relatives is not required to pay token money; instead he must pay $11.00 for his visa.

HITCHHIKING

Not only is it legal to hitchhike in Poland, but the government encourages it. Anyone over the age of seventeen may purchase an auto-stop booklet for approximately $2.00 (U.S.) which also includes accident insurance. You simply stand by the side of the road and hold up the booklet, and drivers will stop and pick you up. You then give the driver a coupon which is inside your booklet. The drivers cash in the coupons for valuable gifts. This system was developed mainly because there was a lack of motor vehicles and an overabundance of people who wanted to travel. The auto-stop booklet is available through Orbis, the Polish Travel Agency.

MONEY CHART

POLAND

MONETARY UNIT: Zloty
22.08 Zloty = $1.00
100 Groszy = 1 Zloty
Code: Zl

Amount of Local Currency You May Enter With	*Amount of Local Currency You May Leave With*	*Coins*	*Notes*	*Conversion Chart $1.00 US ='s*	*Black Market Rates*
None	None	1 Groszy 2 Groszy 5 Groszy 10 Groszy 20 Groszy 50 Groszy 1 Zloty 2 Zloty 5 Zloty 10 Zloty	20 Zloty 50 Zloty 100 Zloty 1000 Zloty	US Zl $1.00 = 22.08 .50 = 11.04 .25 = 5.52 .10 = 2.21 .05 = 1.10	Negotiable

WARSAW—CAPITAL OF POLAND

The tourist information center is located at 28 Aleje Jerozolimskie, or telephone 27-00-00. Directly across the street is a self-service restaurant called Praha. One block from the tourist information center is a student hotel located on Smolna Street.

FURTHER INFORMATION

Orbis, Polish Travel Information Bureau, 500 Fifth Ave., New York, N.Y. 10036. Tel: (212) 524-4152.

Polish Embassy, Consular Section, 2224 Wyoming Ave., N.W., Washington, D.C. 20008.

MAKING IT TO CZECHOSLOVAKIA

VISA

A transit or tourist visa good for one entry costs $5.00. Two photos are required. In organized groups of more than twelve persons the cost of a visa is $2.00 per person. The Czechoslovakia Embassy in Vienna is open for visa applications from 9:00 to 11:30 a.m. only.

MONEY CHART

CZECHOSLOVAKIA

MONETARY UNIT: Koruna
6.55 Korun = $1.00
100 Heller = 1 Koruny
Code: Kr

Amount of Local Currency You May Enter With	*Amount of Local Currency You May Leave With*	*Coins*	*Notes*	*Conversion Chart $1.00 US ='s*	*Black Market Rates*
None	None	1 Heller	3 Koruna	US Kr	Negotiable
		3 Heller	5 Korun	$1.00 = 6.55	
		5 Heller	10 Korun	.50 = 3.28	
		10 Heller	20 Korun	.25 = 1.64	
		25 Heller	25 Korun	.10 = .655	
		50 Heller	50 Korun	.05 = .328	
		1 Koruna	100 Korun		
		3 Korun			
		5 Korun			
		10 Korun			
		25 Korun			
		50 Korun			
		100 Korun			

ARRIVAL AND DEPARTURE

PRAGUE

Prague is easily accessible by land from West Germany and Austria. Many tours leave each weekend from Vienna for approximately $30.00 U.S. (The price of the tour does not include token money and visas.)

In Prague, the capital, the tourist information service is located at 1 Nove Mesto, Na prikope–20, or telephone 54-44-44.

ACCOMMODATIONS

The travel bureau of Czechoslovakian students offers inexpensive accommodations in a student hotel called CKM, located on Jindrisska Street #28, or telephone 23-11-67.

RECOMMENDED PLACE TO RECEIVE MAIL

Czechoslovak Travel Bureau, 10 East 40th Street. New York, N.Y. 10016.

MAKING IT TO HUNGARY

VISA

A transit visa valid for one entry and forty-eight hours costs $3.00 ($5.00 for two entries; $12.00 for multiple entries). A tourist visa valid for one entry and thirty days costs $3.50. Two photos are required.

Travel arrangements can be made though travel agencies with contact Ibusz, the Official Hungarian travel bureau. Along with a visa you will receive a copy of your token money voucher.

Recommended Travel Procedure:

Budapest is easily reached from Vienna. There you can arrange for your visa and complete tour. Many travel agencies including American Express offer a weekend tour to Budapest for approximately $27.00 (bus and hotel)–not including visa and token money, or you can arrange a tour yourself via public transportation (trains, bus etc.).

BUDAPEST

The Danube River runs right through the center of Budapest, the capital, dividing it into Buda and Pest. The tourist information board located at Roosevelt Ter 5, offers a reservation service.

For unique accommodations ask to be booked in the Citadella, a castle which has been converted into a hotel located on top of a mountain overlooking the entire city. The cost is approximately 60¢ U.S. a night. To reach the Citadella, walk across the Lanchid Bridge, which is directly in front of the tourist information center. Once across the bridge, take

MONEY CHART

HUNGARY

MONETARY UNIT: Forint
27.63 Forint = $1.00
100 Filler = 1 Forint
Code: Ft

Amount of Local Currency You May Enter With	*Amount of Local Currency You May Leave With*	*Coins*	*Notes*	*Conversion Chart $1.00 US =’s*		*Black Market Rates*
Ft 200	Ft 200	2 Filler	10 Forint	US	Ft	Negotiable
		10 Filler	20 Forint	$1.00 =	27.63	
		50 Filler	50 Forint	.50 =	13.82	
		1 Forint	100 Forint	.25 =	6.91	
		2 Forint	500 Forint	.10 =	2.76	
		5 Forint		.05 =	1.38	
		10 Forint				

Tram #9 up to the intersection of Bartok Bela and Karinthy Frigyes. From there you can take bus #27 right to the door of the Citadella.

FURTHER INFORMATION

Kovacs International Travel Service, Inc. 81-08 Broadway, Elmhurst, N.Y. 11373 Tel: (212) 651-2494.

Legation of the Hungarian Peoples Republic, 2437 15th St., N.W., Washington, D.C. Tel: (202) DU 7-3800.

MAKING IT TO ROMANIA

VISA

No advance visa is necessary. No charge, no photos. Apply at the border or any port of entry. A tourist visa valid for one entry within six months for a stay of thirty days can be extended ninety days from date of arrival.

MONEY CHART

ROMANIA

MONETARY UNIT: Leu
6 Leu = $1.00
100 Bani = 1 Leu
Code: Leu

Amount of Local Currency You May Enter With	*Amount of Local Currency You May Leave With*	*Coins*	*Notes*	*Conversion Chart $1.00 US ='s*	*Black Market Rates*
None	None	5 Bani	3 Leu	US Leu	Negotiable
		10 Bani	5 Leu	$1.00 = 6	
		1 Leu	10 Leu	.50 = 3	
			25 Leu	.25 = 1.5	
			50 Leu	.10 = .6	
			100 Leu	.05 = .3	
			500 Leu		

ARRIVAL AND DEPARTURE

To really see Romania, you must visit the countryside. If you are *en route* from Europe to Athens or Turkey, an excellent way to see Romania is by bus via Belgrade, the capital of Yugoslavia and across the western Romanian border to the town of Timisoara in the foothills of the Transilvanian Alps. Along the way you will see covered wagons, gypsies and women pulling plows. You can either return to Belgrade or continue on to Bucharest and then head south to Bulgaria.

Bucharest, the capital is rather out-of-the-way and off the main travel trail, but is connected by airlines to most major cities. Roads are adequate and if you have the time en route to Istanbul or Athens—go from Belgrade, Yugoslavia through Romania and Bulgaria.

FURTHER INFORMATION

Romanian National Tourist Office, 500 Fifth Ave., New York, N.Y. 10036 Tel: (212) 524-6951.

MAKING IT TO BULGARIA

Bulgaria is perhaps one of the more conservative Eastern European countries. Recent harrassment of long haired travelers have caused many to avoid this area.

VISA

A visa is required. A transit visa (for a stay of up to twenty-four hours) costs $1.00 for one entry and $2.00 for two entries. An entry visa for a stay of from twenty-four hours to sixty days costs $2.60 at the embassy ($3.00 surcharge if obtained at border). No photos are required.

MONEY CHART

BULGARIA

MONETARY UNIT: Leva
2 Leva = $1.00
100 Stotinki = I Lev
Code: Lev

Amount of Local Currency You May Enter With	*Amount of Local Currency You May Leave With*	*Coins*	*Notes*	*Conversion Chart $1.00 US ='s*	*Black Market Rates*
None	None	1 Stotinki 2 Stotinki 5 Stotinki 10 Stotinki 20 Stotinki 50 Stotinki 1 Leva 2 Leva	1 Leva 2 Leva 5 Leva 10 Leva 20 Leva	US Leva $1.00 = 2 .50 = 1 Sto- tinki .25 = 50 .10 = 20 .05 = 10	Negotiable

ARRIVAL

Most travelers pass through Bulgaria *en route* to Istanbul

and other points east. The tourist information center is located in Sofia, the capital, at #1 Lenin Square. Tel: 877574.

Accommodations and food get cheaper the further you go from Lenin Square.

RECOMMENDED PLACE TO RECEIVE MAIL

Use the American Embassy.

FURTHER INFORMATION

Bulgarian Tourist Office, 50 E. 42nd Street, New York, N.Y. 10017 Tel: (212) 661-5733.

MAKING IT TO YUGOSLAVIA

Although technically considered a Communist country, Yugoslavia, unlike the rest of the Eastern European bloc, seems to be pro-West. Yugoslavia's Adriatic coast has become Europe's Miami Beach.

VISA

No advance visa is necessary. Apply at port of entry or border points for a tourist visa valid up to six months. There is no fee.

MONEY CHART

YUGOSLAVIA

MONETARY UNIT: Dinar
17 Dinar = $1.00
100 Para = 1 Dinar
Code: Yd

Amount of Local Currency You May Enter With	*Amount of Local Currency You May Leave With*	*Coins*	*Notes*	*Conversion Chart $1.00 US ='s*		*Black Market Rates*
				US	Yd	
Yd 100	Yd 100	5 Para	5 Dinar	$1.00	= 17	Negotiable
		10 Para	10 Dinar	.50	= 8.5	
		20 Para	50 Dinar	.25	= 4.25	
		50 Para	100 Dinar	.10	= 1.7	
		1 Dinar	500 Dinar	.05	= .85	
		2 Dinar				
		5 Dinar				

ARRIVAL AND DEPARTURE

You can enter Yugoslavia from Trieste, Italy. Train fare from the Italian border to Rijeka, Yugoslavia, is approximately $1.50. From Rijeka regularly scheduled boats travel south along the Adriatic coast between the big cities and the islands. The fare from Rijeka to Dubrovnik is approximately $5.00 including stopovers *en route*. From Dubrovnik regularly scheduled ferry boats cross over to Brindisi, Italy. All together transportation for the entire trip along the Yugoslavian coast from Trieste, Italy, back to Brindisi, costs approximately $10.00 to $15.00 U.S.

Many travelers pass through Yugoslavia *en route* to Greece and Turkey. Roads are better than adequate and hitchhiking is easy. The fastest road through Yugoslavia to Greece and Turkey is inland via Belgrade. From Belgrade you can head south to Athens, Greece, or east through Bulgaria to Istanbul, Turkey. Avoid hitchhiking along the coast road; there are too many local tourists.

RECOMMENDED PLACE TO RECEIVE MAIL

Belgrade: American Express, c/o Atlas, Yugoslav Travel Agency (R), Mose Pijade 11, Tel: 341-471.

FURTHER INFORMATION

Yugoslav State Tourist Office, 509 Madison Ave., New York, N.Y. 10022.

MAKING IT TO ALBANIA

The U.S. Government is not represented in Albania. For the latest information always check with the nearest American Embassy before departing.

Albania has been removed from the off-limits list for American travelers, however, it is still difficult to gain entry. There are only two cities in Europe where you can obtain a visa for Albania—Rome and Paris. The Americans I have interviewed who went to Albania were not warmly welcomed, and rocks were thrown at some.

Albania is not only not inhospitable to Americans but to many other European nationals as well. In fact, Albania boasts few tourists besides an occasional visitor from Peking.

MAKING IT TO ASIA

MAKING IT TO INDIA VIA ISTANBUL

The majority of travelers passing through this area will be going from Europe through Istanbul on to India and other

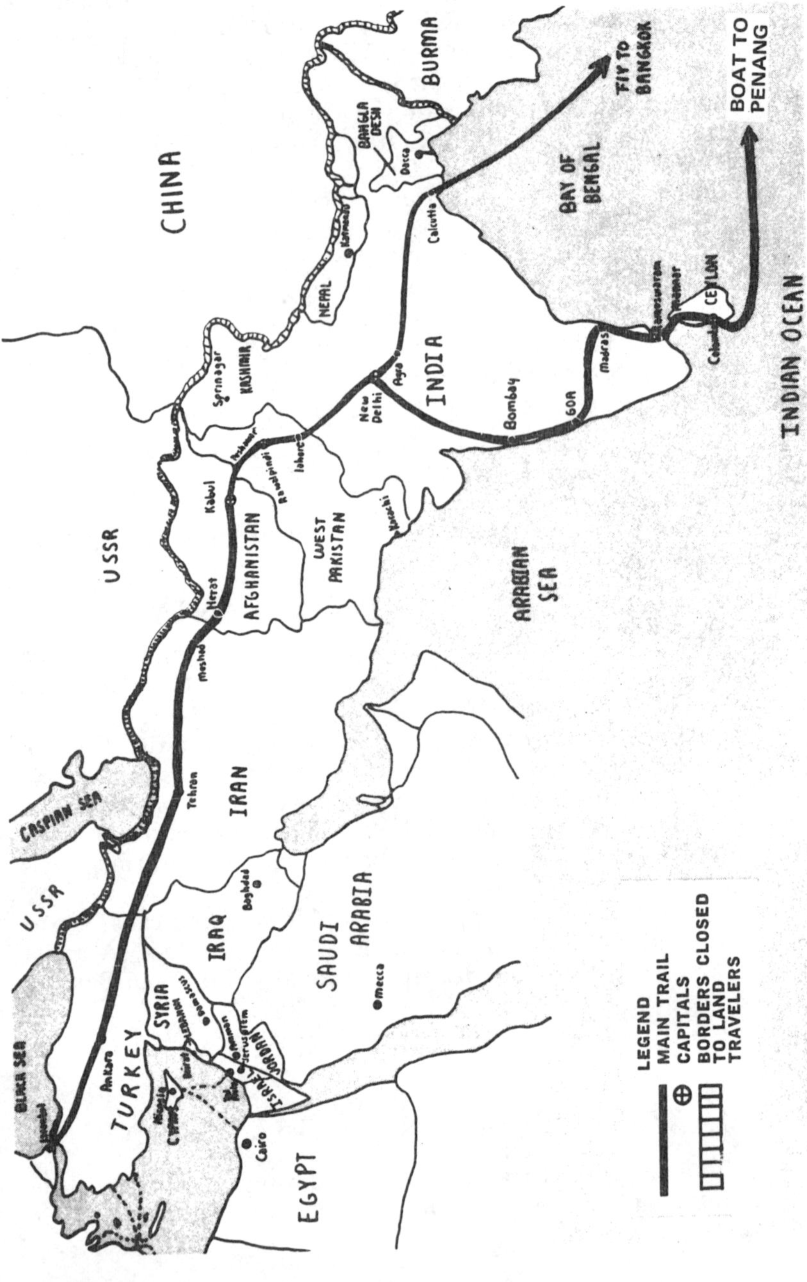
CHINA
USSR
USSR
BURMA
BANGLA DESH
Dacca
NEPAL
KASHMIR
Srinagar
INDIA
New Delhi
Agra
Calcutta
Bombay
GOA
Madras
CEYLON
BAY OF BENGAL
FLY TO BANGKOK
BOAT TO PENANG
INDIAN OCEAN
ARABIAN SEA
WEST PAKISTAN
Karachi
Lahore
Rawalpindi
Peshawar
Kabul
AFGHANISTAN
Herat
IRAN
Tehran
CASPIAN SEA
IRAQ
Baghdad
SAUDI ARABIA
Mecca
SYRIA
Damascus
Amman
Jerusalem
JORDAN
ISRAEL
TURKEY
Ankara
BLACK SEA
Nicosia
EGYPT
Cairo
LEGEND
MAIN TRAIL
CAPITALS
BORDERS CLOSED TO LAND TRAVELERS

parts of Asia. The following information is intended for them. Should you be traveling in the opposite direction, it is still applicable.

Heading to India from Istanbul, you pass through the following countries: Turkey, Iran, Afghanistan and Pakistan. Using third-class public transportation, you can travel from Istanbul to New Delhi for $35 to $45 (not including food and lodging).

Unlike Europe, health requirements in this area vary. Cholera immunization is required throughout Asia, and smallpox immunization is necessary for travel to Pakistan, India and Nepal. Obtain vaccinations before leaving the U.S. or in Europe. Advance visas are required to enter Iran and Afghanistan; it is best to obtain these before venturing into Asia.

When you travel through Asia, you will find yourself part of a massive fraternity of young travelers. All along the travel route in almost every major stop from Istanbul through India to Singapore you will find many meeting places for travelers. These may be a hotel, a cafe or an American Express Office. It is here that you will receive valuable information and travel tips from your fellow travelers that might not only save you money but could save your life. This information is extremely valuable, up to date and not available in any guide books.

The map section on Asia will give you pertinent information collected through extensive research and actual travel experience.

NOTE: The suppress-the-hippie policy is in full force in this area.

MAKING IT TO ISTANBUL (TURKEY)

VISA

ARRIVAL AND DEPARTURE

Situated at the crossroads of Europe and Asia, Istanbul can be easily reached via the Orient express from Paris in four days (cost approximately $66.00 U.S.) or by train from Athens in two days at a cost of approximately $25.00 U.S. Airlines connect Istanbul with almost every major city.

Public transportation schedules are usually maintained. Trains, busses and adequate roads connect Istanbul with Ankara, the capital of Turkey, and eastward to the Iran border. Before leaving Ankara, be sure to have the appropriate visa for Iran. In Turkey and Iran try to travel by train whenever possible. Trains are more comfortable than busses in hot climates and more reliable.

In the past few years European and American hippies have run frequent shuttle busses connecting Istanbul with Kabul, Afghanistan, for approximately $30.00 U.S. From Athens through Istanbul to Kabul the cost is $40.00 U.S., from Istanbul to Amsterdam, Paris or London it may be as low as $20.00 U.S. You can find out more about these bus services by visiting the places in Istanbul recommended below.

Recommended route by car or hitchhiking:

Roads are better than adequate.

Trieste, Italy to Belgrade, Yugoslavia, Belgrade to Sofia, Bulgaria, Sofia to Istanbul *OR* from Belgrade south to Greece then East to Istanbul.

To the traveler heading East to India, Nepal, Afghanistan and other points in Asia, Istanbul is of more strategic importance. It is here that almost everyone on the trail between Europe and Asia will stop. Travelers with busses, cars and vans will pick up others to share expenses. It is also here that you will meet travelers, who have just come from the places you are intending to visit, and you will, therefore, be able to pick up vital information.

The place to go in Istanbul is a section of town called

MONEY CHART

TURKEY

MONETARY UNIT: Lira
14 Lirasi = $1.00
100 Kurus = 1 Lira
Code: Tl

Amount of Local Currency You May Enter With	*Amount of Local Currency You May Leave With*	*Coins*	*Notes*	*Conversion Chart $1.00 US ='s*	*Black Market Rates*
Tl 100	Tl 100	5 Kurus	5 Lirasi	US Tl	17 Tl = $1.00
		10 Kurus	10 Lirasi	$1.00 = 14	
		25 Kurus	20 Lirasi	.50 = 7	
		1 Lira	50 Lirasi	.25 = 3.5	
		2½ Lira	100 Lirasi	.10 = 1.4	
		10 Lira	500 Lirasi	.05 = .7	
			1000 Lirasi		

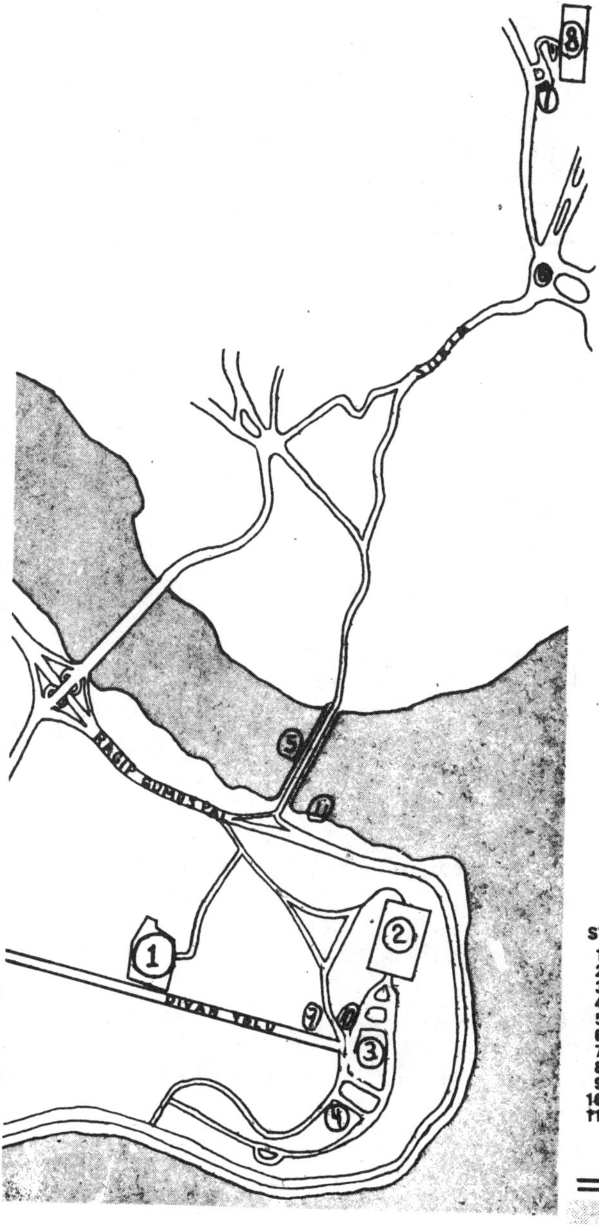

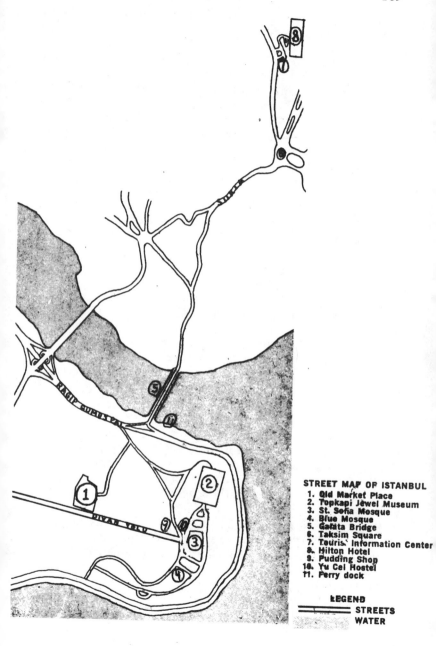

STREET MAP OF ISTANBUL

1. Old Market Place
2. Topkapi Jewel Museum
3. St. Sofia Mosque
4. Blue Mosque
5. Galata Bridge
6. Taksim Square
7. Touris. Information Center
8. Hilton Hotel
9. Pudding Shop
10. Yu Cel Hostel
11. Ferry dock

LEGEND

STREETS

WATER

Sultan Ammet. In this area you will find the Topkapi Jewel Museum (#2), the St. Sofia Mosque (#3) and the Blue Mosque (#4). On Divan Yolu Street is a restaurant specializing in puddings called the Pudding Shop (#9), which is a meeting place for travelers passing through Istanbul. It is here that you will find a bulletin board with advertisements for riders, rides, and other information.

Around the corner from the Pudding Shop across the street from the Blue Mosque is the Yu Cel Hostel (#10) offering clean accommodations for approximately $1.00 a night. In this area between the Pudding Shop and the Yu Cel Hostel are other inexpensive hotels.

Directly up the street from the Pudding Shop is the Old Market Place (#1). It is here you will be able to meet black marketeers as well as shopkeepers and craftsmen who will be able to design and make for you suede and leather clothes. Be extra careful to get what you pay for.

In front of the Pudding Shop you can catch bus #T4 which will take you across the Galata bridge (#5) up to Taksim Square (#6), where the Taksim monument of the Republic is located. From there it is a short walk to the Hilton Hotel (#8). In the Hilton you'll find the American Express, the recommended place to receive mail in Istanbul: c/o American Express Turk Ekspres (R), (Havacilik ve Turizm Ltd.), Istanbul Hilton Hotel, P.O. Box 70. Tel: 48.56.40 and 48.39.05. Directly in front of the Hilton Hotel is the tourist information center (#7). Also on the same street are located all the airline ticket offices.

Right next to the bridge indicated on the map is a ferry dock (#11) where for approximately $1.50 you can take an enjoyable ride up the Bosperous to the Black Sea and visit small fishing villages. For a change of scenery on the return trip take one of the regularly scheduled busses which run inland.

Because of the availability of drugs and the crack-down on the illicit flow from this area, Istanbul is occasionally placed under marshal law. During such periods it is not uncommon to see soldiers armed with machine guns roaming the streets searching out black marketeers and drug dealers.

Many people have complained about being ripped off when dealing with black marketeers. Use the utmost caution even if you are just changing money on the street.

STREET MAP OF TEHRAN, IRAN
1. Tourist Information Center
2. American Express
3. American Embassy
4. Post Office
5. Amier Kabier

FURTHER INFORMATION

Turkish Tourist and Information, 500 Fifth Ave., New York, N.Y. 10036.

MAKING IT TO IRAN

VISA

A tourist visa valid for three months is required. There is no charge, but two photos required. You might be required to show sufficient funds (at least $100.00 U.S.) if you obtain a visa *en route*.

CAPITAL—TEHRAN (See Map)

Most travelers en route to India often stop here. A popular meeting spot for travelers and an inexpensive place to stay is Amier Kabier (cost approximately $1.25 U.S.) located on Amier Kabier Street above a general tire store. Just look for the General Tire sign (#5). For slightly nicer accommodations and a better location try the Cyrus Hotel located at Lalezar Now Street. Tel: 303082. (Cost approximately $1.50 U.S. per night.)

As you can see by the map, The American Embassy (#3), the tourist information center (#1) and American Express (#2) are all located in the same part of town.

MONEY CHART

IRAN

MONETARY UNIT: Rial
75.75 Rials = $1.00
100 Dinars = 1 Rial
Code: Rl

Amount of Local Currency You May Enter With	*Amount of Local Currency You May Leave With*	*Coins*	*Notes*	*Conversion Chart $1.00 US =’s*	*Black Market Rates*
				US Rl	
No limit	Rl 3000	5 Dinars	5 Rials	$1.00 = 75.75	None
		10 Dinars	10 Rials	.50 = 37.88	
		25 Dinars	20 Rials	.25 = 18.94	
		50 Dinars	50 Rials	.10 = 7.58	
		1 Rial	100 Rials	.05 = 3.79	
		2 Rial	200 Rials		
		5 Rial	1000 Rials		
		10 Rial	5000 Rials		

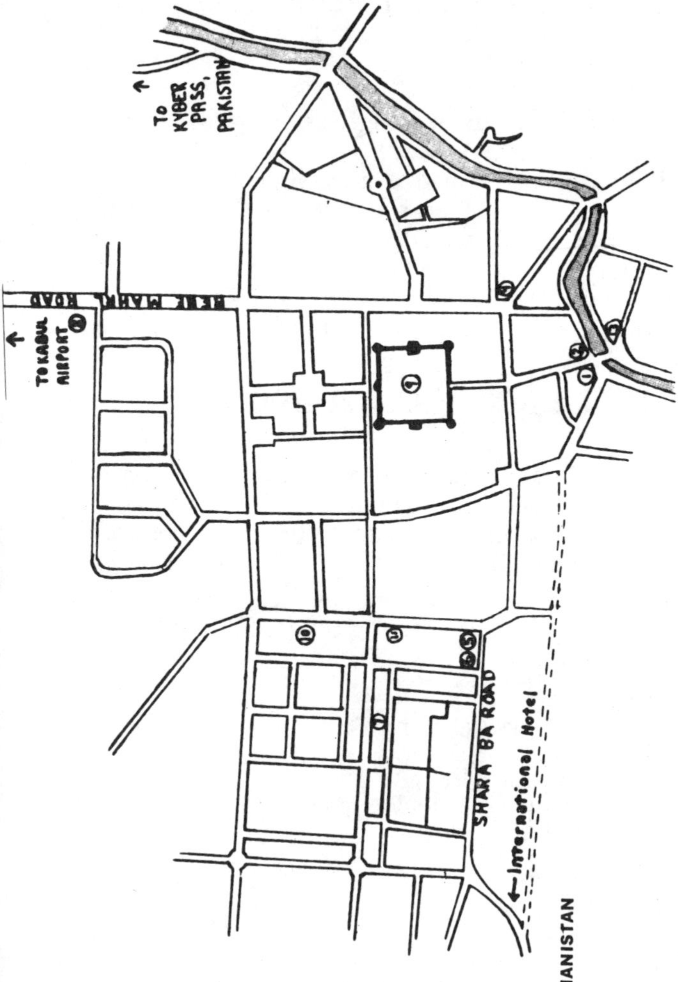

STREET MAP OF KABUL, AFGHANISTAN

1. Spenzar Hotel
2. Hospital
3. Central post office
4. Kiber restaurant
5. Mustaffa Hotel
6. Coat Shop
7. Marco Polo Restaurant
8. American Embassy
9. Royal Palace
10. Airlines Office
11. U.S. Library and Information Agency

LEGEND

MAIN ROAD

UNPAVED ROAD

RIVER

RECOMMENDED PLACE TO RECEIVE MAIL

Tehran: c/o American Express, Near East Tours (R), 130 Takht Jamshid, Tel. 47134/7.

DEPARTURE

Leaving Tehran by train heading East towards Afghanistan, you can go as far as Neshad.

A new rail link from Neshad to the Afghanistan border should be completed in the near future. In the meantime busses are available. Roads are adequate should you be driving or hitchhiking.

FURTHER INFORMATION

Iranian Consulate General, 630 Fifth Ave., N.Y., N.Y. 10020 (212) 541-7270.

MAKING IT TO AFGHANISTAN

VISA

To enter Afghanistan, you must have an advance visa for which there is no charge. Three photos are required.

The last place to obtain a visa coming from the West will be Tehran, the capital of Iran; from the East, New Delhi, capital of India. Most Afghani consulates abroad require the applicant to show that he has at least $100 (U.S.) in currency before issuing a visa.

MONEY CHART

AFGHANISTAN

MONETARY UNIT: Afghani
45 Afghani = $1.00
100 Puls = 1 Afghani
Code: Af

Amount of Local Currency You May Enter With	*Amount of Local Currency You May Leave With*	*Coins*	*Notes*	*Conversion Chart $1.00 US ='s*	*Black Market Rates*
Af 500	Af 500	None	Afghanis	US Af	None*
			10	$1.00 = 45	
			20	.50 = 22.50	
			50	.25 = 11.25	
			100	.10 = 4.50	
			500	.05 = 2.25	
			1000		

* IF ENROUTE TO INDIA: Buy Indian Rupees in Kabul, Afghanistan. As high as 14 Rps. to 100 as opposed to 10 in India.

Kabul, Afghanistan, has become an extremely popular stopping-off place on the main trail from India to Europe. The availability of drugs has also attracted a large number of young travelers. Because of Kabul's popularity the influx of travelers has caused food and lodging prices to rise since last year.

ARRIVAL

Kabul, the capital of Afghanistan, can be approached from the West by air or by land. Kabul's international airport is readily accessible to almost all international airlines (except Pakistan's).

You should be reminded again that the penalty in Iran for taking drugs across the Irani-Afghani border is *DEATH*.

Afghanistan has no railroads, but public busses and private automobiles are available to take you to the major city of Herat and on to Kabul. Although the minor roads in Afghanistan are quite primitive and unpaved in backward areas, the main highways are good and are open most of the year, weather permitting. However, gas stations are few and far between. Your automobile should therefore be in excellent condition, and you should carry extra gasoline.

KABUL–(See Map)

When you arrive in Kabul, you will find a wide variety of accommodations ranging from the Western-style Intercontinental Hotel for the tourist to the dollar-a-night hotel for the budget-minded traveler. Other than the Intercontinental, there are few tourist hotels in the center of town. The Spenzar Hotel (#1) has a small tourist information center in the lobby. Within five blocks of the Spenzar the budget-minded traveler will find a wide selection of low-cost accommodations. But remember: in this part of the world health standards are not what they should be, so don't necessarily settle for the first thing that comes along. Two hotels may cost the same price, but one may be twice as clean as the other. It is best to check out a few.

I found that the Mustaffa Hotel (#5), which is fairly new, has Holiday-Inn type facilities for the same price as some of the older and more run-down buildings in town. (40 Afghanis or 55¢ U.S. for a dorm room, 200 Afghanis–$1.30 U.S. each or $2.60 for a private room.

FOOD

DON'T DRINK THE WATER.

Most tourist hotels from the Spenzar to the Intercontinental will have a varied Western and European tourist menu. Almost every traveler in town can be found at the Kiber restaurant (#4) which is Kabul's version of Horn and Hardart. The Kiber restaurant, which is cafeteria style, serves Western-style, European, meat-and-potato dishes plus some local rice dishes and a wide selection of desserts, all for under $1.00.

The Marco Polo (#7) offers a similarly varied menu but more local color. For extra atmosphere you can sit on soft cushions in the back room and eat at little six-inch tables, Afghani style.

MAIL

It's advisable in Kabul to use the American Embassy (#8) as your mailing address. It's located on the outskirts of town on the main road to the airport.

LOCAL TRANSPORTATION

A taxi ride from the airport to the center of Kabul should cost no more than 50 Afghanis for four people and luggage—12½ Afghanis each—if you bargain with the driver.

Kabul is big enough to get lost in, yet small enough to cover the sightseeing in a day or two on foot. Cars can be hired with a driver at an average price of $5 to $10 a day for four people, depending on how good a bargainer you are. There are local busses in town.

RUMOR

Kabul is filled with numerous unusual shops. Very common is the antique store with its many artifacts from the neighboring villages and towns and souvenirs such as rifles and military equipment dating from the fighting at the Khyber Pass. Rumor has it that these shops are stocked with valuable antique American firearms such as the blunderbust. Actually most of these rifles and guns are of Russian or European manufacture. Travelers contemplating purchasing them should check with U.S. customs before shipping them home.

One of the most popular items purchased by travelers in Afghanistan are the Afghani coats. (See Con Games). One of the larger dealers is Nkjiullah Nourzad (#6), located on the same street as the Mustaffa Hotel. He has a large selection of top-quality merchandise, and if you ask him nicely, he might even take you to the factory where the coats are made. There you can see people of all ages, some only eight or nine years old, embroidering the coats by hand.

DEPARTURE

Continuing on your journey, you can leave Kabul in either of two directions: The first is North towards the U.S.S.R. Four flights a week connect Kabul with Moscow. However, travelers *en route* to the U.S.S.R. should be advised that it takes a week or two to arrange for a visa. It is wiser to do this while you are still in Europe.

If you choose to continue on the main trail between Istanbul and India, you can head due East. A bus from Kabul crosses the border almost daily into Pakistan.

FURTHER INFORMATION

Afghan American Trading Co., 122 West 30th St., New York, N.Y. 10001 Tel: (212) L 5-6494.

MAKING IT TO PAKISTAN

VISA

A visa is no longer obtainable at the border but must be obtained prior to arrival. A transit visa for 14 days or a multiple-entry visa good for 48 months is available at no charge; no pictures are required.

BORDER PASS

To enter or leave Pakistan, you need a border pass. This can be obtained in any Pakistani Consulate in the U.S., Europe or throughout the rest of the world including Kabul, Afghanistan. It is good for one journey and has no time limit.

ARRIVAL

The bus from Kabul, Afghanistan, goes directly to Peshwar, Pakistan. From there you can take a train to Rawalpindi, the capital, and then on to Lahore. In Lahore various low-budget hotels are located near the central railway station. One of the most popular is the YMCA. From Lahore it's only a short hop to the Indian border.

From Rawalpindi the traveler can take a side trip, north to Kashmir or head outh to Karachi. Both are connected by bus and rail.

MONEY CHART

PAKISTAN

MONETARY UNIT: Rupee
4.76 Rupees = $1.00
100 Paisa = 1 Rupee
Code: Prp

Amount of Local Currency You May Enter With	*Amount of Local Currency You May Leave With*	*Coins*	*Notes*	*Conversion Chart $1.00 US ='s*		*Black Market Rates*
				US	Prp	
Prp 80	Prp 20	1 Paisa	1 Rupee	$1.00 =	11.00	10 Rp = $1.00
		5 Paisa	2 Rupee	.50 =	5.50	
		10 Paisa	5 Rupee	.25 =	2.75	
		25 Paisa	10 Rupee	.10 =	1.00	
		50 Paisa	50 Rupee	.05 =	.50	
		1 Rupee				

KASHMIR

From time to time the in-place in this part of the world changes. In the past two years it has moved from Kabul to Katmandu, Goa, Benares, and now Srinagar, Kashmir. For anywhere from 50¢ to $10 a day you can rent a house boat on Srinagar's Dal Lake. Some travelers get by on $1.00 a day including accommodations and meals.

KARACHI

Karachi, a seaport, is one of the largest industrial centers in Pakistan. Pakistan's only international airport is located here. There are no flights between Karachi and Afghanistan, and only international carriers of other countries will fly between Karachi and New Delhi, India. (The airlines of West Pakistan and India do not connect these two countries).

If you fly to or from Pakistan (Karachi), you are entitled to a free ride on the bus which connects the airport with the center of town.

RECOMMENDED PLACE TO RECEIVE MAIL

Rawalpindi: American Express International, Cantonment Bldg., Lawrence Rd., P.O. Box 96, Tel: 5117 and 5128.

FURTHER INFORMATION

The Consulate General of Pakistan, 12 East 65th Street, New York, N.Y. 10021 Tel: (212) 879-5800.

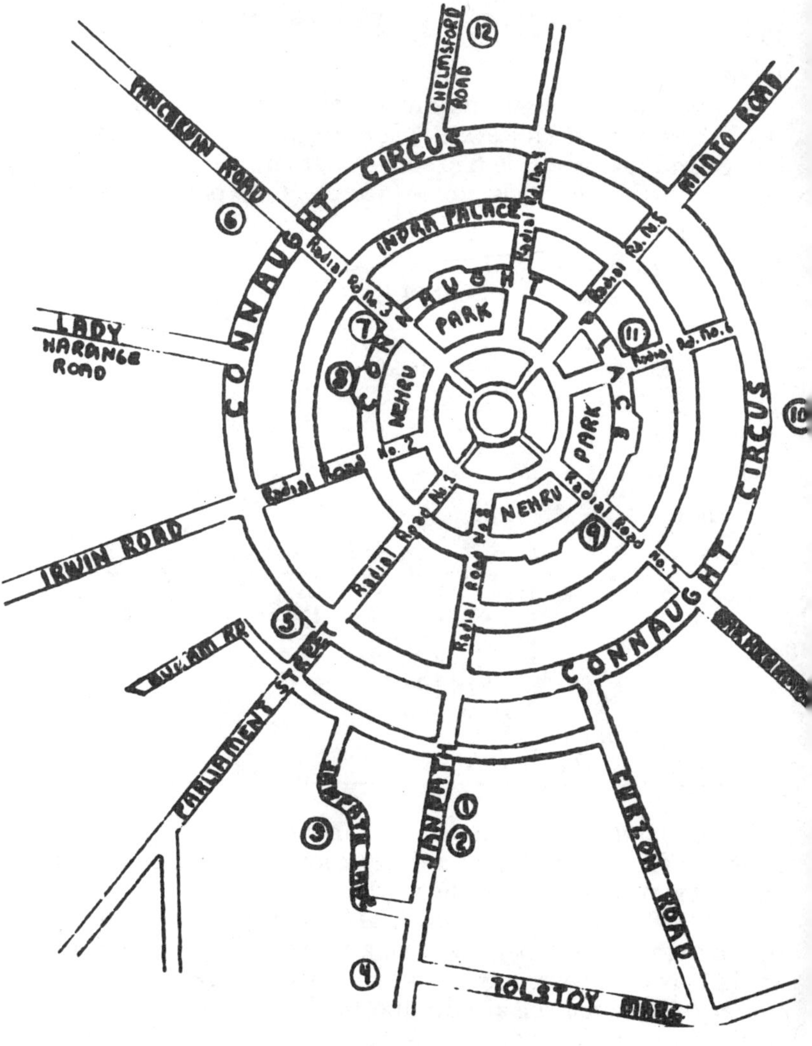

STREET MAP OF NEW DELHI, INDIA

1. Tourist Information Center
2. Indian Airlines Office
3. Mrs. Colaco's Rooming House
4. Pan American (Imperial Hotel)
5. Cellar Restaurant
6. Hospital
7. American Express
8. Post Office
9. First National City Bank
10. Central Market
11. Embassy Restaurant
12. Central Railway Station

MAKING IT TO INDIA

VISA

A visa is not necessary for an American citizen staying less than three weeks. However, if you are planning on staying longer and taking a side trip to Nepal, then it is advisable to get a multiple-entry visa (cost: $2.10). Two photos are required.

MONEY CHART

INDIA

MONETARY UNIT: Rupee
7.27 Rupees = $1.00
100 Paise = 1 Rupee
Code: Rp

Amount of Local Currency You May Enter With	*Amount of Local Currency You May Leave With*	*Coins*	*Notes*	*Conversion Chart $1.00 US ='s*		*Black Market Rates*
				US	Rp	
None	None	Naya Paise	1 Rupee	$1.00 =	7.27	10 Rp = $1.00
		1	2 Rupee	.50 =	3.64	
		2	5 Rupee	.25 =	1.82	
		5	10 Rupee	.10 =	.73	
		10	100 Rupee	.05 =	.36	
		20				
		50				
		1 Rupee				
		10 Rupee				

ARRIVAL

Trains and busses run from Lahore, Pakistan to New Delhi, India. International airlines connect New Delhi with almost every major city in the world.

IMPORTANT NOTE FOR AIR TRAVELERS: Anyone arriving at or departing from an international airport in India may take advantage of Indian Airlines' free bus transportation between the airport and the Indian Airlines Office in the center of the city.

NEW DELHI

Since many nations from around the world have their consulates and representatives stationed in New Delhi, it is an excellent place to acquire visas.

The center of New Delhi is Connaught Place (see Map); everything eminates from this circle. Located on the Circle is the American Express office (#7) in Hamilton House, Block A, Connaught Place, Tel: 43554. One block off Connaught Place is the tourist information center (#1). The central railway station (#12) is only a few blocks on the opposite side of the circle.

ACCOMMODATIONS

Two blocks from Connaught Place is #3 Janpath Lane, Mrs. Colaco's Rooming House (#3), which is *THE* place for the traveler. Mrs. Colaco charges 5 rupees (70¢ U.S.) a night for a room. If she is booked up, Mrs. Johnson's Rooming House is only one block away. The Jayne Guest House, located at Bagot Sein Market, is very popular.

RESTAURANTS

The sidewalk stands in the area are usually the best bet for the money, but there are a number of other places to eat. There is a combination discotheque-restaurant called the Celler (#5), where for 7½ rupees (approximately $1.00 legally) you can get a steak dinner including a baked potato. The Celler, a modern, Western-style discotheque with a juke box, is located right on Connaught Place.

SIGHTSEEING

The Indian government sponsors excellent daily tours in every major city in the country. They are usually inexpensive—only $1.00 or $2.00 apiece, and the guides are quite informative.

The world-renowned Taj Mahal is about a three hour's ride south from New Delhi to Agra. The Taj Express, which is fairly comfortable, leaves the New Delhi train station daily at 7:00 a.m. (Round trip price: 13½ rupees, or approximately $1.85 legally, or in black market money a little over $1.00). The train meets a comfortable tour bus in Agra at approximately 10:00 a.m. Tickets for the bus are sold on the train and cost 8 rupees (a little over $1.00 legally), or about 60¢ in black market money.

The bus leaves at approximately 10:15 or 10:30 a.m. to explore Agra and some of the ancient cities built by the rajahs of centuries ago. After a lunch break at a local restaurant the bus approaches the Taj Mahal a little before sunset, usually around 4:00 o'clock. The bus returns to the train station for the 7:00 p.m. train back to New Delhi, arriving at 10:00 p.m.

If you prefer, you can stop off Agra on your way to Calcutta. It is right on the route. New Delhi's strategic location affords an excellent opportunity to set off in any direction. Many people will head due south for Bombay, one of the larger industrial cities of India or continue south to Goa, which has become one of the larger hippie centers in this part of the world. Last year an estimated 3,000 hippies were living there.

From there the route leads due east to Madras, which is another big tourist spot in southern India, and then north to Calcutta or south to Ceylon.

SHOPPING

Sidewalk merchants offer a wide selection of goods. Be sure to bargain! Or you can play it safer in the government-run department stores just off Connaught Circle. One of the more popular items travelers buy in India is jewels—rubies, star sapphires and other gems. (See Con Games.) Do not buy forged student ID cards in India. The word is out and no one accepts them.

RUMOR

Some claim it is possible to live in India on $1.00 a day, but there is a thin line between living and existing. It is possible if you stay in the simplest of accommodations, eat local food and don't do much traveling, sightseeing, or shopping. However, conditions being what they are, sooner or later you will physically run down. If you do try to get by on such a budget, it is recommended that at least once or twice a week you spend an extra 50¢ and buy yourself a good meal. Limit the usage of drugs and/or selling of blood.

CALCUTTA

Calcutta is a densely overpopulated, slum-ridden city with seven million people, 2½ million of whom sleep on the streets. Most of the inhabitants are unemployed and beg for a living.

India's black market is strongest in Calcutta. You don't have to find it—it will find you. Black marketeers will beg to buy anything you're wearing, but they won't offer you ten cents for it.

Conditions in Calcutta have worsened since the recent uprising in East Pakistan. Since it is not uncommon to see lepers and people infected with smallpox, yellow fever and cholera walking the streets untreated, you must take care to find a safe place to stay.

ACCOMMODATIONS

One of the safest and cleanest is the Salvation Army's Red Shield Inn, which charges only 8.2 rupees per night—a little over a dollar legally—including breakfast and a twenty-four hour guard at the door. Behind a big gate there is a courtyard for guests' vehicles. The water at the Inn is boiled to prevent disease, and dinner (soup, meat, and potato meal, and a choice of dessert for just 2½ rupees) is served on a white tablecloth. Very rarely does the Inn turn away a traveler.

SIGHTSEEING IN CALCUTTA

Anyone with normal 20-20 vision needs only eyes. Don't be alarmed if you see herds of cattle and wild animals roaming the street. In the central park is the rat farm where people walk by and feed rats while begging peasants stand by and starve to death.

Calcutta's city government has arranged an elaborate tour starting at 8:00 a.m. and ending at 5:00 p.m. for a little over $1.00. On this tour you visit the botanical gardens to see the world's largest banyon tree, the Calcutta Zoo to see the albino tiger and to various museums and monuments throughout town, including a bridge where every day two people jump off and commit suicide.

DEPARTURE

If you are heading east to Southeast Asia, there are two ways to bypass the land block of Burma. One is to fly from Calcutta to Bangkok (cost approximately $88.00; $68.00 student fare). The other is via Ceylon.

FURTHER INFORMATION

Government of India Tourist Office, 19 East 49th St., New York, N.Y. Tel: (212) MU 8-2245.

MAKING IT TO CEYLON

VISA

A visa is not required for a stay of up to six months. $500.00 and/or an onward ticket may be required at the border. Hippies have been hassled.

MONEY CHART

CEYLON

MONETARY UNIT: Rupee
5.95 Rupees = $1.00
100 cents = 1 Rupee
Code: Rp

Amount of Local Currency You May Enter With	*Amount of Local Currency You May Leave With*	*Coins*	*Notes*	*Conversion Chart $1.00 US ='s*	*Black Market Rates*
Rp 50	Rp 50	½ Cent	1 Rupee	US Rp	15 Rp = $1.00
		1 Cent	2 Rupee	$1.00 = 5.95	
		5 Cent	5 Rupee	.50 = 2.98	
		10 Cent	10 Rupee	.25 = 1.49	
		25 Cent	50 Rupee	.10 = .595	
		50 Cent	100 Rupee	.05 = .30	
		1 Rupee			
		5 Rupee			

ARRIVAL

The ferry to Ceylon leaves Rameswarm, India, every Monday and Thursday and takes one to two hours to cross the straits. A train connects the port of Mannar with Colombo, the capital of Ceylon, and other major cities on the Island.

ACCOMMODATIONS

YMCA's and youth hostels are available.

DEPARTURE

Colombo is connected by international airlines to every major city in the East. Also a ship to Penang off the coast of Southeast Asia leaves Colombo twice a week (deck class: approximately $45). The trip takes approximately three days. This is one of the two possible routes from India to Southeast Asia. (The landblock of Burma limits the alternatives.)

RECOMMENDED PLACE TO RECEIVE MAIL

Colombo: c/o American Express, Bobby Arnolda & Co., Ltd. (R), Times of Ceylon Bldg., Bristol St., P.O. Box 91. Tel: 29563.

FURTHER INFORMATION

Ceylon Tourist Board, Suite 308, 609 Fifth Ave., New York, N.Y. 10017.

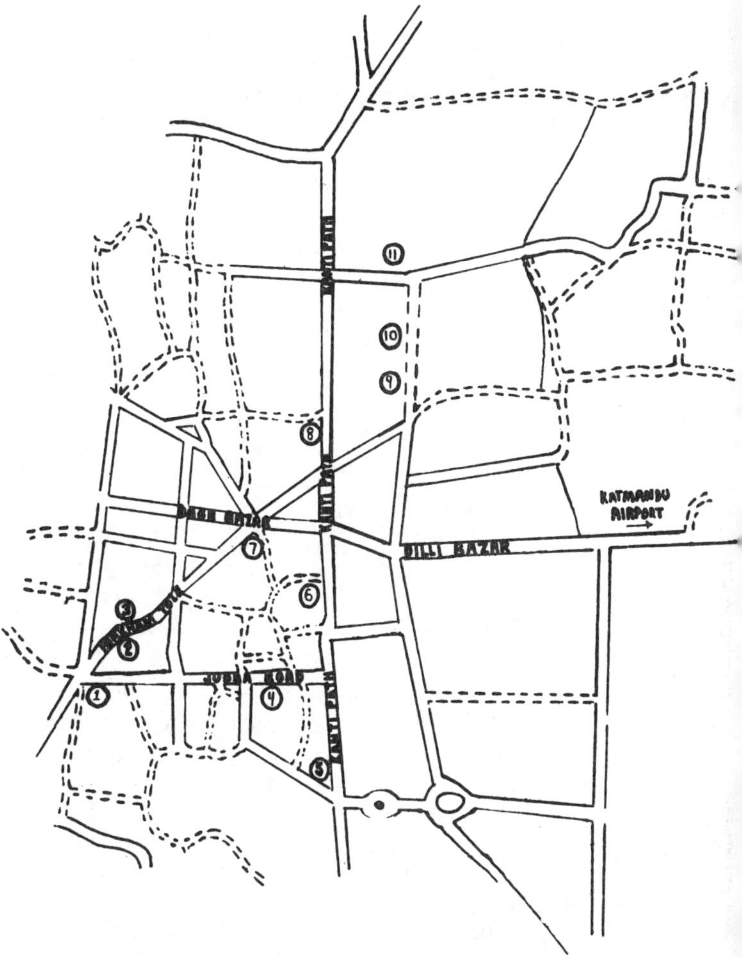

STREET MAP OF KATMANDU, NEPAL

1. Tourist Information Center
2. Hanuman Dhoka (Darbar Square)
3. Police Station
4. Airlines Office
5. Local Post Office
6. Hospital
7. Asan Annapurna Temple
8. American Embassy
9. Hotel Opera
10. Annapurna Hotel
11. Imperial Palace

MAKING IT TO NEPAL

VISA

A visa is required. Cost is $2.00, one picture is necessary.

Nepal's suppress-the-hippie policy may make entry even with a visa difficult or impossible.

MONEY CHART

NEPAL

MONETARY UNIT: Rupee
10.10 Rupees = $1.00
100 Paisa = 1 Rupee
Code: Rp

Amount of Local Currency You May Enter With	*Amount of Local Currency You May Leave With*	*Coins*	*Notes*	*Conversion Chart $1.00 US ='s*	*Black Market Rates*
No limit	None	1 Paisa	1 Rupies	US Rp	14 Rp = $1.00
		5 Paisa	5 Rupies	$1.00 = 10.10	
		10 Paisa	10 Rupies	.50 = 5.05	
		50 Paisa	100 Rupies	.25 = 2.53	
				.10 = 1.01	
				.05 = .51	

ARRIVAL

International carriers connect Katmandu, Napal with major cities including daily flights from New Delhi. If you are entering by road, you must pay a road tax from the Indian border to the capital, Katmandu. It is usually 35 Nepalese rupees (approximately $3.00 U.S.) each way. Free bus transportation from the airport to the Nepalese airline office in the center of town is available. (See Map.)

ACCOMMODATIONS

The travelers who like local color can live amongst the Nepalese people in the center of Katmandu. This part of town consists primarily of unpaved streets and buildings which by American standards would make Harlem look like Beverly Hills. It is recommended only for the hardest of travelers.

Some of the local gathering places for travelers in the center are The Camp (restaurant) and the Oriental Lodge (hotel). There are also many moderately priced hotels which are more comfortable and safer. At the Hotel Opera (#9), which is next to the Annapurna Hotel (#10), travelers who don't like to rough it can live in a much cleaner environment for almost the same price they would pay to live in the center (15 rupees a night including breakfast). The Kathmandu lodge located near the square costs 8 rupees a day with a hot shower.

SIGHTSEEING

Sightseeing in this area is very stimulating. The biggest attraction around, and I use that term literally is Mount Everest. Special sightseeing excursions leaving before dawn provide the opportunity to watch the sun rise in the Himalayas over Mount Everest. The Nepalese government offers various tours costing from $1 to $2. Some of them include Mount Everest on their itinerary; others visit ruins and museums around town and explore backward Tibetan refugee villages and rug-weaving factories.

MAIL

Use the American Embassy (#8). The local post office (#5) in town has rather lax rules and regulations. The mail is very vulnerable to theft because anyone is allowed to sort through it in search of a letter.

DEPARTURE

From Nepal most travelers have to head back to either New Delhi or Calcutta.

FURTHER INFORMATION

Royal Nepalese Consulate, 300 E. 46th St., New York, N.Y. 10017. Tel: (212) 986-1989.

MAKING IT TO BANGLADESH (EAST PAKISTAN)

VISA

An advance visa is necessary. It can be acquired only in New Delhi and Calcutta. There is no charge, three photos are required.

ARRIVAL

The capital of Dacca is connected by international air travel via New Delhi or Calcutta. Adequate roads and rail service connect India with BanglaDesh.

As of this writing calm seems to prevail in the new state of BanglaDesh. A wide variety of accommodations are available.

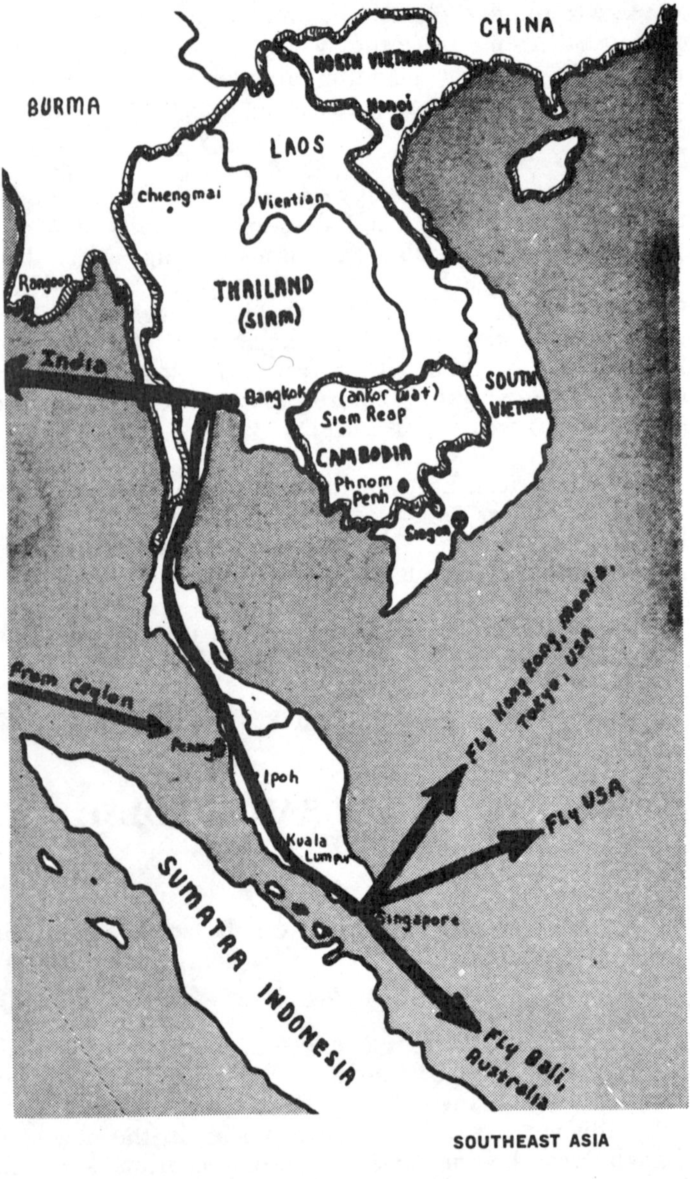

SOUTHEAST ASIA

LEGEND
MAIN TRAIL
BORDERS CLOSED TO LAND TRAVEL
⊕ CAPITAL

MONEY CHART

New official currency of Bangladesh

$1.00 = 7.50 Taka

100 Paista = 1 Taka

COINS	NOTES	
1 Paisa	1 Taka	7.50T = $1.00 US
5	5	3.75T = .50 US
10	10	1.37T = .25 US
50	50	.75T = .10 US
	100	.37T = .05 US
	500	

HEALTH

Smallpox and cholera immunizations are required.

RECOMMENDED PLACE TO RECEIVE MAIL

Dacca: American Express International, American Life Insurance Bldg., 18-19 Motijheel—P.O. Box 420, Tel: 83173, 83193 and 51228.

FURTHER INFORMATION

Bangladesh Consulate, 130 East 40th Street, New York, N.Y. 10016. Tel: (212) 686-5233.

MAKING IT TO SOUTH AND EAST ASIA AND INDONESIA

IMPORTANT NOTE: IT IS IMPOSSIBLE TO TRAVEL TO SOUTHEAST ASIA BY LAND FROM EUROPE VIA INDIA (See Map) BECAUSE THE BORDERS OF BURMA HAVE BEEN CLOSED TO ALL LAND TRAVELERS SINCE 1959. IT IS NOT LIKELY THIS SITUATION WILL CHANGE IN THE NEAR FUTURE.

All capital and other major cities are serviced by international air carriers.

Although the war in Indochina is still making headlines, it is basically confined to Vietnam, Laos and Cambodia. Should you plan to travel in this area, however, you should keep abreast of fluctuating policies due to the war. Airports may be closed at a moments notice. Read the newspapers, and always check with airlines and embassies for the latest information available.

The number of travelers visiting Thailand, Malaysia, Singapore and Indonesia has been increasing annually. Land travel throughout this area is relatively safe providing the traveler obeys laws and curfews. You can easily travel by land from Bangkok to Singapore (or vice versa) by using public transportation (train, bus or hired car). Hitchhiking is relatively safe, but to avoid hassles, hitchhikers are advised to take public transportation across borders, since the suppress-the-hippie movement is in full swing in this area. The following facts and statistical information broken down country by country should help you avoid hassles and enjoy a safe journey.

MAKING IT TO BURMA

Although crossing Burma's borders by land is not permitted, an American traveler may enter by air.

VISA

An advance transit visa–valid up to twenty-four hours, costs $2.10 when purchased in the U.S.; often more if purchased *en route*. Two photos are required, and you must leave Burma traveling in the same direction as on arrival with visas and confirmed plane reservation for destination beyond Burma.

An advance tourist visa valid up to seventy-two hours for one entry costs $6.30 if purchased in the U.S.; $7.50 *en route*. Four photos and an onward ticket are required.

A visa for a stay of up to one week is also available. Check with embassy.

ARRIVAL

Once in Burma, you are free to travel as far as your time will allow. There is a road to Mandalay, but it is not the same one Hope and Crosby took. This one goes all the way to Peking.

RUMORS

There are two rumors purporting to explain why you cannot cross the Burmese border by land.

(1) An unstable political situation and guerrilla fighting make it unsafe.

MONEY CHART

BURMA

MONETARY UNIT: Kyat
5.34 Kyat = $1.00
100 Pyas = 1 Kyat
Code: Ky

Amount of Local Currency You May Enter With	*Amount of Local Currency You May Leave With*	*Coins*	*Notes*	*Conversion Chart $1.00 US =’s*	*Black Market Rates*
None	None	1 Pya	1 Kyat	US Ky	25 Ky = $1.00
		5 Pya	5 Kyat	$1.00 = 5.34	
		10 Pya	10 Kyat	.50 = 2.67	
		25 Pya	20 Kyat	.25 = 1.34	
		50 Pya		.10 = .53	
		1 Kyat		.05 = .27	

(2) Inadequate roads prevent passage. This rumor seems to have some facts behind it. Peter Townsend, British WW II flying ace, was one of the last to drive through Burma from Europe to Asia in 1959. He had to hack his way through thick jungles with a machette. However I have been advised that adequate roads now connect Burmese cities.

FURTHER INFORMATION

Consulate of the Union of Burma, 10 East 77th Street, New York, N.Y. 10021. Tel: (212) LE 5-1310.

MAKING IT TO THAILAND

VISA

A tourist visa is not required. The embassy here in America will advise you that a visa is not required for a stay of thirty days. However, when you arrive at the port of entry in Thailand, you will only receive a 15-day entry stamp. Extension is possible for an additional 15 days, but reasonable means of support and an onward ticket are very helpful and will cut the red tape.

IONEY CHART

THAILAND

IONETARY UNIT: Baht
20.80 Bahts = $1.00
100 Stang = 1 Baht
Code: Baht

Amount of Local Currency You May Enter With	*Amount of Local Currency You May Leave With*	*Coins*	*Notes*	*Conversion Chart $1.00 US ='s*	*Black Market Rates*
Baht 500	Baht 500	5 Stang	1 Baht	US Baht	100 Baht =
		10 Stang	5 Baht	$1.00 = 20.80	$4.70
		25 Stang	10 Baht	.50 = 10.40	21.28 Baht =
		50 Stang	20 Baht	.25 = 5.20	$1.00
		1 Baht	100 Baht	.10 = 2.08	
				.05 = 1.04	

IRRIVAL AND DEPARTURE

With the exception of the few who travel from Singapore on the Malay penninsula to Thailand, Americans normally enter the country by plane via Bangkok. A great majority of he land travelers coming from Europe via India fly from Calcutta to Bangkok.

The Bangkok airport is about thirty miles from town. Taxicabs from the airport to town charge approximately 30 baht or $1.50 U.S., but a hundred yards from the airport terminal there is a bus-stop on the main highway. For 1 baht or 5¢ U.S. you can take bus #29 to the central station in Bangkok. (Often an additional ½ Baht is charged for luggage.)

When you arrive at the airport, you will find canvasses, or 'pimps," if you like, who will offer free transportation into town and to their hotels.

BANGKOK

Thailand is a modern, almost Westernized society which has economically surpassed all her neighbors. Bangkok has become a major stop for the fast-growing tourist trade in Asia and is a favorite R & R (rest and recuperation) center for American G.I.'s. Because of this, numerous first-class hotels have sprung up.

However, there are still some inexpensive places for budget-minded travelers to stay. The Thai Song Kit (pronounced in English "Ti Song Creet") Hotel, located at 247 Rama IV

Road a few blocks from the central railway station has become a local hangout for young travelers in the past few years. This hotel will supply you with a single room for $1.00 a night, but because it is known to be popular with hippies, it is not a good idea to name it when border officials ask you where you will be staying.

There are more modern hotels in Bangkok, such as the Reno or the Atlanta. The latter offers a swimming pool for the same price. To get to the Atlanta, take bus #45 from the Central Railway Station to Nano North Lane, and walk back one block.

The YMCA at 27 South Sathorn Road offers a bed, breakfast and supper for 40 baht ($2.00 U.S.) per night.

Because Bangkok is centrally located in Southeast Asia, you can make this city home base and take interesting side trips, such as:

BY TRAIN

	Second-class One-way
Bangkok to Vientiane, Laos (daily)	$12.00
Bangkok to Chang Mi (daily) (an ancient, provincial capital in the North)	$13.00
Bangkok to Penang (leaves Mondays, Wednesdays & Saturdays)	$20.00
Bangkok to Kuala Lumpur (leaves Wednesdays)	$30.00
Bangkok to Singapore (daily)	$40.00

BY PLANE

Bangkok to Phnom Penh, Cambodia	$44.30

(All prices are approximate and subject to change.)

SIGHTSEEING IN BANGKOK

The Tourist Organization of Thailand is located in Bangkok at the corner of Rajadamnern Avenue and Dim Saw Road on the traffic circle of the Democracy Monument one block from the Majestic Hotel (Tel: 24641).

Ask for information about some of the more popular attractions, such as the Sunday Market, the Floating Market and Thai boxing.

RECOMMENDED PLACE TO RECEIVE MAIL

Bangkok: c/o American Express, World Travel Service Ltd. (R), 1053 Charoen Krung Rd., Tel: 35901.

FURTHER INFORMATION

Tourist Organization of Thailand, 20 E. 82nd Street, New York, N.Y. 10028. Tel: (212) 628-7900.

MAKING IT TO LAOS

VISA

A tourist visa valid for one entry for a stay of up to fourteen days and good for three months from date of issue is required. It may be extended for an additional fourteen days after arrival. If purchased in the U.S., it costs $5.00. Three photos and an onward ticket are required.

To purchase a visa *en route* (for example, in Singapore, Bangkok or Hong Kong), apply at the Laotian Embassy. If none is available, apply at the French Embassy. The cost abroad is $2.25, and two pictures are required. (Travelers who resemble hippies may be denied entry even with a visa.)

Technically you are allowed a fourteen-day stay. However, upon entry you will be asked how long you wish to stay. If you say four days, that will be marked on your passport, and you must leave within that time. To avoid hassles and red tape should you wish to extend your visa, always request the fourteen-day visa.

ARRIVAL AND DEPARTURE

Because of the onward ticket requirement the only way to enter Laos is by plane from Bangkok, Hong Kong or another major city or by train from Bangkok. Almost all entries must be made through Vientiane, the capital of Laos.

Good roads connect Bangkok with Vientiane, and hitchhiking in Thailand is better than average but not advisable near the borders of Laos. Once you reach the Laotian border by road, you cannot walk across to Vientiane. To enter Laos, you must purchase a round-trip train or bus ticket. At the Laos-Thailand border you must cross the Mekong River via a passenger ferry. The fare is 100 kip (20¢ U.S.). Ferries run continuously from sunrise until 5:00 p.m. No traffic is permitted on the river after dark and border guards tend to be trigger happy.

After your stay you may walk across the border to Thailand, sell the remaining half of your train ticket if you wish and continue hitchhiking back to Bangkok.

Once in Vientiane, you may find that because of occasional flare-ups in the Indo-China war, you may not be allowed to leave the capital. Before entering Laos you should check with both Laotian and American embassies to determine whether entry is possible. An excellent way to confirm

MONEY CHART

LAOS

MONETARY UNIT: Kip
600 Kip = $1.00
100 At = 1 Kip
Code: Kip

Amount of Local Currency You May Enter With	*Amount of Local Currency You May Leave With*	*Coins*	*Notes*	*Conversion Chart $1.00 US ='s*	*Black Market Rates*
No limit	Kip 500	None	5 Kip 10 Kip 20 Kip 50 Kip 100 Kip 200 Kip 500 Kip 1000 Kip	US Kip $1.00 = 600 .50 = 300 .25 = 150 .10 = 60 .05 = 30	1000 Kip = $1.65

the information is to call a passenger airline. As long as passenger carriers are flying in and out of a war-torn country, tourists are allowed. Should anything happen while you are in this country, tourists will be the first to be evacuated.

RUMOR

Until a few years ago Laos was a haven for young Americans, because drugs, such as marajuana, were not illegal and were readily available. More than 2,000 young Americans congregated in and around Vientiane. However, with the heightening of the war in Southeast Asia, Laos is no longer attracting large crowds. Rumor has it that about two years ago in the middle of a busy street in broad daylight, two members of the CIA walked over to two hippies and point-blank shot them in the head.

When I arrived in Vientiane last year, I found only a few hundred young Americans. Two Peace Corps members advised me to be careful to whom I spoke. They told me many young Americans in Laos were either Peace Corps workers or spies, and they were not sure who was who. They also told me the two hippies who were supposedly shot by the CIA were actually double agents.

All and all, given the uncertain political situation, the high price of hotel rooms ($3 to $4 at the cheapest) and lack of interesting sights to see, I would advise young Americans to avoid this area.

FURTHER INFORMATION

Laositan Mission to the U.N., 321 E. 45th Street, New York, N.Y. 10017. (Tel: 212-446-0227.)

MAKING IT TO CAMBODIA

VISA

A tourist visa valid for three months from date of issue for a stay of seven days is required. If purchased in U.S., the visa costs $4.30. Two photos are required. If purchased *en route* (for example, in Singapore, Hong Kong or Bangkok), a visa costs $4.25, and three photos are required.

ARRIVAL

Because of the war in Southeast Asia travelers will find that the only access to Cambodia is from Bangkok and then again only by air. The Cambodian border cannot be crossed by land from South Vietnam or Thailand. Once you are in Cambodia, you may occasionally cross the border into Thailand by land. Always check beforehand.

Because of the war, as in Laos, airports are often closed at a moment's notice. Therefore, it is not a good idea to take a leisurely sightseeing trip through Cambodia. However, most travelers think it worth the risk if only to see the ruins at Ankorwatt. Access is easy because they are located near Siemrep, which has an international jetport.

MONEY CHART

CAMBODIA

MONETARY UNIT: Riel
140 Riels = $1.00
Code: Rl

Amount of Local Currency You May Enter With	*Amount of Local Currency You May Leave With*	*Coins*	*Notes*	*Conversion Chart $1.00 US =’s*		*Black Market Rates*
				US	Rl	
None	None	—	1 Riel	$1.00 =	140	.90 Rl = $1.00
			5 Riels	.50 =	70	
			10 Riels	.25 =	35	
			20 Riels	.10 =	14	
			50 Riels	.05 =	7	
			100 Riels			
			500 Riels			

Direct flights from Bangkok to Siemrep leave frequently and cost $40.00 one way. All other connections must be made through Phnom Penh, the capital of Cambodia. ($44.30 one way.) From Phnom Pehn you can share a taxicab to Siemrep for approximately $4.00.

ACCOMMODATIONS

In Siemrep the safest place to stay is the New Siemrep Hotel, which offers everything from private rooms to sleeping on the roof for 50¢ a night. It is only a few miles from the hotel to the ruins of Ankorwatt. You can get there via taxi or bus or rent a bicycle for 35¢. Because of the jungle heat it is best to rise early in the morning, proceed to the ruins and return by noon. After you have seen what you came for, take the next available plane back to Bangkok.

FURTHER INFORMATION

Cambodia Mission to the U.N., 845 Third Ave., New York, N.Y. 10022.

MAKING IT TO VIETNAM

NORTH VIETNAM—OFF LIMITS TO AMERICAN TOURISTS

SOUTH VIETNAM

I do not recommend visiting South Vietnam for the following reasons:

1. First and most important, if your passport has been stamped by South Vietnam, you will be denied entry to Cambodia, the U.S.S.R., most Eastern European countries and other Soviet satellite countries.

2. Because of the war economy, prices are extremely high; for example, the price of a hamburger can be as high as $1.50 and a coke, 70¢, not to mention the price of accommodations. I cannot see spending this much money to see bombed buildings and be antagonized by people with anti-American feelings.

3. Even though South Vietnam and Cambodia have been fighting side by side in the Indo-China war, they have been social enemies for centuries. It is, therefore, physically impossible for an American traveler to fly directly from Saigon to Phnom Penh without making special costly and time-consuming arrangements.

VISA

Despite the war any American with a valid passport can stay seven days without a visa. The only requirement is that you have prepaid transportation to the next country on your itinerary and proof of means of support ($100 U.S. or more).

If your passport has been stamped in any Communist country or Cambodia, or you have visited same, or such a country is your next destination, you must have an entry/exit visa for South Vietnam.

It is extremely difficult to arrange a visa for South Vietnam while you are in the U.S. In Hong Kong or Singapore you may easily obtain:

1. *A transit visa* valid for fifteen days for $2.50.
2. *A tourist visa* valid for seven to fifteen days for $2.50. Two photos are required.
3. An entry visa valid for one entry for fifteen days to three months for $5.00.

An exit permit is required for any stay over one week.

Penalties are imposed for noncompliance with the law and overstaying your visit. Check with the embassy or a consulate for specific requirements.

MONEY CHART

SOUTH VIETNAM

MONETARY UNIT: Piastre
400 Piastres = $1.00
100 Dongs = 1 Piastre
Code: Pt

Amount of Local Currency You May Enter With	*Amount of Local Currency You May Leave With*	*Coins*	*Notes*	*Conversion Chart $1.00 US ='s*	*Black Market Rates*
Pt 500	Pt 500	1 Dongs	5 Piastre	US Pt	450 Pt = $1.00
		5 Dongs	10 Piastre	$1.00 = 400	
		10 Dongs	20 Piastre	.50 = 200	
		20 Dongs	100 Piastre	.25 = 100	
			500 Piastre	.10 = 40	
				.05 = 20	

ARRIVAL AND DEPARTURE

There are no direct flights from the U.S. to Saigon. Connections can be made via Singapore or Hong Kong.

FURTHER INFORMATION

Embassy of South Vietnam, 2251 "R" Street, N.W. Washington, D. C. 20008.

MAKING IT TO MALAYSIA

VISA

No advance tourist visa is necessary for a stay of up to thirty days.

ARRIVAL AND DEPARTURE

Entrance from Thailand or Singapore is easy. However, should you have long hair, proof of reasonable means of support and an onward ticket may be required.

LOCAL TRANSPORTATION

Travel within Malaysia, for the most part, is easy. Trains, busses and taxicabs connect all major cities. Roads are better than average, and hitchhiking is very pleasant. Local inhabitants will often buy your meals during long drives.

Hitchhikers should take a bus through Kuala Lumpur to

MONEY CHART

MALAYSIA

MONETARY UNIT: Dollar
2.82 Dollars = $1.00 US
100 Cents = 1 Dollar
Code: M$

Amount of Local Currency You May Enter With	*Amount of Local Currency You May Leave With*	*Coins*	*Notes*	*Conversion Chart $1.00 US ='s*	*Black Market Rates*
No limit	M$500	10 Cents	1 Dollar	US M$	None
		20 Cents	5 Dollars	$1.00 = 2.82	
		50 Cents	10 Dollars	.50 = 1.41	
			50 Dollars	.25 = .71	
			100 Dollars	.10 = .28	
				.05 = .14	

the other side of town for your next ride. Hitchhiking within this city is difficult.

Many travelers will merely pass through Malaysia *en route* to Singapore, Bangkok or Penang. You should be warned, however, that a curfew which bans pedestrians and automobiles at certain times is enforced. At last check curfew was enforced between 2:00 and 4:00 a.m. At the state borders within Malaysia a military road block haults traffic, but papers are not checked. Border guards at these crossings have occasionally stopped hitchhikers and made them wait while the guards themselves asked motorists to give them a lift.

ACCOMMODATIONS

It takes about two days to pass through the country. Most travelers stay overnight at Kuala Lumpur. A youth hostel and other inexpensive lodgings are available.

RUMORS

Hippies have been getting jumped and have had their long hair cut.

FACT: Thus far only native Malaysian and Singapore hippies have been harassed—not Americans.

RECOMMENDED PLACE TO RECEIVE MAIL

Kuala Lumpur: c/o American Express, K.C. Dat SDN Berhad (R), 54-B Jalan Bukit Bintang, Tel: 22212 and 22214.

FURTHER INFORMATION

Pacific Area Travel Association, 228 Grant Ave., San Francisco, Cal. 94108.

MAKING IT TO PENANG

VISA

No visa is required.

MONEY—(SEE MALAYSIA)

ARRIVAL AND DEPARTURE

Penang is an island located off the coast of Malaysia. A ferry boat for vehicles and pedestrians runs continuously between Malaysia and Penang. The ride to the island is free, and it takes only a few minutes. Costs about 45 Malaysian cents (15¢ U.S.) to return to the mainland.

A boat from Ceylon via India arrives in Penang twice a week. Passengers must clear customs, and proof of reasonable means of support and an onward ticket may be required.

Since Penang is the half-way point between Bangkok and Singapore, most travelers stop mid trip just to look around.

SIGHTSEEING

Once you are on the island, there is much to do and lots to see. For an excellent do-it-yourself sightseeing tour take a ride on a blue bus which encircles the entire island in three to four hours, climbing steep mountains and crossing gorges. (Price: approximately $1.50 U.S.). A ride in a cable car up Penang Hill costs only 80 Malaysian cents (about 27¢ U.S.), and the 2500-foot verticle climb to a small village on top of the mountain affords a beautiful view of the ocean. The beaches on Penang are exquisite. Also on the island a snake temple houses drugged snakes which perch on bushes and shelves.

ACCOMMODATIONS

A short walk from the ferry pier is a youth hostel on Farquhar Street, costing 3 Malaysian dollars ($1.00 U.S.). It is run by an Indian and his family who serve snacks and beverages and do your laundry for a reasonable price. There is also a YMCA on the Island and many inexpensive hotels for $2.00 a night and up.

AT NIGHT

The main street in Penang, Penang Road comes alive at night. Movie theatres show first-run American films for about 60¢ U.S. However, you must buy your ticket early. Many of the local kids pick up spending money as scalpers. Since movies are popular with the Chinese inhabitants of the island, theatres are usually sold out, and the young scalpers make a tidy sum selling tickets to latecomers. Open markets and sidewalk restaurants contribute to a pleasant evening spent wandering the streets.

FURTHER INFORMATION

Pacific Area T-ravel Association, 228 Grant Ave., San Francisco, Calif. 94108.

MAKING IT TO SINGAPORE

VISA

In 1968 Singapore separated from Malaysia to form its own independent nation, The Republic of Singapore. No advance visa is required; however, onward transportation and proof of reasonable means of support are necessary. In most cases the more funds you have, the longer the stay you will be granted. The maximum is thirty days for which you must show $10 a day, or $300.00 total (which you are not required to spend).

With a thirty-day visa you will be allowed to make a trip to Penang or Malaysia and return without going through additional red tape if you have not exceeded the visa's time limit. Know your rights. If you have the requirements, demand your thirty-day visa (politely).

Because of American involvement in Southeast Asia, Singapore has now become the economic stronghold of this area. In order to attract outside investors, she has not only tried to clean up the Charlie Chan atmosphere and turn herself into a modern metropolis, but hippies are strictly barred to preserve Singapore's clean-cut image.

ARRIVAL AND DEPARTURE

Singapore is connected by international air travel to almost every major city.

Singapore–Hong Kong	$150.20 (one way)
Singapore–Djkarta	$ 60.90 " "
Singapore–Darwin, Australia . .	$206.00 " "

Shipping companies, including large passenger lines, of most countries service Singapore. Do not rely on announced boat schedules from Singapore to Indonesia. They often change without notice.

Passenger ships from Singapore to Hong Kong offer deck class to local inhabitants first, then to Westerners. However, very rarely is there room; you must usually take the next class available.

MONEY CHART

SINGAPORE

MONETARY UNIT: Dollar
2.82 Dollars = $1.00 US
100 Cents = 1 Dollar
Code: S$

Amount of Local Currency You May Enter With	*Amount of Local Currency You May Leave With*	*Coins*	*Notes*	*Conversion Chart $1.00 US ='s*	*Black Market Rates*
S$500	S$500	1 Cent	1 Dollar	US S$	None
		5 Cent	5 Dollar	$1.00 = 2.82	
		10 Cent	10 Dollar	.50 = 1.41	
		20 Cent	50 Dollar	.25 = .71	
		50 Cent	100 Dollar	.10 = .28	
		1 Dollar	1000 Dollar	.05 = .14	

For example:

Singapore–Hong Kong (deck class) . . .	$50.00
(next class) . . .	$70.00

Singapore and Malaysia are connected by a land bridge. You can get a bus to cross the border from Johore Bahru, Malaysia, for 80¢ Malaysian (27¢ U.S.) that lets you off in the center of Singapore.

Once you have reached Singapore, you must decide whether to return by land via Asia and Europe, go island-hopping through Indonesia to Australia or go north to Hong Kong, Taiwan, Japan and back to the U.S. The information in this chapter will help you decide. By this time you should know approximately how much it has cost you to arrive in Singapore, so you will have some idea of approximately how much it will cost you to return home.

ACCOMMODATIONS

To get further information, talk to your fellow travelers. An excellent place to meet them and a good place to stay is at 44 Sam Leon Road, which is 2 blocks from the amusement park called New World. Here you will find clean accommodations $3 Singapore ($1.00 U.S.) with a twenty-four hour cafe across the street where travelers exchange information. Because 44 Sam Leon Road is such a popular hangout, it is not recommended that you name it at your port of entry when asked where you will be staying in Singapore. If Sam Leon Road is booked up, ask the proprietor or your fellow travelers about other places to stay in this area.

SIGHTSEEING AND SHOPPING

Sam Leon Road is a short bus ride to the downtown area where you will find the general post office, tourist information center, Pan Am and American Express all within a few blocks of each other. Two blocks from the post office is a place called Change Ally, a fascinating market place with hundreds of tiny shops where you can buy almost anything and meet the local black marketeers to change money.

Most of the better hotels, foreign embassies, and large department stores are located in the Orchard Row area. A few department stores handle radio equipment with large record libraries. All you have to do is buy a blank cartridge tape, and select as many as three or four albums you like. For 50¢ each they will be taped for you.

Singapore is an excellent place to buy watches, camera equipment and clothing. You can often get better buys than in Hong Kong, but be careful. Only buy from reputable, authorized dealers. (See Con Games.)

RECOMMENDED PLACE TO RECEIVE MAIL

Singapore: American Express International, Inc., American International Bldg., 6th Floor, 1 Robinson Road. Tel: 71221/4.

FURTHER INFORMATION

Singapore Tourist Promotion Board, 251 Post St., San Francisco, Cal. 94108.

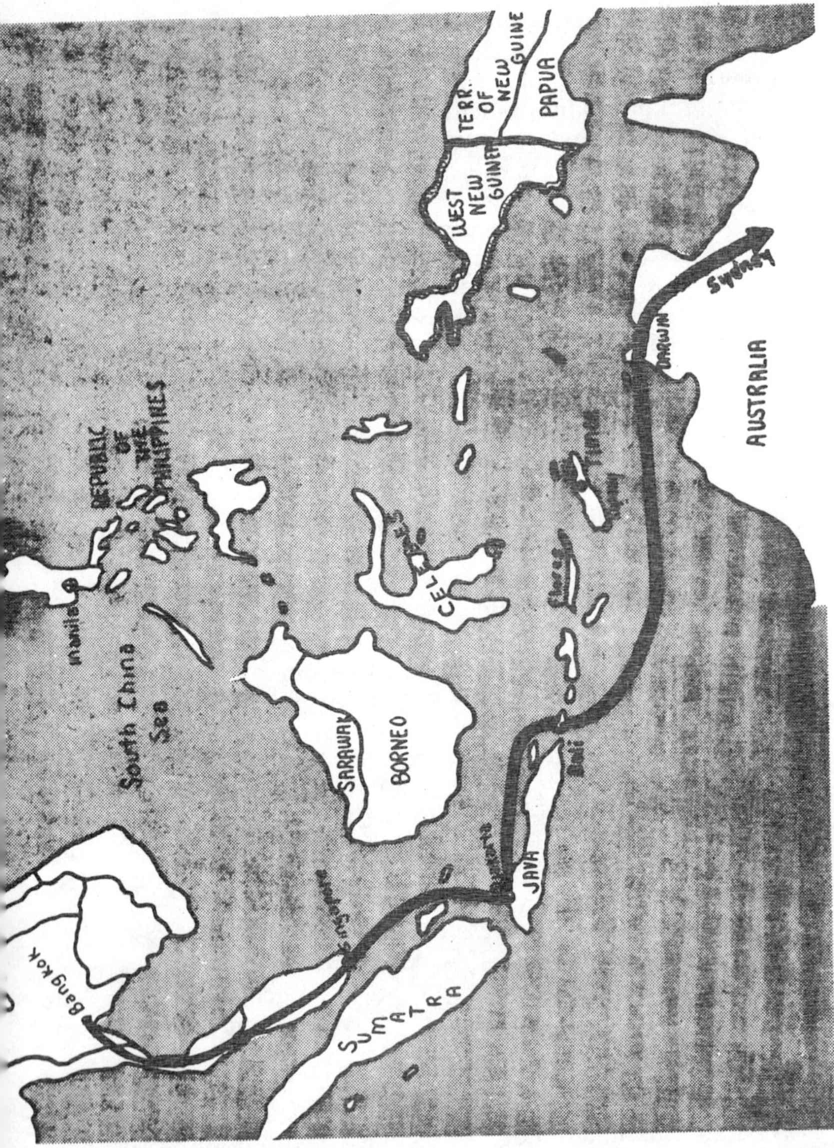

INDONESIA

LEGEND

- MAIN TRAIL
- ⊕ CAPITALS
- BORDERS CLOSED

MAKING IT TO INDONESIA

VISA

A tourist visa good for one entry and a stay of up to one month is required. In the U.S. the visa costs $3.50. Two photos and proof of reasonable means of support and onward transportation are required. If purchased *en route* (in Sydney, Australia; Singapore, etc.) the visa costs approximately $3.50, and three photos and the above proof are required. This visa is not valid for travel to Irian (the Indonesian portion of New Guinea).

It is extremely difficult and expensive to extend your visa. The fee is $15 U.S., and you must show $10 a day for each day of extension, though you are not required to spend any amount of money.

NOTE: Indonesia is the third most densely populated area in the world. One hundred and thirty-eight million people live on a few islands. The capital, Djkarta, has experienced the worst of this overcrowding. Here you will find mass unemployment and the largest civilian military reserve force in the world. Watch your possessions carefully. Thieves abound. Take care not to engage in any political conversations with strangers.

The suppress-the-hippie policy is strictly enforced.

MONEY CHART

INDONESIA

MONETARY UNIT: Rupiah
415 Rupiah = $1.00
Code: Rp

Amount of Local Currency You May Local With	*Amount of Local Currency You May Leave With*	*Coins*	*Notes*	*Conversion Chart $1.00 US ='s*	*Black Market Rates*
Rp 2500	Rp 2500	1 Rupiah	Rupiah	US Rp	415 Rp =
		2 Rupiah	1	$1.00 = 415	$1.00
		5 Rupiah	2½	.50 = 208	Negotiable
			5	.25 = 104	
			10	.10 = 41.5	
			25	.05 = 21	
			50		
			100		
			500		
			1000		
			5000		
			10000		

ARRIVAL AND DEPARTURE

Most young Americans go to Indonesia for two reasons: (1) to island hop and sample the exotic life of tropical paradises such as Bali, (2) to complete their journey from Singapore to Australia.

You can travel through Indonesia in two ways:

(1) by plane to Australia with stop-overs in Djkarta and Bali,

(2) by trains, busses, ferries and planes.

The short validity period of your visas will make it impossible for you to island-hop without taking some flights, and even then it is very difficult and expensive.

SINGAPORE TO DJKARTA

The first leg of the journey is from Singapore to Djkarta either by direct plane (price: $66.00 U.S.) or by ferry boat from Malaya to the island of Sumatra ($17.00 U.S.). The boat takes six hours. Then you must take a train to the southern end of Sumatra and another ferry boat to the island of Java and a train or bus to Djkarta. All of this takes two or three days and costs approximately $30 for transportation alone.

DJKARTA TO BALI

The train, bus and ferry trips from Djkarta to Bali and the flight to the island of Timor cost another $45.00 U.S. If you miss the connection from Kopand to Dilli, the Portuguese side of Timor (the plane from Kopang to Dilli leaves only once a week on Thursday), you are out of luck. All that is available is a three-day transit visa to the Portuguese side of the island. During the rainy season the roads may be closed. Regardless, the flight from Dilli to Darwin costs $40 U.S., bringing the total travel expenses to more than $150 not to mention the cost of food and lodging along the way, the Portuguese visa and airport taxes. For only $198 you can fly direct from Singapore to Darwin with stop-overs in Djkarta and Bali and avoid a lot of hassles and the danger of getting stranded.

Most hotels in Djkarta which are safe cost at least $5.00 a night and up, but there is a youth hostel for $1.00 a night located a few blocks behind the central railway station.

BALI

The conditions in Djkarta and every other major city on the Island of Java cause most young Americans to head for the Island of Bali. Advance train reservations are necessary, as the station master will seat all Westerners together. A third-class train with cane mesh seats leaves Djkarta's central railway station at 4:00 p.m. daily and arrives in Seribora before noon the following day. The fare is approximately $3.00 U.S. but the train is recommended for only the heartiest travelers. A first-class, air-conditioned sleeper costs upwards of $10 U.S.

A daily bus connects Seribora with a ferry to Bali and leaves at approximately 9:00 p.m. The fare is 850 rupea (approximately $2.00 U.S.). The bus arrives at the dock at 6:00 a.m. The bus and its passengers are ferried across the strait and arrive in Denpassar, the capital city of Bali before noon.

In Denpassar the local people will flock around you at the bus station offering to take you to a hotel. Two hotels are recommended for their cheap ($1.00 U.S. a night), clean, comfortable accommodations and as meeting places for young travelers. First is Adyassa, located near the center of town. Just ask anyone. The other is Ami, approximately a ten-minute walk from Adyassa.

Adyassa is better located and is much more popular. One reason is that directly across the street is the Three Sisters Restaurant offering fresh Indonesian food as well as fruit, salads, omelettes and fried rice. Here you will meet other travelers who will give you vital information about the area.

Since it is ridiculous to go to a tropical island and stay in a city, sooner or later everyone heads to Kuta Beach, approximately eight miles from Denpassar. The easiest way to get there is by Bemo Taxicab, a little three or four wheeled pick-up truck with benches in the back. If you flag down a Bemo, the driver will demand 500 rupea (approximately $1.50 U.S.) to make the trip. By American standards this is cheap for an eight-mile cab ride. However, if you walk down the main street of town to the intersection where the Gruda and Zanrad airlines offices are and make a left, you will find the main road to Kuta Beach. By flagging a regularly scheduled Bemo there, you will pay the same price as a local inhabitant—approximately 30 rupea (10¢ U.S.).

The Bemo cab will let you off at the intersection of a dirt road, where the main highway makes a sharp left. One-half mile down the dirt road from the intersection is the beach. At this intersection is located the village of Kuta with three or four food stands. The little hut to the right of the dirt road makes out-of-sight fried bananas topped with shredded coconut and maple syrup (two for 5¢ U.S.). The shop on the left hand side of the road makes the best fried rice in town. Be sure to specify "no" meat in your fried rice. Meat here is not refrigerated and often spoiled.

Halfway down the dirt road on the left hand side is a small colony of bungalows. Two or three people can share one for 250 to 350 rupea total per night. Other bungalows are available all around this area. Sharing a bungalow and cab to and from town, you can eat well and still get by on $1.00 to $1.25 a day.

SIGHTSEEING

Bali is known as the Island of Festivals. Each day of the year is a different religious holiday. Unless you stumble on a festival by accident, you will probably hear about it only after it is over. Twice a week in the village of Kapal you can see cock fights held in an arena-like building.

A trip to the village of Mass, the source of the wood and bone carvings sold in the city makes an interesting excursion. Small motorcycles can be rented for as little as $3 a day. The rental agencies in town require a large deposit or your passport as security. When you return the bike, the agent will often claim that repairs are needed, and you will be forced to pay in order to retrieve your passport.

MAIL

Because the price of a stamp equals that of a day's pay for many Indonesians, it is just a matter of luck if your mail gets through (Stamps are usually peeled off the envelope and resold on the black market). To send mail from Indonesia, take your letter directly to the post office, and have the clerk cancel the stamp in your presence.

If you must receive mail here, have it sent care of Pan American, Hotel Indonesia or American Express in Djkarta.

FURTHER INFORMATION

Indonesian Consulate, 5 East 68th Street, New York, N.Y. 10021. Tel: (212) 879-0600.

Indonesian Tourist Information Office, 909 Third Ave., New York, N.Y. 10022. Tel: (212) 421-8146.

MAKING IT TO EAST ASIA

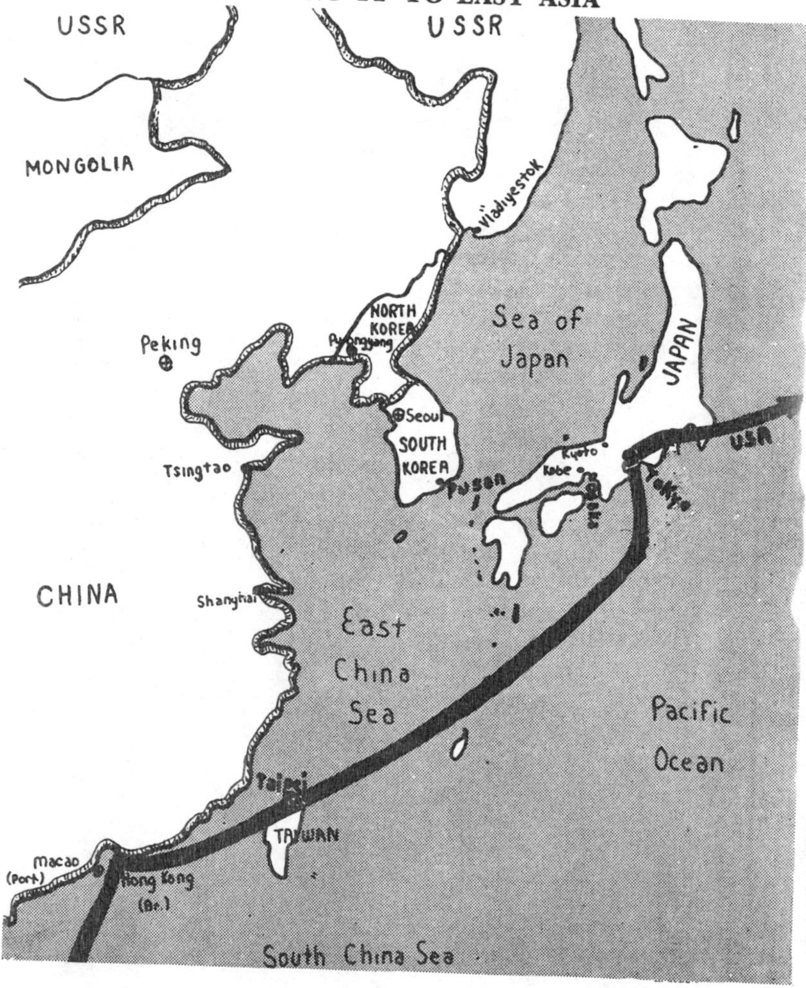

EAST ASIA

LEGEND
MAIN TRAILS
CAPITALS
BORDERS CLOSED TO LAND TRAVEL

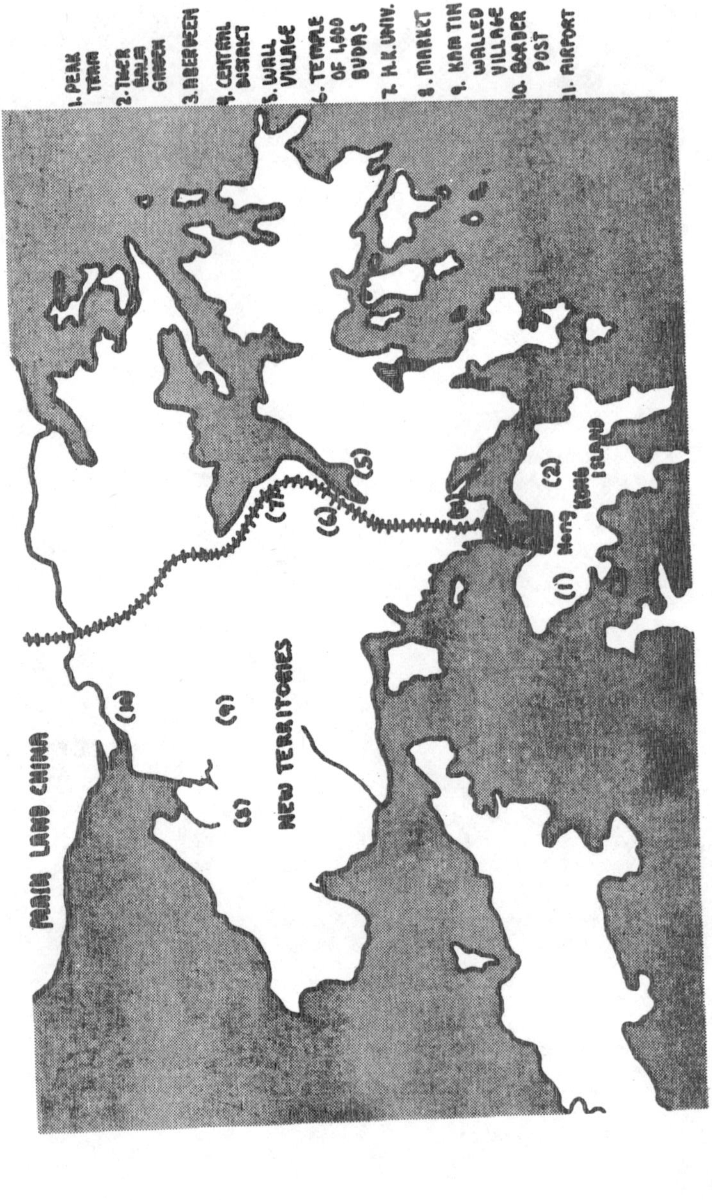
1. PEAK TRAM
2. TIGER BALM GARDEN
3. ABERDEEN
4. CENTRAL DISTRICT
5. WALL VILLAGE
6. TEMPLE
BUDAS
7. H.K. UNIV.
8. MARKET
9. KAM TIN WALLED VILLAGE
10. BORDER POST
11. AIRPORT
MAIN LAND CHINA
NEW TERRITORIES
Hong Kong ISLAND

MAKING IT TO HONG KONG

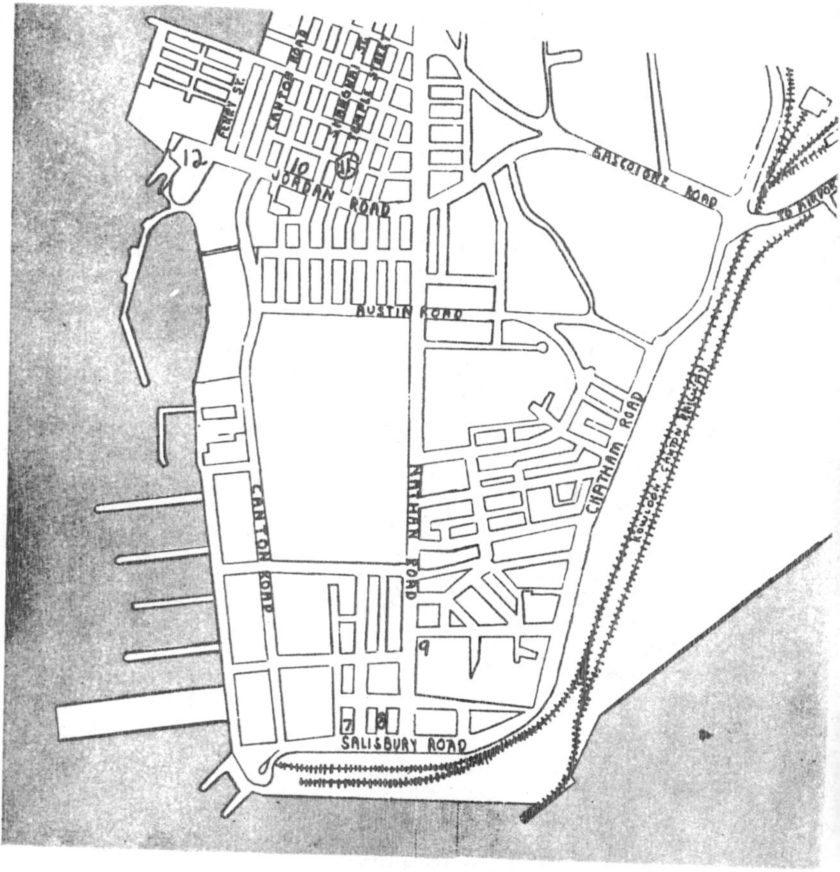

STREET MAP OF HONG KONG (KOWLOON)

7. Y.M.C.A.
8. Penninsular Hotel
9. Chungking Mansion—Guest House
10. Michael Chan's Youth Hostel
11. Temple Street Market
12. Jordan Road Bus Terminal

LEGEND

WATER

RAILROAD

CENTRAL BUSINESS DISTRICT

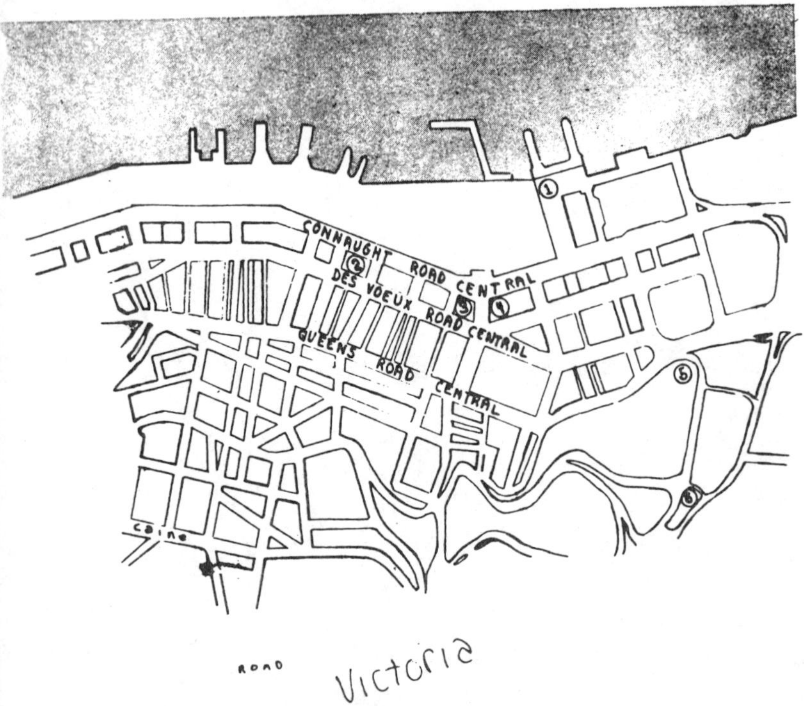

1. Star Ferry
2. Tourist Information Center
3. General Post Office
4. American Express
5. Hilton Hotel
6. Peak Tram Station

MAKING IT TO HONG KONG

What is Hong Kong?

As you can see by the map on page 226, Hong Kong consists of two parts, an island called Victoria and new territories leased to Hong Kong by Mainland China which are known as Kowloon.

VISA

No visa is necessary for a tourist stay of up to one month with onward or return ticket.

MONEY CHART

HONG KONG

MONETARY UNIT: Dollars
5.60 Dollars = $1.00 US
100 Cents = 1 Dollar
Code: HK$

Amount of Local Currency You May Enter With	*Amount of Local Currency You May Leave With*	*Coins*	*Notes*	*Conversion Chart $1.00 US ='s*		*Black Market Rates*
				US	HK$	
No limit	No limit	5 Cents	5 Dollars	$1.00 =	5.60	None*
		10 Cents	10 Dollars	.50 =	2.80	
		50 Cents	50 Dollars	.25 =	1.40	
		1 Dollar	100 Dollars	.10 =	.56	
			500 Dollars	.05 =	.28	

* Excellent place to buy foreign currencies.

ARRIVAL

When you arrive in Hong Kong either by air or sea, you will land on the Kowloon side. There you will find most of the tourist shops, hotels and general business area. Because Hong Kong is a duty-free port, it attracts many Americans looking for fantastic bargains. Also, when tourism begins Hong Kong will become the tourist gateway to Mainland China.

Because of its location it is impossible to reach Hong Kong by land. If you are traveling eastward from Europe through Asia to Singapore, you can complete your trip around the world by flying from Singapore back to the States with stopovers in Hong Kong, Taiwan and Japan. Whether you return by land through Asia and Europe or fly across the Pacific with stopovers, the cost is the same—approximately $500.00. A stopover in Hong Kong is almost always included in tours of the Pacific area.

ACCOMMODATIONS

Because Hong Kong is an international commercial city, most accommodations are designed for businessmen on expense accounts. Even a room in the YMCA located next to the Penninsular Hotel costs $4.00 a night. For budget travellers Micyael Chan's Foreign Youth Service Hostel at #10 Jordan Road is conveniently located right in the center of the Kowloon District and near all the tourist sights. Another popular centrally located place for budget-minded travelers is Chung King Mansion on Nathan Road. Here are a number of guest houses which offer rooms for $3.00 and $4.00 a night or by the week.

FOOD

Hong Kong offers a wide variety of Western dishes as well as local seafood specialties. Restaurants such as Richards, located on Jordan Avenue near Temple Street, offer a special tourist menu. For $5.00 Hong Kong (approximately 86¢ U.S.) you can select from a variety of dishes and enjoy a full five-course dinner. The local street venders offer the best bargains in seafood delicacies as well as other Chinese dishes.

LOCAL TRANSPORTATION

Since Hong Kong is a very compact area, it is relatively easy to walk to any destination. Taxicabs are very inexpensive. The Star Ferry connects Hong Kong Island with the Kowloon section and runs every few minutes; the fare is approximately 15¢ to 20¢ Hong Kong (5¢ U.S.).

SIGHTSEEING

In addition to the points of interest listed on the map of Hong Kong there are other attractions, such as the Temple Street Market, located near Jordan and Nathan Road. (See street map of Kolowoon). After sundown all traffic stops and hundreds of tiny push cart type shops fill the streets. Here you can buy almost anything.

Movie theatres showing first-run American films are located throughout Hong Kong. Prices are very reasonable averaging 50¢ to $1.00 U.S.

For a do-it-yourself sightseeing trip, take a bus to the new territories or the border for a view of Communist China.

The bus leaves regularly from the station near the Star Ferry near the end of Jordan Road. If you prefer, you can return via Canton Express after it comes through the Chinese border. It stops in front of the Penninsular Hotel near the Star Ferry.

RECOMMENDED PLACE TO RECEIVE MAIL

American Express International, Inc., Union House, 8 Connaught Rd., Central. Tel: 243151.

FURTHER INFORMATION

Hong Kong Tourist Association, 548 Fifth Ave., New York, N.Y. 10036 (212) 947–5008.

Hong Kong Tourist Association, Suite 401, 291 Geary St., San Francisco, Cal. 94102.

MAKING IT TO TAIWAN

(Also known as Formosa and the Republic of China)

VISA

Taiwan requires an advance visa. A multiple-entry, tourist visa valid for forty-eight months or life of passport is available free. Two pictures are required.

MONEY CHART

TAIWAN

MONETARY UNIT: NT Dollars
40 NT Dollars = $1.00
100 Cents = 1 NT Dollar
Code: NT$

Amount of Local Currency You May Enter With	*Amount of Local Currency You May Leave With*	*Coins*	*Notes*	*Conversion Chart $1.00 US ='s*	*Black Market Rates*
NT$1000	NT$1000	10 Cents	NT Dollars	US NT$	100 NT$ = $2.20
		20 Cents	5	$1.00 = 40	45.5 NT = $1.00
		50 Cents	10	.50 = 20	
		1 NT Dollar	50	.25 = 10	
			100	.10 = 4	
				.05 = 2	

ARRIVAL AND DEPARTURE

Taiwan is often a free stopover *en route* from Hong Kong to Tokyo by either plane or ship. Most people will arrive at the capital city of Taipei.

ACCOMMODATIONS

Because of the influx of tourists and G.I.'s on R & R, western-style hotels have sprung up through Taipei.

Most of the budget hotels are situated around the central railway station.

SHOPPING

Since Taiwan does not subscribe to international copyright laws, "forgery" shops have sprung up all over the island. At these shops $10 record albums can be purchased for as little as 35¢ and $50 Webster's dictionaries for $4.00.

RUMORS

Taiwan has long been known as a man's paradise. This is not merely a rumor but is in fact true. Taiwan has legalized prostitution. The resort hotels high in the mountains offer hot spring baths and cater to tourists and G.I.'s. When you check into a hotel, you can expect to get room and board.

Because its prostitution is government-controlled, Taiwan has managed to curtail the spread of venereal disease much more effectively than other countries which do not legally control it.

RECOMMENDED PLACE TO RECEIVE MAIL

Taipei: c/o American Express, China Travel Service (Taiwan) (R), 46A Nanking East Rd., Sect. 1, P.O. Box 378. Tel: 55933.

FURTHER INFORMATION

Chinese Information Service, 100 W. 32nd St., New York, N.Y. 10001 (212) 594-0440.

MAKING IT TO JAPAN

Japan's climate is much like that of the Northern U.S. The best times of the year to visit are in the spring and summer.

VISA

A visa is required for Americans. A multiple-entry, tourist visa valid for forty-eight months or life of passport is usually issued. There is no charge and no pictures are required.

MONEY CHART

JAPAN

MONETARY UNIT: Yen
308 Yen = $1.00
100 Sen = 1 Yen
Code: Yen

Amount of Local Currency You May Enter With	*Amount of Local Currency You May Leave With*	*Coins*	*Notes*	*Conversion Chart $1.00 US ='s*		*Black Market Rates*
No limit	Yen 20,000	1 Yen	100 Yen	US	Yen	315 Yen = $1.00
		5 Yen	500 Yen	$1.00 =	308	
		10 Yen	1000 Yen	.50 =	154	
		50 Yen	5000 Yen	.25 =	77	
		100 Yen	10000 Yen	.10 =	31	
				.05 =	15	

ARRIVAL

Because Japan is the third largest industrial power in the world, it is on almost all major freighter and passenger shipping routes. It is accessible by air directly from the U.S. and is a very popular stopover *en route* to Hong Kong or Southeast Asia.

The majority of Americans will enter Japan via Tokyo. Even here the suppress-the-hippie policy is in effect, and you will find it a great deal easier to enter by air than by ship.

From the Tokyo airport a monorail will take you into Tokyo Station in the central district known as Ginza. The tourist information center is located right near Ginza on a street called Hibiya, across from the Nikkatsu Hotel.

In the central area you will also find the general post office and American Express located at Tokyo Chamber of Commerce Bld., 2-2 Marunouchi 3-chome, Chiyoda-ku, C.P.O. 115. Tel: 211-0481. (Use American Express to receive your mail.)

ACCOMMODATIONS

You will find lodging in Japan is very expensive. Ask the tourist information center to send you to Okabo House located in Shinakobo Station. There you will find a Japanese-style hotel (the take-off-your-shoes type). You will sleep on a mat and take hot baths for only $1.00 a night. If you arrive at Okabo House and find it booked, the proprietor will steer you to other places in the neighborhood with comparably priced accommodations.

SIGHTSEEING

Just a short walk from Okabo House is Shinsuko Station, which is the Times Square area of Tokyo, where you will find movie theatres and gambling houses. The Chamber of Commerce offers bus tours throughout the city of Tokyo, but get a map from the tourist information center, and go on your own. It's more exciting. The Japanese people are very warm and friendly and will bend over backwards to help you find your way.

FOOD

In most large cities you can find Western as well as national dishes, but food is expensive. Sukiyaki is very rarely eaten even in the Japanese homes because of the high price of meat. Tampora (fried shrimp floating in soup) is very popular. You will also find the Japanese are ice cream freaks.

Don't worry if you can't read the menu. Most restaurants have a showcase in the window with sample dishes of food made of plaster which look identical to that served inside. Point to the platter you like in the window, and they'll serve you the real thing.

LOCAL TRANSPORTATION

Hitchhiking in and around Tokyo and throughout the rest of Japan is the easiest in the world.

Transportation within Japan is comparable to that in America—subways, busses, taxicabs and, of course, traffic jams. For the trip to Osaka, almost 300 miles from Tokyo, a computerized train called the Bullet, leaves Tokyo every twenty minutes for Osaka, almost 300 miles away, traveling at a speed of 120 miles an hour.

Once in Osaka, you will find accommodations are expensive but, a little over a half hour away by train in Kyoto, an ancient city which has changed very little over the past centuries. The tourist information center is located right outside the railway station. Ask for directions to Okaga house, which is similar to Okabo house in Tokyo. Here you will find Japanese-style accommodations for $1.00 a night.

There are over 1,000 youth hostels throughout Japan, but regulations are strictly enforced.

The seaport of Kobe is half an hour's train ride from Osaka. From there boats leave twice a week for Pusan, South

Korea. The trip takes two days and costs about $38.00 third class (sleeping on mats on the floor and eating soy bean soup and rice). Second- and first-class are more expensive but include sleeping births, however, the food isn't much better.

RUMOR

Can a high school dropout teach English in Japan?

I have met many young Americans *en route* to Japan with the dream of getting a job teaching English in order to support themselves. Years ago this might have been the case. Since Japan's businessmen must learn English for economic reasons, English schools have sprouted up all over Japan. At one time any English-speaking person could teach conversational English for $7.00 an hour, more than enough to sustain someone in Japan if he only worked about five hours a week.

Recently, however, there have been more teachers than students. The English schools that do exist require someone to stay for six months to a year and one must be qualified to take such a position and obtain a work visa. In order to do this you must leave the country of Japan and apply at a Japanese embassy in South Korea, Taiwan or elsewhere. The Japanese government has been cracking down on English teaching schools and weeding out their employees without work visas.

It is technically possible to get jobs teaching English on your own by placing an ad in the local newspapers. However, it takes quite a while to build up a clientele. All and all it is not a good idea to go to Japan with the impression that you will be able to get a job teaching English to sustain yourself. People who are lucky enough to get such a job will find that the pay is only between $2.00 and $3.00 an hour, and you must work more than just five or ten hours a week to support yourself.

FURTHER INFORMATION

Japan National Tourist Organization, 45 Rockefeller Plaza, New York, N.Y. 10020. Tel: (212) PL 7-5640.

MAKING IT TO KOREA

NORTH KOREA

OFF LIMITS TO AMERICANS.

SOUTH KOREA

VISA

A visa is required. A multiple-entry, tourist visa valid for forty-eight months of life of passport is good for sixty days at a time. There is no charge, but two photos are required.

MONEY CHART

SOUTH KOREA

MONETARY UNIT: Won
370 Won = $1.00
100 Chon = 1 Won
Code: Won

Amount of Local Currency You May Enter With	*Amount of Local Currency You May Leave With*	*Coins*	*Notes*	*Conversion Chart $1.00 US ='s*		*Black Market Rates*
Won	Won	1 Won	10 Won	US	Won	1000 Won =
64,200	64,200	5 Won	50 Won	$1.00 =	370	$2.50
		10 Won	100 Won	.50 =	185	
			500 Won	.25 =	93	
				.10 =	37	
				.05 =	19	

ARRIVAL AND DEPARTURE

If you are not flying directly to Seoul, the capital of South Korea, the next best way to enter is through the port city of Pusan on a boat which leaves Kobe, Japan, twice a week. The boat is called the Aerian, and the two-day trip costs $33 U.S.

Food on the boat consists of soy bean soup and rice, and you sleep on mats on the floor in the hull. It is advised only for the heartiest travelers.

Once in Pusan only a few blocks from the pier is the Seamen's Club, which serves American food. A few blocks from the Seamen's Club is the Mido Hotel which offers clean accommodations for approximately $2.00 a night.

Texas Street is where it's happening. G.I.'s and tourists flock to the bars and clubs. Black marketeers are prevalent.

The train fare from Pusan to Seoul is only $3.00.

RECOMMENDED PLACE TO RECEIVE MAIL

Seoul: c/o American Express, Chunusa Travel Service (R), Sokong Bldg., Room 201, I.P.O. Box 1330, Tel: 22-9648 and 23-3120.

FURTHER INFORMATION

Korea Tourist Office, 48 W. 48th Street, New York, N.Y. 10036. Tel: (212) 247-3726.

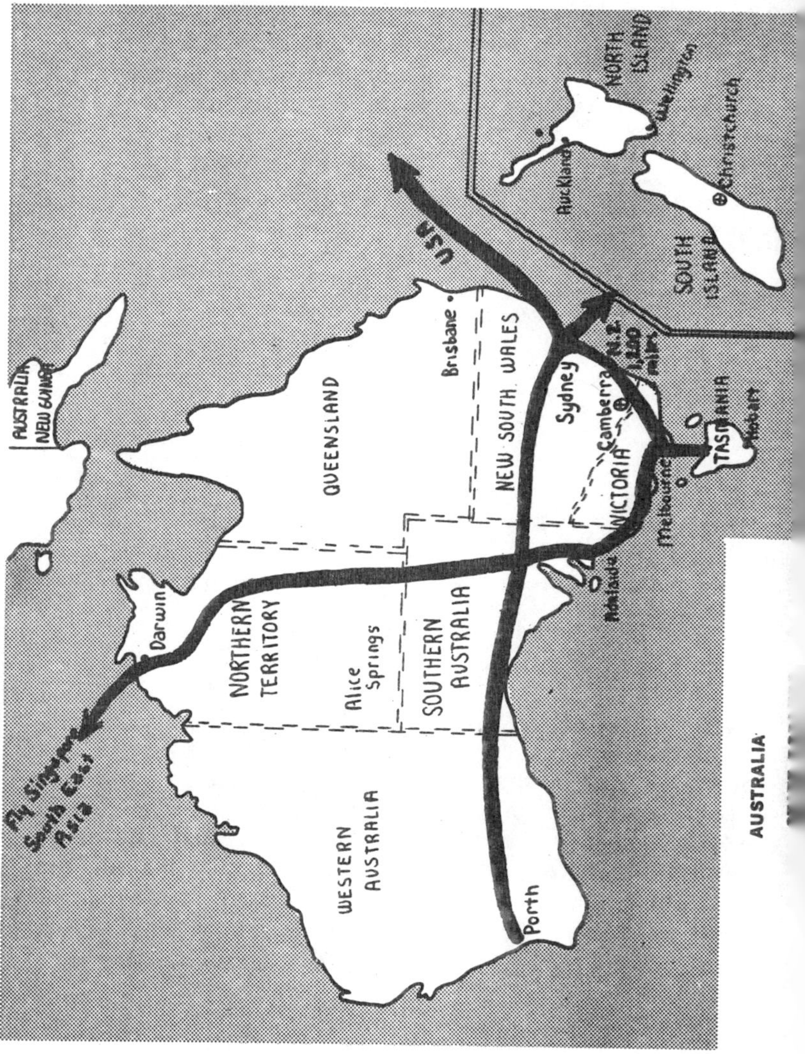

AUSTRALIA

MAKING IT TO AUSTRALIA

VISA

A visa must be obtained prior to arrival in Australia. It is advisable to get one before leaving the U.S. There is no fee, but you need three photos, proof of reasonable means of support and proof of onward transportation.

Once you are in Australia, it is extremely easy to get work visas and to extend tourist visas which are valid for six months at a time. A multiple-entry visa valid for forty-eight months or life of passport, whichever is shorter, is also available. A transit visa for a stay of up to seventy-two hours is not required.

HEALTH

A smallpox immunization is required.

MONEY CHART

AUSTRALIA

MONETARY UNIT: Dollar
1 Australian Dollar = $1.19
100 Cents = 1 Australian Dollar
Code: A$

Amount of Local Currency You May Enter With	*Amount of Local Currency You May Leave With*	*Coins*	*Notes*	*Conversion Chart $1.00 US ='s*	*Black Market Rates*
No limit	A$100	1 Cent	1 Dollar	US A$	None
		2 Cents	2 Dollars	$1.00 = .84	
		5 Cents	5 Dollars	.50 = .42	
		10 Cents	10 Dollars	.25 = .21	
		20 Cents	20 Dollars	.10 = .08	
		50 Cents		.05 = .04	

ARRIVAL AND DEPARTURE

Australia is located on most major shipping routes. Average travel time by ship from the U.S. is three to five weeks depending on the route. Flying time from San Francisco is 18½ hours. Most major airlines land in Sydney and allow stopovers *en route;* the more popular include Hawaii, the Fiji Islands, and New Zealand. The average round-trip air fare is approximately $1200. (See "Overland Route to Australia".)

ACCOMMODATIONS

Bed-and-Breakfast Hotels

One of the most common types of accommodations are the bed-and-breakfast hotels where you can find a comfortable room and a substantial breakfast for $2–$4 a night and up, or, by the week, from $15 up. In Sydney a very popular bed-and-breakfast chain called Gould's Hotels can be found throughout the Kings Cross area. (see map)

Youth Hostels

The Australian Youth Hostel Handbook is practically a must for details about locations and access. The charge per night ranges from $A.20 to $A. 50. For further information contact the Australian Youth Hostels Association, 184 Sussex St., Sydney, N.S.W. 2000 (local telephone 29-5068).

TASMANIA

Tasmania is the island state of Australia. It lies 140 miles south of Melbourne and is accessible either by ship or airplane. Smallest of the seven Australian States, it is considered by many to be the most beautiful. Hobart, the capital of Tasmania, is as modern and westernized as any of the other leading Australian cities. Yet compared to the mainland, Tasmania seems much richer and greener, spoating everything from orchids to peaceful tree lined beaches. Because of this, many Australians from the mainland spend their vacations here.

Because Tasmania is agriculturally rich, many Australians as well as American travelers head there during harvest time (December thru March) to work as migrant farm hands.

NEW GUINEA

New Guinea is divided into three political territories. The western section is governed by the Netherlands. The two eastern sectors, Northeast New Guinea and the territory of Papua, are both governed by Australia.

Located just south of the Equator, New Guinea has a tropical climate with an average temperature of 80° fahrenheit. New Guinea's rugged mountains, wild jungles and friendly natives whose life style has not changed in hundreds of years offer the tourist an excellent opportunity to explore beyond the beaten path of Western civilization.

For further information contact any Australian National Tourist Agency (address at end of chapter).

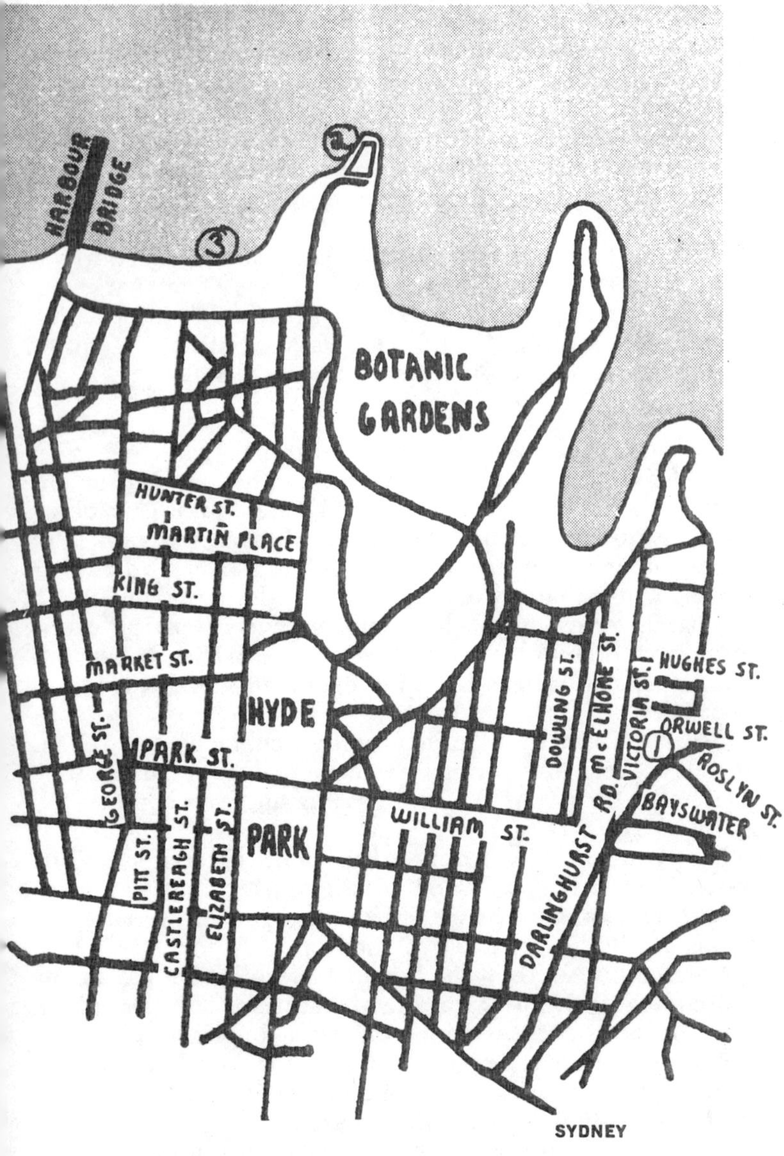

SYDNEY

1. KINGS CROSS
2. OPERA HOUSE
3. FERRIES TO OTHER PARTS OF SYDNEY

RUMORS

Free Passage to Australia

The Australian government will not pay your entire fare to Australia. For example, it will pay approximately 25%, or about $150 of the $600 one-way fare from New York City to Sydney, Australia. The traveler must agree to stay for two years. Should you decide to leave before the two years are up, you must repay the $150 before you are allowed to leave.

Once you are in Australia, the government will assist you in the following ways. (1) If you are arriving as an immigrant, they will put you up temporarily and lodge you until you get on your feet. (2) They will help you to find a job. The rest is up to you.

Free Land

Nobody gives away anything for free, not even the Australian government. However, government land grants are available. Under the terms of a land grant the purchaser must agree to make improvements and develop the land within a specified amount of time. The land offered under these grants is situated in the middle of the country where desert-like conditions exist. Most of the really valuable land in Australia was claimed a long time ago, mostly for agricultural purposes.

In recent years some of this worthless desert land has proved to be rich in mineral deposits. Many Australians have taken up prospecting as a hobby. Land can be leased for this purpose for $1.00 an acre per year.

Real estate in and around the major cities has become expensive, and its value is proportionate to that in America.

Six Girls to Every Guy! Five Guys to Every Girl!

Both of these rumors have been circulating for years, and much to your dismay you will find they are both true. Working conditions and salaries are not equal for men and women in Australia. Since good-paying jobs for women are hard to find in the rural areas, they flock to the cities. At the same time many men trying to seek their fortunes in this developing country flock to the outback. This has created a great inbalance with a shortage of women in the outback and a shortage of men in the cities.

Nevertheless, if you go to Australia, do not think that the overabundance of one sex in any part of the country is going to make the pickings easy. Remember, it's not what you have; it's what you can do with it. If you cannot make it here in America, it will not be any easier in a foreign country.

White Australian Policy

For many years rumors have circulated that Australians are racially prejudiced and try to enforce the White Australian Policy by denying entry to Orientals, Negroes or any minorities not of European descent. After careful research I have found that Australian people have no more racial prejudice than Americans have.

The rumor that no Orientals or Negroes are allowed to live in Australia is also not true. Many thousands of Orientals have been living there since before WW II. And may I remind you that the black race of people known as the Aborigines were Australia's earliest citizens. For the last 25 years or so since WW II, Australia has tried to control the immigration of large numbers of non-European peoples.

After careful investigation I have discovered the reason for this policy. Although Australia is a country the size of America, its population is equal to that of the New York City metropolitan area. There are approximately 12½ million people in the entire country of Australia, and she is trying to profit by the mistakes of other world powers which are now having racial problems. Despite rapid economic growth and a labor shortage, Australia, in order to avoid social problems, still prefers to limit her immigrants and take a few more years to attain the status of a world leader.

Australia is located south of Indonesia, which is a stepping stone to Southeast Asia. In recent years many millions of Chinese have immigrated to various countries in Asia. If Australia opened her doors to any and all people, many millions of Asians, Africans and South Americans would certainly take advantage of the offer. Within a few years the native Australian would be a minority in his own homeland.

Australia's policy towards immigration of American Negroes has been extremely rigid. Until recently American Negro G.I.'s visiting Australia and marrying Australian girls were denied permission to return to live with their wives. A very popular female American Negro entertainer who married an Australian was denied permission to live in Australia.

However, a recent article in *The New York Times* stated that within the last year 250 American Negroes have been allowed to immigrate to Australia. It is the opinion of this author that these immigrants were professional people and/or skilled workers who would be productive members of society and assets to Australia.

It is also the opinion of the author that since Australia is suffering from a severe labor shortage, it will only be a matter of time before immigration standards will have to be changed to let in a limited number of non-Europeans to fill the void in the labor market.

ABORIGINES

The natives of Australia, like our American Indians, now live on reservations. A stop at one of these reservations is included on almost every sightseeing excursion to the outback.

RECOMMENDED PLACES TO RECEIVE MAIL

The General Post Office, downtown Sydney located at Martin and George Streets, or American Express, AWA Building, 47 York Street, GPO Box 7006. Tel: 29 59 91.

FURTHER INFORMATION

Australian Tourist Commission, 630 Fifth Ave., New York, N.Y. 10020. Tel. (212) CI 9-4000.

Australian Tourist Commission, 1 Post St., San Francisco, Calif. 94104

Australian Tourist Commission, 3600 Wilshire Blvd., Los Angeles, Calif. 90005.

THE OVERLAND ROUTE TO AUSTRALIA

For years traveling to Australia has been the dream of many people. The average round-trip air fare from New York to Sydney, Australia, is approximately $1200. but anyone can just hop on a plane and fly direct. But if you play your cards right for approximately $600.00 U.S. you can travel through 30 countries in Europe and Asia on your way to the land down under.

As you can see on the map on page 127 it's possible to travel by land from London to Singapore (except for crossing Burma, see Making it to Burma), and from there it's a short hop to Australia.

The following three basic steps will give you the logistics for this overland route to Australia Refer to the appropriate maps and chapters for each country for more detailed information.

Step 1. *London to Istanbul* (See maps on pages 127 and 128) no matter what your port of entry to the European continent, whether it be London, Amsterdam or Luxembourg, you will find that getting to Istanbul is a relatively simple matter. Boads are better than adequate, and it is relatively easy to drive from any point in Europe to Istanbul. Hitchhiking is extremely easy throughout most of the continent to Istanbul, but it is not recommended during the winter months, and you should use caution when hitchhiking through Yugoslavia and Bulgaria (See the respective chapters.) Many people team up in London or Amsterdam, buy used cars and try to make the entire trip. I do not recommend using automobiles as a mode of travel for the overland route to Australia. As mentioned in the chapter on transportation, they are extremely inconvenient, especially when travelling to our-of-the-way places where gasoline and repairs are hard to come by. I have found that a majority of travelers rely on public transportation throughout Asia. It is usually safer, a lot more reliable and in the long run less expensive. During the spring and summer months you will find a large number of vans, busses and trucks leaving London and Amsterdam for Istanbul. Here you can meet people to share driving expenses for around $30.00 per person.

From Paris the Orient Express costs approximately $66.00 and takes three or four days to reach Istanbul.

If you are spending the summer in Europe using a Eurailpass and planning on making it to Istanbul, Indian and on to Australia, wail until the Eurailpass is ready to expire and head toward Trieste, Italy. From there you simply cross the border, and for about $24.00 by train you can go through Yugoslavia and Bulgaria to Istanbul. Regularly scheduled trains and busses leave from almost every country in Europe and connect with busses and trains going to Istanbul.

Step 2. *Istanbul to India* (See map on page 182) Istanbul is in an extremely stragetic location. It is here that you will arrange for visas for passing through most of the Asian countries (See the respective chapters.) By hanging around the section of town called Sultan Amid and especially the Pudding Shop, you will meet people with busses, vans and trucks going to India. Occasionally, hippie busses leave for India and Nepal.

It is possible using public transportation (basically third class rail) to make it from Istanbul to India for $35.00 not including food. Trains are much more reliable and comfortable in the hot climate than busses. As you can see by the map on page 182, the path from Istanbul leads from Ankara, Turkey; to Teheran, Iran; to Kabul, Afghanistan; to New Delhi, India. From there you can make a decision whether you want to take a side trip to Kathmandu, Nepal; and then end up in Calcutta, India. As you can see in the chapter "Making it to Burma", Calcutta is the farthest east you can go by land because of the closing of the Burmese border. You must make the decision to fly from Calcutta to Bangkok or go south to Ceylon and take a boat to Penang. Calcutta to Bangkok is the recommended route, for it is less expensive and less tiring than the boat.

Step 3. *Bangkok to Singapore* (See map on page 204) Once in Bangkok you will find that hitchhiking is easy down the Maylay Penninsula to Singapore. Regularly schedule trains and busses also connect both cities. Half way down the Penninsula stop at Penang; the "Pearl of the Orient."

Step 4. *Singapore to Australia* (See map on page 220) Singapore is a stragetic city at the other end of the line, for it is here you must make a decision to head back by land or continue through Indonesia to Australia. It is here you must also make a financial decision and arrange for your visa to Australia, for in most cases you will not be allowed to enter unless you have a ticket to leave — usually a ticket back to the U.S. or a return ticket to Singapore. A one way ticket from Singapore to Darwin, Australia, with stopovers in Bali and Djkarta, Indonesia is approximately $200.00 one way. Since the round-trip fare is about $400, it may be cheaper to fly for $500 or $600 back to America. The only other alternative would be to return overland through Asia and Europe. By this time you should have calculated how much it has cost you to get to Singapore, and you will therefore know how much it will cost to return overland.

Many people try to island-hop through Indonesia. This is physically possible if you make the correct connections. However, it may take longer than the term of your visa. For example, if you have a two-week visa, it may not be long enough for you to go by land through the islands to Australia. The Indonesian government is reluctant to give out one-month visas unless you show sufficient funds. Therefore, I recommend a direct flight from Singapore to Australia with perhaps a stopover on the island of Bali in Indonesia.

ENCOUNTER OVERLAND

For those who do not know where they are going there are various organizations in London which arrange for guided camping tours through Europe and Asia as far as India. These usually range from six to eight weeks and can cost as much as $700 depending on the itinery. Encounter Overland runs one of the most reputable tours with modern facilities on specially equipped trucks. Parties camp out most of the way and avoid the major metropolises which have become tourist traps. Encounter Overland will take you as far east as India. From there they will help you with reservations and airline tickets which are a lot cheaper booked through Encounter Overland than if you buy them yourself.

Contact: Encounter Overland
12 Egerton Gardens
London S.W. 3
Tel: 01 584-2810

AROUND THE WORLD, THROUGH ASIA AND EUROPE ON $3.00 A DAY

There is a thin line between *living* and *existing,* and one must have the desire to accept the challenge of living on an extremely tight budget. If you have the discipline to live on a budget of $1.00 a night for a room and $2.00 a day for food and miscellaneous espenses, I feel that you will enjoy your experience tenfold. I personally have traveled through fifty countries and have lived on $3.00 a day. This is, however, an average cost per day. In some countries I spent as much as $4.00 a day while in others I spent under $2.00, but this was only after subtracting the cost of transportation. Even such guidebooks as *Europe on $5 a Day* do not include the cost of transportation to and from Europe in their budgeting. Likewise, when I talk about traveling around the world on $3 a day, this is the daily cost of living abroad and does not include the cost of transportation.

You cannot possibly live on such a tight budget by going to the hotels and restaurants recommended in popular guidebooks. If a million other people in Europe also have the same name and address, the hotel will either be booked up before you arrive, or the price will be higher than you expected.

You will find it easier to take one big trip to many countries than to take a small trip to a few countries. The cost of getting there will be the same either way. The cost of a round-the-world airline ticket is very inexpensive — often less than a round-trip fare overseas. Once you have paid the transportation cost, you can then budget all your remaining funds for room, board and miscellaneous expenses according to the length of your trip.

What is a round-the-world airline ticket?

ROUND-THE-WORLD TICKETS

Round-the-World Tickets

Airplanes can be less expensive than ships, and it is now very inexpensive to fly around the world. For a basic fare of $1,250.00 a traveler can fly all the way around the world, stopping in as many places as he wants. For example, leaving New York heading west, you can stop in Chicago, Las Vegas, Los Angeles, Hawaii, Tokyo, Hongkong, Bangkok, New Delhi and so on around the world. Once you pick your direction, you cannot backtrack, nor can you go too far north or too far south, or you will use up too much of your mileage. However, because you are buying mileage in quantity, you get a bonus. This enables you to buy an additional 25% of the original mileage at a reduced rate which is approximately 40% of the list price.

These tickets are a must for anyone who is going around the world.

1. The initial cost of $1,250 is less than the cost of flying across oceans and hitchhiking by land. As you can see in the map section of this book, certain borders are closed to land travel, and travelers must take planes or boats to circumvent these obstacles. Delays will also occur in crossing land borders. However, when entertaining a country via an international airport, a traveler is rarely delayed, providing all his documents are in order.

2. The second most important reason is visa requirements. Most countries in Asia and Eastern Europe will not allow you to enter unless you have pre-paid transportation to leave. In most cases an airline ticket carries a lot of weight. People using this round-the-world ticket have very few problems entering countries.

3. This ticket is like having an insurance policy in your pocket. Should you have to go home for any reason or get sick and have to move on to another country, you need not wait for funds or tickets to be sent to you.

4. This round-the-world ticket is good for one year and is broken up into segments, for example, San Francisco to Honolulu, Honolulu to Tokyo, etc. There are no dates or names of carriers on any ticket. When you decide to move on to the next point, you make a reservation on the flight of your choice. This same procedure can also be used for small excursions to three or four countries throughout Europe.

5. Itineraries for round-the-world flights can easily be changed. If you do not exceed the mileage allowance, there will be no extra charge.

SAMPLE ITINERARY

New York - Los Angeles - Hawaii - Japan - Taiwan - Hong Kong - Singapore - Bangkok - Calcutta - Nepal - New Delhi - Kabul - Teheran - Istanbul - Athens - Rome - Paris - Amsterdam - London - New York.

Cost: $1250 approximately plus $300 including Australia for a total of $1550.

As you can see by this sample, round-the-world itinerary, the plane lands in each country at an international airport (in most cases, the capital of the country). From there you are on your own to travel around the rest of that country via public transportation or by hitchhiking. In Europe it is a good idea to use a Eurailpass and sleep on night trains to save the hotel costs. It is also wise to travel in warm weather or follow summer, so you can sleep out.

Try to divide your spending money into four segments for the journey. If you find you are exceeding your budget for the first segment, leave for the next stop on your trip.

Don't carry all your money with you — especially if your trip takes many months to a year. Send money ahead, and have it waiting at local banks in strategic stops, so you won't exceed your budget.

There are many other money-saving hints and tips in each individual chapter of this book.

Mark Atlas attempts to keep abreast of the latest information of interest to travelers, but it is physically impossible for any one person annually to cover each of the fifty countries mentioned in MAKING IT ABROAD. Therefore, the author requests that the travelers themselves add to, comment on and help update the information for each edition. The attached post card is for your convenience. If you feel you have any vital information which will aid your fellow travelers, please write to the following address:

MAKING IT ABROAD
P.O. BOX 5847
GRAND CENTRAL STATION
NEW YORK, N.Y. 10017